DOCTRINE AND DEED

EXPOUNDED AND ILLUSTRATED

IN SEVENTEEN SERMONS

Preached in the Broadway Tabernacle,
New York City

BY

CHARLES EDWARD JEFFERSON

NEW YORK
THOMAS Y. CROWELL & CO.
PUBLISHERS

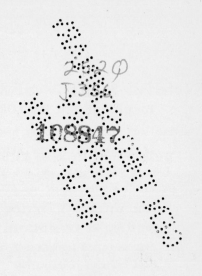

To MRS. JESSIE TAYLOR

REVERED AND BELOVED BY ALL THE MEMBERS OF

THE BROADWAY TABERNACLE CHURCH

FOR HER WORTH'S SAKE AND HER WORK

AND ALSO FOR THE SAKE OF HER HUSBAND

DR. WILLIAM M. TAYLOR

WHOSE ELOQUENCE AND SAINTLINESS ARE

HELD IN LOVING REMEMBRANCE BY

A GRATEFUL CONGREGATION

These Sermons are Affectionately Dedicated

BY HER PASTOR

TABLE OF CONTENTS

THE ACTUAL AND THE IDEAL

THE ACTUAL AND THE IDEAL

"But now we see not yet all things put under him, but we see Jesus." — Heb. 2 : 8–9.

WHO is writing? We do not know. But whoever he is, he is undoubtedly a Hebrew. His memory is filled with the treasures of Hebrew history and his style is saturated with the spirit of Hebrew thought. He falls back continually upon Hebrew literature for illustrations with which to body forth his ideas and illuminate his argument. He has been quoting the 8th Psalm, a Psalm which we ourselves are in the habit of quoting. He has given the most familiar part of it. "What is man, that thou art mindful of him? and the son of man that thou visitest him? For thou hast made him a little lower than the angels, and hast crowned him with glory and honor. Thou madest him to have dominion over the works of thy hands; thou hast put all things under his feet." When he reaches that point he is startled by the size of the word "all." He pauses to explain what it means. He declares that when the Psalmist says *all* he means *all*. If God has put in subjection all things under man, then nothing is left that is not put under him. But this does not tally with the condition of things

as it exists to-day. " But now we see not yet all
things put under him, but we see Jesus." We see
the ideal and we see the actual, and we see the
chasm which separates the two. But there is no
room for despair, for the actual will most certainly work itself into the ideal, and man shall
some day be undisputed monarch of the earth.

The history of our race is the story of the progressive conquest of man over forces exterior to
himself. Man is by nature a conqueror. His brow
was created to wear the laurel. His hand was
fashioned to hold the sceptre. He has travelled
through the deeps of time, passing from victory to
victory. He is the lord of all the world, and his
place is on a throne. This was the conviction of
the man who wrote the first chapter in the book of
Genesis. He represents God as saying to man
immediately after man's creation, " Replenish the
earth and subdue it, and have dominion over the
fish of the sea, and over the fowl of the air, and
over every living thing that moveth upon the
earth." In the second chapter he sketches us a
picture of the beginnings of this conquest. He
represents the entire animal creation moving
toward the feet of man, each animal looking up
into man's face to find what its name shall be.
Whatsoever man called every living creature that
was the name thereof.

This picture haunted the Hebrew imagination
through all the centuries of Hebrew history.
The Hebrew poets never grew weary of rejoic-

ing in the fact that man is the master of the animal creation. The writer of the 8th Psalm, after declaring that the Almighty has placed all things under man's feet, goes on to give an illustration of what this means. It means that man's feet are on all created things: " All sheep and oxen, yea, and the beasts of the field; the fowl of the air, and the fish of the sea, and whatsoever passeth through the paths of the sea." The same note of triumph is heard in the New Testament. The most unpoetical man in the New Testament is probably the apostle James. He has very little of the poet in him, but even his soul is thrilled by the thought that man is lord of the entire animal world. Listen to him as he writes to the Christians of the first century: " Every kind of beasts, and of birds, and of serpents, and of things of the sea, is tamed, and hath been tamed of mankind." That is the 8th Psalm worked out into flat-footed, unadorned prose.

We can repeat the words of James with an emphasis and an accent which he was not master of. The animal creation has at last been utterly subdued. There is no sea upon the face of the earth across which man is afraid to travel for fear of any sea monster lurking there. There is no jungle so dark and dense into which man dare not penetrate for fear of ravenous beasts which make it their home. All fear has been driven from man's heart, and he goes everywhere, the unquestioned lord of the animal creation. It is for him to say what animals shall live and what animals shall perish. It is he who says what birds shall multiply and what birds shall disappear. The animal creation lies completely at his mercy. Whatever he calls a living creature, that is the name thereof.

But this conquest of the animal world is only prophetic of more difficult conquests and vaster. The animal forces are only a small fraction of the vast aggregate of forces which constitute the world. To lord it over beasts and birds is comparatively easy. There are forces other than those which throb and burn in the veins of living things; there are forces in the water and in the air and in the clouds compared with which the forces of even the greatest animals count as nothing. The 19th century will be forever memorable among the centuries of human history as being the century in which mighty cosmic forces came forth and threw themselves at the feet of man. That is a wonderful picture which stands on the first page of our book of Genesis, but he would paint a far grander picture who could paint what has been going on in these recent times. Under the first picture, representing the conquest of man in the first centuries of human history, we should place the words, "Conquest over the Animal Creation"; but under the picture which the 19th century has painted we should place the words, "Conquest of Man over Matter." The procession pictured by the Genesis writer, of oxen, sheep, and beasts of the field, is picturesque and striking; but it is nothing compared with that procession which has passed before man in the century which has recently reached its close. In this modern procession what mighty forces march! Fire and water, wind and wave, that strange power called gravitation, that mighty spirit called steam, that weird genius known as electricity, that white-robed angel known as light: out of the earth and out of the sky they have come, a band of Titans, a group of genii, a company of archangels, to cast themselves at man's feet. And whatsoever man has called every one of these cosmic forces, that is the name thereof. The most dazzling feature of the 19th century was the conquest of man over matter. It was a century of inventions. More conquests were made within that century over the forces that lie hidden in the pockets of the natural world than were made by all the generations that went before us. If you should start out with a magic broom to sweep off the earth everything that was discovered or invented or created during the 19th century, what a job you would have on hand. After you had completed your sweeping, the world would seem to be as bare and naked as a beggar's garret. You would in the first place sweep off of all the continents every mile of railroad and every railway train and every electric car, and you would sweep off of every sea every vessel moved by steam. How strange the world would seem without a railway train, without a steamship. And with your broom you would sweep down every mile of telegraph wire, and you would sweep away all the telephones and all the phonographs and grapho-phones. Passing into the office of the physician, you would sweep out all the anæsthetics and anti-septics, and all the hundred different and myste-rious contrivances by means of which he carries on his heroic warfare against disease. You would pass into the laboratory and sweep out al-most all the marvellous apparatus by which the biologist and the chemist have been able to make the discoveries which have thrilled and blessed the modern world. And after you had done all this work it would be necessary for you to sweep out all the machinery that thunders and roars in its work of performing miracles, almost as wonderful as the miracles which Jesus wrought, in the facto-ries and foundries and mills and steel plants in all the world's great manufacturing centres. And after you had swept out all of this machinery, the present industrial order would come crashing down on your head, for it is upon this machinery that the present industrial world has been con-structed. Coming into the home, you would sweep out all the gas jets and electric lights, and the sewing machine and the photograph album, and a hundred other of the comforts and luxuries which minister to our domestic life. If the Psalm-ist could say : " Thou hast put all things under his feet, all sheep and oxen, yea, and the beasts of the field, and the fowl of the air, and the fish of the sea, and whatsoever passeth through the paths of the seas. O Lord, our Lord, how excellent is thy name in all the earth!" much more have we occasion for rejoicing who can say: Thou hast put under man's feet fire and water, wind and wave, steam and electricity, the sunbeam and the thunder-cloud, the powers of the air and the powers of the sea, and whatsoever passeth through the substance of the earth. O Lord, our Lord, how excellent is thy name in all the earth!

But right at this point we are obliged to make a confession. We must here take up the words of the writer to the Hebrews, and say, " We see not yet all things put under him." We must make the confession which James made 1900 years ago. " Every sort of beast and bird and serpent has been tamed, but the tongue no man can tame." The tongue is the organ of the heart, the heart is the centre of that mesh of forces which we call human nature. Human nature is not yet subdued, the great conquest of human history is still ahead of us. These are three pictures then: first, the conquest of man over the animal creation; second, the conquest of man over matter; and third, the conquest of man over human nature. The first picture is completed, the second picture is approaching completion, the third picture is only well begun. Uncounted ages must elapse before the finishing touches are put on. The forces of the animal world are docile, and so also are the great cosmic forces; but human appetite and human passion, the impulses and the inclinations, the soaring aspirations and the vaulting ambitions, the burning thirsts and the insatiable hungers, the devouring greeds and the fiery lusts, the implacable furies and the uncontrollable manias — all the diabolical impulses that are hell-born in the human soul — these are still in insurrection.

"We see not yet all things put under him." We are not able to use with wisdom any of the good things which the Almighty has showered upon the present generation. Ours is an age of wealth. Never since history began has so much wealth been created and accumulated. In a single century we have accumulated three times as much wealth as was accumulated in the preceding 1800 years. And we are the greatest money-makers among all the nations. We have more gold in our vaults than has any other nation on earth. We started the 19th century poor, but we closed the century jingling more dollars in our pockets than the oldest and richest of empires. But we have not yet learned how to use our wealth. Our wealth has brought on us fearful curses. It has converted thousands of young men into loafers and thousands of young women into butterflies, and sent hundreds of American homes to perdition. It has spread demoralization and ruin through large sections of the political and commercial worlds. Ours has been a century of knowledge. Men have never known so many things as they know to-day. The knowledge has been dumped before us in mountainous heaps, and the immediate effect of this expanded knowledge has been distressing. Many men know so many things that they do not know what they know. They are all bewildered and confused. They are not able to use their knowledge. As Tennyson says " Knowledge comes, but wisdom lingers." We lack the wisdom to use our knowledge. Many a man does not know in what direction to turn, and many a fixed star of hope has been dissipated into mist. We have received an enormous increase of power, but we do not use our power as the sons of God ought to use it. We have the power to travel as no other people have ever travelled. We travel swiftly and in the greatest luxury, but no other generation has been more weary than the generation living now. We have the power to print as no preceding century was ever able to print. What greater miracle than the miracle of the modern printing-press! But these printing-presses have in large numbers been seized by godless men, who use them to vitiate the public taste and debauch the public conscience, and to demoralize all our social and our religious life. We have power to produce clothing in almost unmeasured quantities; there should be no nakedness anywhere upon the earth. In four of the leading nations of the earth steam power is doing the work of five hundred and fifty millions of men. But we do not know how to direct and control this power.

Go into the mill towns of New England and the south of England or the Continent, and everywhere you find squalor and degradation. A father is working in one mill, a mother in another, while little children are locked up at home, through the long and dreary day, waiting for the mother's return at night. Home life in all our great manufacturing centres is torn to shreds between the wheels of our machinery. Those of you who have travelled down the Ohio River, beginning at Wheeling, will undoubtedly still remember the wonderful scenes which are presented to the traveller on both banks of the river. Great chimneys belching volumes of black smoke, long lines of ovens with tongues of flame reminding one of the pits of fire in Dante's Hell; all the air filled with soot and dust, and smoke hiding all the finer and sweeter and diviner aspects of our human life. You who have travelled across the continent must have felt, after leaving Omaha that you were passing into another world. One can almost feel the soil rising little by little, creeping inch by inch higher up over the soul of man, until at last, in some of the little towns in the shadow of the Rocky Mountains, one feels that the supremacy of matter over mind has reached completeness, and the soul of man is submerged completely beneath the sand. How true it is, " We see not yet all things put under him."

What shall be the effect of this picture of mingled defeat and conquest on our heart? Shall we be optimists or pessimists? Many of the most thoughtful men now alive are pessimistic in their estimates of current life. An English scientist in writing of the marvels of the 19th century devotes more pages to the failures than he gives to the successes. An English philosopher has recently written an article on " Christianity at the Grave of the 19th Century." He begins it with a moan and ends it with something between a groan and a growl. There are many who see little that is bright in the immediate future. One of the saddest-hearted of the English prophets is the distinguished artist, George Frederick Watts. One of his latest pictures is most suggestive and most depressing. At the centre of the picture there stands a great tree. A heavy robe of gold has broken down its largest limb. On one side upon the ground lies a broken cog-wheel. In the grass a champagne glass glimmers. In another place there lie two horses' hoofs filled with dice. Under the broken bough there is a skeleton, and underneath the skeleton these words are written, " Shall the dead bones rise again? " According to the interpretation of Mr. Watts the tree represents life. The heavy robe which has broken down the tree is wealth. The broken cog-wheel represents interrupted industry. The champagne glass stands for intoxication. The two horses' hoofs filled with dice suggest gambling. That, says George Frederick Watts, is my opinion of the civilization of the present time. When some of his friends suggested that it was pessimistic, he said, " Of course it is, because I cannot see how the tendency of our age toward mammonism is ever to be overcome." I do not like the hopeless pessimism of George Frederick Watts. If I were a painter and could paint the 19th century, I should paint it after this fashion : I should paint a vast and complicated machine with innumerable wheels and belts and pistons and cylinders, and I should endeavor to crowd into this one vast machine the miracles that have sprung from the brains of all the inventors that have lived through the hundred years. I should say that the machine is the embodiment of the spirit of our time. Underneath the machine I should place the figure of a man, one of his legs pinned to the earth by a part of the machine. I should make one of his hands torn and bleeding, caught between the cogs of the turning wheels, but his other hand should be outstretched, reaching upward toward a hand reaching downward from the heavens. And in his eyes I should not paint despair, but rather the light of a glorious hope caught from the eyes that closed on Calvary to open upon all the centuries as guiding stars. That should be my picture, and underneath it I should write, " But now we see not yet all things put under him, but we see Jesus."

Some men go into the new century with a shout. They gather up all the inventions and discoveries and blessings and triumphs of a

hundred years, and say: " Hurrah! What wonderful men we are!" There are others who face
the future with a whine. They rake together all
the wars, and all the savageries, and all the bar-
barities, and all the injustices, and all the agonies,
and all the Diveses with purple and fine linen,
and all the Lazaruses with their running sores —
and pointing to these, they moan, What an awful
world this is! We ought not to go into a new
century giggling over our toys or moaning over
our failures. We should not be afraid to face the
actual, but we should not lose sight of the ideal,
and we should dare to believe that by and by the
actual shall work itself into the ideal. Instead of
laughing or crying, we should go into the new
century thankful for whatsoever triumphs have
come to us, and believing that, with the help of
God, we shall win triumphs greater still. "We
see not yet all things put under him, but we see
Jesus," — the ideal man, the man in whom humanity reached its highest triumph, and who
stands as the living prophecy of what all men
shall some day be. We see Jesus, to whom every
appetite was a servant, and every passion a slave,
and who brought every impulse and every inclination into swift subjection to the law of God;
we see Jesus, who dispensed with money and reputation and ease, and all the things which men hold
dear, and still was blessed. Let us then go into
the new century, not looking at our failures, but
looking unto him! He held the 19th century

more completely in his grasp than any other century that has ever been, and he will hold the 20th century still more completely in the hollow of his hand. All centuries do round him circle, and unto him all nations, tribes, and peoples shall finally come, for he has tasted death for every man, and it is God's decree that every knee shall bow to him, and that every tongue shall some day confess that he is King of kings and Lord of lords.

GOD MANIFEST IN FLESH

GOD MANIFEST IN FLESH

"No man hath seen God at any time; the only begotten Son, which is in the bosom of the Father, he hath declared him." — John i. 18.

It is a Hebrew who says that, an illustrious representative of a race which had come the nearest to the Almighty, a man perfectly familiar with the Old Testament from its first page to its last, a man versed in the old traditions of Abraham and Isaac and Jacob, and of Moses and Elijah and Isaiah, a man who had been with Jesus of Nazareth in his deepest and most glorious experiences. He had been with Jesus on the Mount of Transfiguration, he had been with him in the upper chamber on the night in which he said, "He that hath seen me hath seen the Father." He had been with him in the Garden of Gethsemane, and also in the upper room on the evening in which Thomas exclaimed, "My Lord, and my God!" He had been present on that great day when Jesus had risen above his disciples' heads and a cloud had received him out of their sight. This is the man who says that no man hath seen God at any time. He makes it both positive and sweeping. His statement is as wide as humanity — "no man" — and as broad as history — "at any time."

If this is true, then the existence of God is uncertain and debatable. If no man has seen him at any time, then we cannot be certain that he is. We are left to wander in a region of uncertainties and shadows. Religion becomes a group of speculations and guesses. There is no longer any solid ground on which to stand. In dealing with religious beliefs we are simply walking on the clouds. Why not then let religion go, and devote ourselves exclusively to science? Science deals with things which are tangible and real. Science has a foundation on which to build, and is able to bring indisputable proofs to the support of all her hypotheses. Religion is a world of clouds, while science is solid and unmovable as rock.

So many men have said, and so many men are thinking now, but men who think so are not thinking wisely. The things with which religion has to do are just as solid and substantial as those with which science deals. A Christian is obliged to walk by faith, and so also is a scientist. A scientist cannot do anything without faith in the universe with which he experiments. Sir Isaac Newton laid it down as one of the laws of nature that every particle of matter attracts every other particle in such and such a manner. "Every particle" is rather a large expression for any man to use unless he is a man of faith. What does a scientist know about "every particle" of matter? Has he come in contact with every particle of matter? He has had a few particles of matter under his observation, and from what he has discovered in these few particles he leaps to the conclusion that all particles of matter everywhere are going to observe the same laws which he has discovered in the matter beneath his eye. This is a stupendous act of faith. Because matter does thus and thus upon the earth, the scientist has sufficient faith in the vast system of created things to say that every particle of matter, even to creation's outmost rim, will obey the same law which is dominant in the matter of our earth. The scientist says that the sun will rise at such and such a time to-morrow morning. How do you know, Mr. Scientist, that the sun is going to rise? The scientist has no answer to give, excepting that "yesterday the sun rose at such an hour, and that for thousands of years it has been rising in accordance with a certain law," and because of what the sun has been doing in other days the scientist declares by an act of faith that the sun to-morrow morning is going to be still obedient to an unchanging law. The scientist does not know that the sun will rise. He believes it will, and his belief is an act of faith. Surely no Christian should ever be disturbed by the fact that he is obliged to deal with things that are invisible; the scientist is all the time doing that. There is a mysterious something which he calls the "luminiferous ether." Without assuming the existence of this ether, he finds it impossible to account for a great many phenomena on the earth, and still more phenomena in the heavens. But the luminiferous ether is not visible, and nothing in the whole range of Christian thought could possibly be more mysterious than just this invisible, intangible something of which the scientist is always talking.

" No man at any time," of course not. No man hath seen gravitation at any time. Who knows what gravitation looks like? What is the color of it, or the odor of it, or the shape of it, or the size of it? No man at any time has gotten his eyes upon it. No man has seen heat at any time, nor electricity, nor magnetism. No force is visible to the naked eye, and of all the forces which go to make up the universe in which we live it can be truly said, no man hath seen this force at any time. God is the supreme force of the universe, why should we expect to see him when even lesser forces are hidden from our eyes. No man hath seen man at any time. We see a man's body, but not the man. A man dies, and his body is placed in the casket, and men as they look upon the cold face say: " He is gone. He is gone." The body still is there, but the man is gone. No man has ever seen a man. Who has seen the human memory? How many ounces will it weigh? Who has seen the human imagination? How many pounds will it come to? Who has seen the human reason? How many inches will it measure? Who has seen a human affection, or a human motive, or a human aspiration? How many yards are these in circumference or diameter? No man hath at any time seen a soul; how then can we expect to see the supreme person of the universe? When we say we cannot see God, we are simply saying what science is continually saying of the most common and the most indisputable realities with which scientific men have to do.

But St. John did not close his sentence when he had stated that no man had seen God at any time. He went on to say that the only begotten Son, which is in the bosom of the Father, he hath declared him. And therefore we can know God, even though we have not seen him. We cannot see a spiritual essence, but we can know its nature from its manifestations. No man hath seen gravitation at any time, but the rolling stars, the flowing rivers, the falling apple, — all these declare it. No man hath seen heat at any time, but the burning coal, the roaring furnace, the red-hot iron — these have declared it. No man hath seen electricity at any time, but the click of the instrument in the telegrapher's office, and the miles of moving cars, and the flash of a million electric lights,—all these have declared it. No man hath seen a man at any time, but his words and actions, these declare him. No man hath seen God at any time, but the only begotten Son who is in the bosom of the Father, he hath declared him.

We must, therefore, come to Jesus for our conception of the Almighty. We cannot see God in his essence, but we may study him in his manifes-

tations.   Electricity is everywhere, but we study
it where it manifests itself.   Gravitation is at
work everywhere, but we study it where it reveals
itself.   Just so it must be with our study of deity.
He is everywhere, but if we wish to know him we
must study him in his greatest act of self-revela-
tion, and that is the life and character of Jesus.

All through the 19th century the thinking
world was working its way out into a new conception of God.   The greatest revolution that took
place in all the century was the revolution in
men's conception of deity.   Men talk about the
progress of the century and hurrah over its marvellous achievements, but most of them ignore the
most marvellous movement of the century, and
that was a movement toward a clearer conception
of God as revealed in Jesus of Nazareth.   Recently one of our most enterprising papers published a remarkable series of thirty-six essays on
the progress and achievement of the 19th century.   These essays were written by experts gathered together from both sides the sea, and their
contributions are most interesting reading.   There
is one paper on the progress of astronomy, another
on geology, and another on psychological re-
search, another on photography, another on the
manufacture of steel, another on the progress of
medicine, and another on law.   There are papers
on every branch of industry and achievement, but
there is no paper on the greatest movement of the
whole century, the one which will have the widest

influence on the life of the centuries to come. Only one paper is devoted to religious conceptions, and that paper was written by a man who, because of his intense prejudices and his spiritual limitations, is totally unfit to write upon the theme assigned him. It is only another illustration of a fact which we all lament, that the public press on the whole deals with religious subjects in a very shabby and unsatisfactory manner. He who fails to understand the revolution which has been taking place in men's conception of the deity, fails to grasp the greatest fact of modern history. There are other things which appeal more strongly to the imagination, but this is the thing which goes deepest into human life, and which will most powerfully affect the future. Anybody can see the progress made in the mechanical arts. When we bring out the old stage-coach and put it down by the side of the limited express, we are ready to clap our hands like little children rejoicing over some new-bought toy. When we take Robert Fulton's steamboat, that puffed its way at the beginning of the century up the Hudson to Albany, and put it down by the side of the Oceanic, we are ready to shout out, What wonderful men we are! When we bring out the old spinning-wheel, which is still kept as a curiosity in many an American home, and put it down in the midst of the machinery that thunders and roars in our great mills, we are ready to say, What miracles men have wrought! When we compare the tallow dip with the electric light, or the telescope of Herschel with the telescope at the Lick Observatory, we are led to exclaim, No other century was half so glorious as the marvellous century which has just closed. But all these things, however wonderful, are simply bubbles floating on the stream. They do not touch the springs of life. They do not sway the hearts of men or determine the destinies of nations. What does a nation think of God? That is far more important than in what kind of carriage does it ride, or with what sort of lamp does it light its streets, or through what kind of a telescope does it view the stars. It is the conception of God which cleanses the springs of feeling, and furnishes fresh motives, and carves out new ideals, and creates the stores of knowledge by means of which humanity achieves its destiny. Through the last hundred years thinking men have been working their way out into a conception of God which is going to leave its impress on civilization and renew the life of the next thousand years.

Many of us who are not acquainted with the nature or existence of this revolution, know that something has been going on. Certain things have been presented to our eyes which we have not been able to account for because we have not understood the currents which are flowing swiftly beneath the surface of our modern life. No man can understand the present age unless he understands the nature of this revolution in the idea of

God. It is continually being asserted that the ancient creeds have lost their grip on thinking men. This is undoubtedly true. Nowhere do the creeds of the Christian church retain their hold on men with anything like the grip which they had fifty years ago. The amount of scepticism even in the Christian church is appalling. It is a kind of scepticism which is peculiar to our own day and generation. It is not the loud-mouthed, vindictive scepticism which was rampant in France in the days of Voltaire, it is not the supercilious, patronizing scepticism which filled all England in the days of Bishop Butler. It is not the coarse, brutal scepticism of Bradlaugh or Ingersoll; it is the scepticism that is quiet and silent, a scepticism that does not utter itself, but which pervades all society and honeycombs the whole body of the Christian church. That is the scepticism which we have in New York City. Outwardly the Christian church in New York City is loyal to the old faith, but inwardly it is full of scepticism. Men do not talk their scepticism here with half the freedom that is manifest in many another city, but the scepticism none the less exists and is the root cause of all our troubles. It does not openly attack the Christian faith, it has no word of scorn for Christ or for any of his teachings. It is a scepticism which manifests itself in apathy and indifference. It silently ignores the great problems which Christianity presents. Men and women are interested in other things. They are preoccupied, and little room is left in their crowded weeks for the great mysteries of the Christian faith. The great masses of professing Christians are outwardly respectful to the old traditions, but within them there are doubts to which they do not give expression. What is the cause of this scepticism? The world is discarding the old conception of deity, and is working itself into the newer and larger idea. We are in a transition age, and all transition ages are filled with perplexities and confusions. What is the matter with our seminaries? The life in every one of them is troubled. In some of them the commotion is manifest and notorious, in others it is carefully hidden, but in every seminary throughout the land the same forces are ceaselessly at work. There is a sputtering and an effervescing, and now and then an explosion. What does it all mean? It means that the scholars of the Christian world are working their way out into a new conception of God. And with this new conception it is necessary to rewrite our whole system of divinity. Along with the old conception of God the whole fabric which was built upon it must go. With the new conception of God it is necessary to restate the whole doctrine of inspiration, the doctrine of the atonement, and the doctrine of the incarnation. Christ has said to our age, " Behold, I make all things new."

And now let us endeavor to see just what is

the nature of this transformation which has been taking place in men's conception of the deity. The process has been a long one, and only the general outlines of the movement can be sketched. To state the entire movement in a sentence, we may say that in the 19th century the world passed from the conception of a God outside the universe to the conception of a God who is the indwelling life of his creation. For convenience we may call the first conception the Augustinian conception. Augustine was a Roman of the 5th century of the Christian era — a man of burning passion and marvellous intellect, who by the strength of his genius stamped his ideas upon the entire Western church. His influence has continued to the present hour. All of us grew up under the influence of the Augustinian theology. I say all of us, because Calvinism is nothing more than Augustinianism elaborated and worked out to its logical conclusion. According to the Augustinian theology, God is outside the universe. In Carlyle's phrase, "An absentee God outside the world, watching it go." Augustine got his conception of deity from the gnostics, who were the philosophers of his day. According to their idea God is infinitely removed from our humanity, and in order to bridge the chasm they conceived a long series of supernatural beings which they called "æons" stretching from man all the way up to God. The gnostics had gotten their ideas from Plato, who in one of his most remarkable works pictures God in a far-off heaven, separated by an infinite distance from vile matter, the matter with which it is necessary for him to work. That was the idea not only of Plato, but also of Epicurus, and many others of the greatest of the Greek philosophers. The conception of Plato was taken up by Augustine and worked out into a marvellous theology. That conception of deity was dominant in Christendom for 1500 years. You will find it in all the theologians from Thomas Aquinas to Charles Hodge. Augustinianism is the theology of Dante in his "Divine Comedy." It is the theology of John Milton in his "Paradise Lost." It is the theology of John Bunyan in his "Pilgrim's Progress." In all these immortal masterpieces of the human mind God is a Being separated from our humanity by a chasm which it is necessary to bridge.

But this is a conception of deity which the modern world is no longer able to retain. The "Divine Comedy" is interesting, but its theology has no attraction for us. Bunyan's "Pilgrim's Progress" will always have a fascination because of its fidelity to human nature, but it does not teach the central doctrine of the New Testament. The Augustinian theology is responsible for a large amount of the confusion and the doubt of the present age, and our only deliverance lies in following the leadership of the Christian church, which through the last hundred years has been working its way up to the conception of God which was given to the world by Jesus of Nazareth.

This movement toward Christ began near the beginning of the century. At the opening of the century there stood four young men, all of them about thirty years of age, two in Germany and two in England, — which four may be considered the fathers of modern thought. The first of the four was Schleiermacher, the greatest theologian of the 19th century — a man who turned the current of all theological discussion, and has left his mark on almost every thoughtful minister who has lived within the last fifty years. Schleiermacher saw that the Augustinian conception of deity was untenable, and boldly travelled back beyond the Latin theologians until he came to Origen and Clement of Alexandria. To him God was the indwelling life of the world, not separated by a chasm from humanity, but the Being in whom all created things exist. The other young man in Germany was Hegel, the greatest philosopher of the 19th century. The central idea of his entire philosophical system is that God is immanent in his creation. The two young men in England were Wordsworth and Coleridge, — the first a poet and the second a theologian. All high poetry for a hundred years has testified to the influence of Wordsworth, and the deepest theology has borne the impress of the genius of Coleridge. Both these men saw God in his world. The most illustrious disciple of Coleridge was Frederick

Denison Maurice, the figure that fills the centre of the century with glory. Principal Tulloch says that he was the most God-intoxicated man since Spinoza, and William E. Gladstone called him a "spiritual splendor." All of the theology of Maurice is organized around the great thought that every man is created in Christ. It was about forty years ago that science came to the rescue with its idea of development. Ever since the publication of Darwin's epoch-making book, "The Origin of Species," leaders in the scientific world have been furnishing new illustrations of the fact that God is the indwelling life of nature. It was first supposed that the doctrine of evolution was going to undermine the foundations of all religious faith, but in the hands of Professor Drummond in the Old World and Mr. John Fiske in our own country, the doctrine has become a powerful ally of the Christian faith. Matter is no longer dead, matter is alive. We used to speak of the "dead clod" — nobody would speak so nowadays. A clod is not dead, it throbs and pulsates with energy. A clod is a living thing, so also is all matter. Matter is a form of energy, and all energy proceeds from God. In the light of the teachings of the latest science the old idea of a God outside the world, seeing it go, is absolutely untenable. God is in the world. God is in humanity. All leaders of thought everywhere are going back to the theology of the early Greek church — to sit at the feet of Athanasius and Origen and Clement of Alexandria. They are going back beyond these theologians and teachers to John, the beloved disciple. The world is coming back to the New Testament. Augustine has had his day, henceforth we are going to listen to Jesus. The conception which science supports, and the conception which the latest theology holds, is the conception announced by John in the first chapter of his Gospel. " All things were made by him, and without him was not anything made that was made." " In him was life, and the life was the light of men. That was the true light which lights every man that cometh into the world. He was in the world, and the world was made by him, and the world knew him not. He came unto his own, and his own received him not. The Word was made flesh, and dwelt among us full of grace and truth." Where did John get his conception? He got it from Jesus of Nazareth. Listen to the carpenter of Nazareth, as he says to the woman at the well, " God is a spirit, and they that worship him must worship in spirit and truth." Listen to him as he says to his disciples, " I am the vine, ye are the branches." Listen to him as he says in the upper chamber on the night in which he was betrayed, " I in you, and you in me." It was the teaching of Jesus that God is in his world. Not a sparrow falls to the ground without his notice. Not a hair of a man's head remains uncounted. Because all these things exist in God. If God is indeed in his creation, then the whole doctrine of

the incarnation becomes natural and credible.
According to the old idea, at a certain point in
human history the Son of God left the shining
court of heaven and came down through the infinite spaces to this little earth, lived here for thirty-
three years, and then disappeared into space again.
The whole story could be believed so long as men
thought the earth to be the centre of the universe;
but when modern science revealed the fact that
the earth is but a grain of sand upon an infinite
shore, one tiny wave upon a boundless sea, when
she uncovered to our eyes vast systems of worlds
stretching out into infinite spaces, men were no
longer able to accept the old story of the Son of
God coming down to dwell with men.   But suppose that God is in his world, and that he has always been in it; suppose that Christ is the name of
this eternal God; suppose that in him all men
from the beginning have had their life, that man's
reason derives its light from the infinite reason;
suppose that ever since man began to live upon the
earth, deity has dwelt in him, and that all man's
aspirations and hopes and dreams have been the
creation of the Eternal Spirit; suppose that God
has been in human history through all the centuries, — why should it be deemed incredible that
at a certain point he should flash upon the world
with a new and unique glory? If he has been present in the life of humanity from the beginning,
why should not his life break out in articulate utterance, and why should not his purpose become

clear and glorious in a man chosen to be the organ
of his will? If God is the indwelling life of men,
then an incarnation is only what might have been
expected. As soon as Jesus had lived his life, all
preceding centuries turned round and looked at
him, and said, " Ah, here we find the realization
of all our aspirations and the consummation of all
our dreams." And ever since his day all succeed-
ing centuries have looked toward him and acknowledged that in his mind and heart they behold
the ideal toward which humanity must work.
Not only was Christ always in the world before
he was manifested in flesh in Galilee, but he never
went away. Christ has not left the earth. God
cannot leave the world. He is in the world, has
always been in it, and will remain in it until the
end. It is said that a cloud received Jesus out of
men's sight, but the New Testament does not say
that a cloud took him out of men's lives. Did
not Jesus expressly say, that " Where two or three
are assembled there am I in their midst "? Did
he not say, " Lo, I am with you alway, even unto
the end of the world "? He is the indwelling life
of our humanity, and " In him," as Paul says,
" all things consist," and without him we should
have no life, no light, no love.

If, then, we are to come to Jesus for our conception of the deity, we are to think of God first of
all as present in his world. There is no chasm between humanity and God. Epicurus was mistaken, and so was Plato, and so were the gnostics,

and so was Augustine. There is not an infinite chasm between deity and the human soul. Human nature is God's nature, God's nature is human nature. God has always been human. He did not become human 1900 years ago. Our nature is what it is because God's nature is what it is. God can manifest himself in the form of man because his nature is human, and can express itself under the limitations of our humanity. The central truth of the Christian religion is that God is human, and that we, as the Scriptures say, are created in the image of God.

Not only is God in the world as the source of its life, but he is in humanity as a comforter and guide. He is the friend of publicans and sinners. It was the teaching of Epicurus that God is indifferent to the woes and wants of men. He lives in ideal blessedness, unresponsive to the cries that come up from tortured hearts. But according to the teachings of Jesus, God is in the world. He is with sinners, with men that have lost the way, with men that are burdened, perplexed, discouraged. He is interested in men, sympathizes with them, bears their burdens, heals their wounds. He is not a God afar off, but a God who sympathizes with us in all our experiences, and yearns to make us one with him.

Read history in the light of this conception, and every page of it becomes the page of a vast Bible in whose glowing sentences we read the will of the Almighty. Read nature in the light of this conception, and the whole universe becomes a burning bush, and the ground on which we stand is holy. Let us read our own life in the light of this conception, and our body becomes the temple of the spirit of the Eternal God. All our troubles become endurable, and our heart comes into the possession of peace and joy. God is with us — Immanuel: God in us and we in him.

THE RECONCILIATION

THE RECONCILIATION

"Christ died for our sins." — I Cor. xv. 3.

I WANT to think with you this morning about
the doctrine of the Atonement. Having used
that word *atonement* once, I now wish to drop it.
It is not a New Testament word, and is apt to
lead one into confusion. You will not find it in
your New Testament at all, providing you use
the Revised Version. It is found in the King
James Version only once, and that is in the fifth
chapter of Paul's Letter to the Romans, but a few
years ago, when the revisers went to work, they
rubbed out the word and would allow it no place
whatever in the entire New Testament. They
substituted for it a better word — *reconciliation*
— and that is the word that will probably be used
in the future theology of the church. It is my
purpose, then, this morning, to think with you
about the doctrine of the reconciliation, or, to put
it in a way that will be intelligible to all the boys
and girls, I want to think with you about the
" making up " between God and man.

Christianity is distinctively a religion of redemption. Its fundamental purpose is to recover
men from the guilt and power of sin. All of its

39

history and its teachings must be studied in the
light of that dominating purpose. We are told
sometimes that Jesus was a great teacher, and so
he was, but the apostles never gloried in that fact.
We are constantly reminded that he was a great
reformer, and so he was, but Peter and John and
Paul seemed to be altogether unconscious of that
fact. It is asserted that he was a great philan-
thropist, a man intensely interested in the bodies
and the homes of men, and so of course he was,
but the New Testament does not seem to care for
that. It has often been declared that he was a
great martyr, a man who laid down his life in
devotion to the truth, and so he was and so he
did, but the Bible never looks at him from that
standpoint or regards him in that light. It refuses
to enroll him among the teachers or reformers or
philanthropists or the martyrs of our race.
According to the apostolic writers, Jesus is the
world's Redeemer, he was manifested to take
away sin. He is the Lamb of God that taketh
away the sin of the world. The vast and awful
fact that broke the apostles' hearts and sent them
out into the world to baptize the nations into his
name, was the fact which Paul was all the time
asserting, " He died for our sins."

No one can read the New Testament without
seeing that its central and most conspicuous fact
is the death of Jesus. Take, for instance, the
Gospels, and you will find that over one-quarter
of their pages are devoted to the story of his

death. Very strange is this indeed, if Jesus was nothing but an illustrious teacher. A thousand interesting events of his career are passed over, a thousand discourses are never mentioned, in order that there may be abundant room for the telling of his death. Or take the Letters which make up the last half of the New Testament; in these Letters there is scarcely a quotation from the lips of Jesus. Strange indeed is this if Jesus is only the world's greatest teacher. The Letters seem to ignore that he was a teacher or reformer, but every letter is soaked in the pathos of his death. There must be a deep and providential reason for all this. The character of the Gospels and the Letters must have been due to something that Jesus said or that the Holy Spirit inbreathed. A study of the New Testament will convince us that Jesus had trained his disciples to see in his sufferings and death the climax of God's crowning revelation to the world. The keynote of the whole Gospel story is struck by John the Baptist in his bold declaration, " Behold the Lamb of God, which taketh away the sin of the world." In that declaration there was a reference to his death, for the " lamb " in Palestine lived only to be slain. As soon as Jesus began his public career he began to refer in enigmatic phrases to his death. He did not declare his death openly, but the thought of it was wrapped up inside of all he said. Nicodemus comes to him at night to have a talk with him about his work, and among other things, Jesus says, " As Moses lifted up the serpent in the wilderness, so shall the Son of Man be lifted up." Nicodemus did not know what he meant, — we know. He goes into the temple and drives out the men who have made it a den of thieves, and when an angry mob surrounds him he calmly says, " Destroy this temple, and in three days I will raise it up." They did not know what he meant, — we know. He goes into the city of Capernaum, and is surrounded by a great crowd who seem to be eager to know the way of life. He begins to talk to them about the bread that comes down from heaven, and among other things he says, " The bread which I will give is my flesh, which I will give for the life of the world." They did not understand what he said, — we understand it now. One day in the city of Jerusalem he utters a great discourse upon the good shepherd. " I am the good shepherd," he says; " the good shepherd giveth his life for the sheep." They did not understand him, — we do. In the last week of his earthly life it was reported that a company of Greeks had come to see him. He falls at once into a thoughtful mood, and when at last he speaks it is to say that " I, if I be lifted up, will draw all men unto me." The men standing by did not understand what he said, — we understand. All along his journey, from the Jordan to the cross, he dropped such expressions as this, " I have a baptism to be baptized with; and how am I straitened till it be accomplished." Men did not know what he was saying, — it is all clear now.

But while he did not talk openly to the world about his death, he did not hesitate to speak about it to his nearest friends. As soon as he found a man willing to confess that he was indeed the world's Messiah, the Son of the Living God, he began to initiate his disciples into the deeper mysteries of his mission. " From that time," Matthew says, " he began to show, to unfold, to set forth, the fact that he must suffer many things and be killed." Peter tried to check him in this disclosure, but Jesus could not be checked. It is surprising how many times it is stated in the Gospels that Jesus told his disciples he must be killed. Matthew says that while they were travelling in Galilee, on a certain day when the disciples were much elated over the marvellous things which he was doing, he took them aside and said, " Let these words sink into your ears : I am going to Jerusalem to be killed." Later on, when they were going through Perea, Jesus took them aside and said, " The Son of Man must suffer many things, and at last be put to death." On nearing Jerusalem his disciples became impatient for a disclosure of his power and glory. He began to tell them about the grace of humility. " The Son of Man," he said, " is come, not to be ministered unto, but to minister, and to give his life a ransom for many." On the last Tuesday of his earthly life he sat with his disciples on the

slope of the Mount of Olives, and in the midst
of his high and solemn teaching he said, "It
is only two days now until I shall be crucified." And on the last Thursday of his life,
on the evening of his betrayal, he took his disciples
into an upper room, and taking the bread and
blessing it, he gave it to these men, saying, "This
is my body which is given for you." Likewise
after supper he took the cup, and when he had
blessed it he gave it to them, saying, "This is my
blood of the covenant which is shed for you and
for many for the remission of sins. Do this in remembrance of me." It would seem from this that
the one thing which Jesus was desirous that all his
followers should remember was the fact that he
had laid down his life for them. One cannot read
the Gospels without feeling that he is being borne
steadily and irresistibly toward the cross.

When we get out of the Gospels into the Epistles we find ourselves face to face with the same
tragic and glorious fact. Peter's first letter is not
a theological treatise. He is not writing a disser-
tation on the person of Christ, or attempting to
give any interpretation of the death of Jesus; he is
dealing with very practical matters. He exhorts
the Christians who are discouraged and down-
hearted to hold up their heads and to be brave.
It is interesting to see how again and again he
puts the cross behind them in order to keep them
from slipping back. "Endure," he says, "because Christ suffered for us. Who his own self

bore our sins in his own body on the tree." The Christians of that day had been overtaken by furious persecution. They were suffering all sorts of hardships and disappointments. But " suffer," he says, " because Christ has once suffered for sins, the just for the unjust, that he might bring us to God." Certainly the Gospel, according to St. Peter, was: Christ died for our sins.

Read the first Letter of St. John, and everywhere it breathes the same spirit which we have found in the Gospels and in St. Peter. John punctuates almost every paragraph with some reference to the cross. In the first chapter he is talking about sin. " The blood of Jesus Christ," he says, " cleanses us from all sins." In the second chapter he is talking about forgiveness, and this leads him to think at once of Jesus Christ, the righteous, " who is the propitiation for our sins, and not for ours only, but for the sins of the whole world." In the third chapter he is talking about brotherly love. He is urging the members of the church to lay down their lives, one for another. " Hereby perceive we the love of God, because he laid down his life for us." In the fourth chapter he tells of the great mystery of Christ's love: " Herein is love, not that we loved God, but that he loved us, and sent his Son to be the propitiation for our sins." To the beloved disciple, evidently, the great fact of the Christian revelation is that Christ died for our sins.

But it is in the Letters of Paul that we find the

fullest and most emphatic assertion of this transcendent fact. It will not be possible for me to
quote to you even a half of what he said on the
subject. If you should cut out of his Letters all
the references to the cross, you would leave his
Letters in tatters. Listen to him as he talks to his
converts in Corinth: " First of all I delivered unto
you that which I also received, how that Christ
died for our sins." That was the foremost fact
to be stated in every letter, and to be unfolded in
every sermon. To Saul of Tarsus, Jesus is not
an illustrious Rabbi whose sentences are to be
treasured up and repeated to listening congregations; he is everywhere and always the world's
Redeemer. And throughout all of Paul's epistles
one hears the same jubilant, triumphant declaration, " I live by the faith of the Son of God, who
loved me and gave himself for me."

Let us now turn to the last book of the New
Testament, the Book of the Revelation. What
does this prophet on the Isle of Patmos see and
hear, as he looks out into future ages and coming
worlds? The book begins with a doxology:
" Unto him that loved us, and washed us from
our sins in his own blood, to him be glory and
dominion forever and ever." John looks, and
beholds a great company of the redeemed. He
asks who these are, and the reply comes back,
" These are they who have washed their robes
and made them white in the blood of the Lamb."
He listens, and the song that goes up from the

throats of the redeemed is, " Worthy art thou to take the book, and to open the seals thereof; for thou wast slain and didst purchase us for God with thy blood." At the centre of the great vision which bursts upon the soul of the exiled apostle, there is a lamb that was slain. Whatever we may think of Jesus of Nazareth, there is no question concerning what the men who wrote the New Testament thought. To the men who wrote this book Jesus was not a Socrates or a Seneca, a Martin Luther or an Abraham Lincoln. His life was not an incident in the process of evolution, his death was not an episode in the dark and dreadful tragedy of human history. His life is God's greatest gift to men, his death is the climax and the crowning revelation of the heart of the eternal. You cannot open the New Testament anywhere without the idea flying into your face, " Christ died for our sins."

How different all this is from the atmosphere of the modern church. When you go into the average church to-day, what great idea meets you? Do you find yourselves face to face with the fact that Christ died for our sins? I do not think you will often hear that great truth preached. In all probability you will hear a sermon dealing with the domestic graces, or with business obligations, or with political duties and complications. You may hear a sermon on city missions, or on foreign missions; you may hear a man dealing with some great evil, or pointing out

some alarming danger, or discussing some interesting social problem, or urging upon men's consciences the performance of some duty. It is not
often in these modern days that you will hear a
sermon dealing with the thought that set the
apostles blazing and turned the world upside
down. And right there, I think, lies one of the
causes of the weaknesses of the modern church.
We have been so busy attending to the things that
ought to be done, we have had no time to feed the
springs that keep alive these mighty hopes which
make us Christian men. What is the secret of
the strength of the Roman Catholic church?
How is it that she pursues her conquering way, in
spite of stupidities and blunders that would have
killed any other institution? I know the explanations that are usually offered, but it seems to
me they are far from adequate. Somebody says,
but the Roman Catholic church does not hold any
but the ignorant. That is not true. It may be
true of certain localities in America, but it is not
true in the nations across the sea. In Europe she
holds entire nations in the hollow of her hand.
Not only the ignorant, but the learned, not only
the low, but the high, not only the rude, but the
cultured, the noble, and the mighty. It will not
do to say that the Roman Catholic church holds
nobody but the ignorant. But even if it were
true, it would still be interesting to ascertain how
she exercises such an influence over the minds and
hearts of ignorant people — for ignorant people

are the hardest of all to hold. When you say that
the church can hold ignorant men, you are giving
her the very highest compliment, for you are
acknowledging that she is in the possession of a
power which demands an explanation. The very
fact that she is able to bring out such hosts of
wage-earning men and women in the early hours
of Sunday morning, men and women who have
worked hard through the week, and many of them
far into the night, but who are willing on the
Lord's Day to wend their way to the House of
God and engage in religious worship, is a phenomenon which is worth thinking about. How
does the Roman Catholic church do it? Somebody says she does it all by appealing to men's
fears, she scares men into penitence and devotion. Do you think that that is a fair explanation? I do not think so. I can conceive how she
might frighten people for one generation, or for
two, but I cannot conceive how she could frighten
a dozen generations. One would suppose that the
spell would wear off by and by. There is a deeper
explanation than that. The explanation is to be
found in the spiritual nature of man. The Roman
Catholic leaders, notwithstanding their blunders
and their awful sins, have always seen that the
central fact of the Christian revelation is the
death of Jesus, and around that fact they have
organized all their worship. Roman Catholics go
to mass — what is the mass? It is the celebra-
tion of the Lord's Supper. What is the Lord's

Supper? It is the ceremony that proclaims our Lord's death until he comes. The hosts of worshippers that fill our streets in the early Sunday morning hours are not going to church to hear some man discuss an interesting problem, nor are they going to listen to a few singers sing; they are going to celebrate once more the death of the Saviour of the world. In all her cathedrals Catholicism places the stations of the cross that they may tell to the eye the story of the stages of his dying. On all her altars she keeps the crucifix. Before the eyes of every faithful Catholic that crucifix is held until his eyes close in death. A Catholic goes out of the world thinking of Jesus crucified. So long as a church holds on to that great fact, she will have a grip on human minds and hearts that cannot be broken. The cross, as St. Paul said, a stumbling-block to the Jews, and foolishness to the Greeks, is the power of God unto salvation to every one that believes. The Catholic church has picked up the fact of Jesus' death and held it aloft like a burning torch. Around the torch she has thrown all sorts of dark philosophies, but through the philosophies the light has streamed into the hearts and homes of millions of God's children.

Protestantism has prospered just in proportion as she has kept the cross at the forefront of all her preaching. The missionaries bring back the same report from every field, that it is the story of Jesus' death that opens the hearts of the pagan world. Every now and then a denomination has started, determined to get rid of the cross of Jesus, or at least to pay scant attention to it, and in every case those denominations have been at the end of the third or fourth generation either decaying or dead. There is no interpretation of the Christian religion that has in it redeeming power which ignores or belittles the death of Christ.

If Protestantism to-day is not doing what it ought to do, and is manifesting symptoms which are alarming to Christian leaders, it is because she has in these recent years been engaged so largely in practical duties as to forget to drink inspiration from the great doctrines which must forever furnish life and strength and hope. If you will allow me to prophesy this morning, I predict that the preaching of the next fifty years will be far more doctrinal than the preaching of the last fifty years has been. I imagine some of you will shudder at that. You say you do not like doctrinal preaching, you want preaching that is practical. Well, pray, what is practical preaching? Practical preaching is preaching that accomplishes the object for which preaching is done, and the primary object of all Christian preaching is to reconcile men to God. The experience of 1900 years proves that it is only doctrinal preaching that reconciles the heart to God. If, then, you really want practical preaching, the only preaching that is deserving the name is preaching that deals with the great Christian doctrines. But

somebody says, I do not like doctrinal preaching.
A great many people have said that within recent
years. I do not believe they mean what they say.
They are not expressing with accuracy what is
in their mind. They do like doctrinal preaching
if they are intelligent, faithful Christians, for
doctrinal preaching is bread to hearts that have
been born again. When people say they do not
like doctrinal preaching, they often mean that
they do not like preaching which belongs to the
eighteenth or seventeenth or sixteenth centuries.
They are not to be blamed for this. There is nothing that gets stale so soon as preaching. We
cannot live upon the preaching of a bygone age.
If preachers bring out the interpretations and
phraseology which were current a hundred years
ago, people must of necessity say, "Oh, please
do not give us that, we do not like such doctrinal
preaching." But doctrinal preaching need not be
antiquated or belated, it may be fresh, it may be
couched in the language in which men were born,
it may use for its illustrations the images and
figures and analogies which are uppermost in
men's imagination. And whenever it does this
there is no preaching which is so thrilling and up-
lifting and mighty as the preaching which deals
with the great fundamental doctrines.

In one sense, the Christian religion never
changes, in another sense it is changing all the
time. The facts of Christianity never change, the
interpretations of those facts alter from age to

age. It is with religion as it is with the stars, the stars never change. They move in their orbits in our night sky as they moved in the night sky of Abraham when he left his old Chaldean home. The constellations are the same at the opening of our century as they were when David watched his flocks on the old Judean hills. But the interpretations of the stars have always changed, must always change. Pick up the old charts which the astrologers made and compare them with the charts of astronomers of our day. How vast the difference! Listen to our astronomers talk about the magnitudes and distances and composition of the stars, and compare with their story that which was written in the astronomy of a few centuries ago. The stellar universe has not changed, but men's conceptions have changed amazingly. The facts of the human body do not change. Our heart beats as the heart of Homer beat, our blood flows as the blood of Julius Cæsar flowed, our muscles and nerves live and die as the nerves and muscles have lived and died in the bodies of men in all the generations — and yet, how the theories of medicine have been altered from time to time. A doctor does not want to hear a medical lecturer speak who persists in using the phraseology and conceptions which were accepted by the medical science of fifty years ago. Conceptions become too narrow to fit the growing mind of the world, and when once outgrown they must be thrown aside. As it is in science, so it is in religion. The facts of Christianity never change, they are fixed stars in the firmament of moral truth.   Forever and forever it will be true that Christ died for our sins, but the interpretations of this fact must be determined by the intelligence of the age.   Men will never be content with simple facts, they must go behind them to find out an explanation of them.   Man is a rational being, he must think, he will not sit down calmly in front of a fact and be content with looking it in the face, he will go behind it and ask how came it to be and what are its relations to other facts.   That is what man has always been doing with the facts of the Christian revelation, he has been going behind them and bringing out interpretations which will account for them.   The interpretations are good for a little while, and then they are outgrown and cast aside.

A good illustration of the progressive nature of theology is found in the doctrine of the atonement.   All of the apostles taught distinctly that Christ died for our sins.   The early Christians did not attempt to go behind that fact, but by and by men began to attempt explanations.   In the second century a man by the name of Irenæus seized upon the word " ransom " in the sentence, " The Son of man is come to give his life a ransom for many " and found in that word " ransom " the keyword of the whole problem. The explanation of Irenæus was taken up in the third century by a distinguished preacher, Origen.   And in the fourth century the teaching of

Origen was elaborated by Gregory of Nyssa. According to the interpretation of these men, Jesus was the price paid for the redemption of men. Paul frequently used the word redemption, and the word had definite meanings to people who lived in the first four centuries of the Christian era. If Christ was indeed a ransom, the question naturally arose, who paid the price? The answer was, God. A ransom must be paid to somebody — to whom was this ransom paid? The answer was, the Devil. According to Origen and to Gregory, God paid the Devil the life of Jesus in order that the Devil might let humanity go free. The Devil, by deceit, had tricked man, and man had become his slave — God now plays a trick upon the Devil, and by offering him the life of Jesus, secures the release of man. That was the interpretation held by many theologians for almost a thousand years, but in the eleventh century there arose a man who was not satisfied with the old interpretation. The world had outgrown it. To many it seemed ridiculous, to some it seemed blasphemous. There was an Italian by the name of Anselm who was an earnest student of the Scriptures, and he seized upon the word " debt " as the keyword of the problem. He wrote a book, one of the epoch-making books of Christendom, which he called " Cur deus homo." In this book Anselm elaborated his interpretation of the reconciliation. " Sin," he said, " is debt, and sin against an infinite being is an infinite debt. A finite being cannot pay an infinite debt, hence an infinite being must become man in order that the debt may be paid. The Son of God, therefore, assumes the form of man, and by his sufferings on the cross pays the debt which allows humanity to go free." The interpretation was an advance upon that of Origen and Gregory, but it was not final. It was repudiated by men of the twelfth and thirteenth centuries, and finally, in the day of the Reformation, it was either modified or cast away altogether. Martin Luther, Calvin, and the other reformers seized upon the word " propitiation," and made that the starting-point of their interpretation. According to these men, God is a great governor and man has broken the divine law — transgressors must be punished — if the man who breaks the law is not punished, somebody else must be punished in his stead. The Son of God, therefore, comes to earth to suffer in his person the punishment that rightly belongs to sinners. He is not guilty, but the sins of humanity are imputed to him, and God wreaks upon him the penalty which rightfully should have fallen on the heads of sinners. That is known as " the penal substitution theory." It was not altogether satisfactory, many men revolted from it, and in the seventeenth century a Dutchman, Hugo Grotius, a lawyer, brought forth another interpretation, which is known in theology as " the governmental theory." He would not admit that Christ was punished. His sufferings were not penal, but illustrative. " God is the moral governor," said Grotius, " his government must be maintained, law cannot be broken with impunity. Unless sin is punished the dignity of God's government would be destroyed. Therefore, that man may see how hot is God's displeasure against sin, Christ comes into the world and suffers the consequences of the transgressions of the race. The cross is an exhibition of what God thinks of sin." That governmental theory was carried into England and became the established doctrine of the English church for almost three hundred years. It was carried across the ocean and became the dominant theory in the New Haven school of theologians, as represented by Jonathan Edwards, Dwight, and Taylor. The Princeton school of theology still clung to the penal substitution theory, and it was the clashing of the New Haven school and the Princeton school which caused such a commotion in the Presbyterian church of sixty years ago. But all of these theories have been outgrown. They are antiquated. They are too little. They seem mechanical, artificial, trivial. We can say of the governmental theory what Dr. Hodge said, " It degrades the work of Christ to the level of a governmental contrivance." If I should attempt to preach to you the governmental theory as it was preached by theologians fifty years ago, you would not be interested in it. There is nothing in you that would respond to it. You would

simply say, " I do not like doctrinal preaching."
Or if I should go back and take up the penal substitution theory in all its nakedness and hideous-
ness, and attempt to give it to you as the correct
interpretation of the Gospel, you would rise up in
open rebellion and say, " We will not listen to such
preaching." If I should go back and take up the
Anselmic theory and attempt to show how an
infinite debt must be paid by infinite suffering,
you would say: " Stop, you are converting God
into a Shylock, who is demanding his pound of
flesh. We prefer to think of him as our Heavenly
Father." If I should go farther back and take
up the old ransom theory of Origen and Gregory,
I suspect that some of you would want to laugh.
You could not accept an interpretation which
represents God as playing a trick upon Satan in
order to get humanity out of his grasp. No, those
theories have all been outgrown. We have come
out into larger and grander times. We have
higher conceptions of the Almighty than the
ancients ever had. We see far deeper into the
Christian revelation than Martin Luther or John
Calvin ever saw. These old interpretations are
simply husks, and men and women will not listen
to the preaching of them. If, now and then, a
belated preacher attempts to preach them, the
people say, " If that is doctrinal preaching, please
give us something practical."

And so the church is to-day slowly working
out a new interpretation of the great fact that

Christ died for our sins. The interpretation has not yet been completed, and will not be for many years. I should like this morning simply to outline in a general way some of the more prominent features of the new interpretation. The Holy Ghost is at work. He is taking the things of Christ and showing them unto us. The interpretation of the reconciliation of the future will be superior in every point to any of the interpretations of the past.

I. The new interpretation is going to be simple, straightforward, and natural. The death of Christ is not going to be made something artificial, mechanical, or theatrical. It is going to be the natural conception of the outflowing life of God.

II. The new interpretation is going to start from the fatherhood of God. The old theories were all born in the counting-room, or the court-house. Jesus went into the home to find his illustrations for the conduct of the Heavenly Father. He never went into the court-house, nor can we go there for analogies with which to image forth his dealings with our race. It was his custom to say, " If you, being evil, know how to give good gifts unto your children, how much more shall your Father which is in heaven give good things to them that ask him."

III. The new interpretation is going to be comprehensive. It is going to be built, not on a single metaphor, but on everything that Jesus and the

apostles said. Right there is where the old interpretations went astray. They seized upon one
figure of speech and made that the determining
factor in the entire interpretation. Jesus said
many things, and so did his apostles, and all of
them must contribute to the final interpretation.

IV. Two things are to be hereafter made very
clear: The first is that God reveals himself in
Jesus Christ. The old views were always losing
sight of that great fact. There was always a
dualism between God and Christ. I remember
what my conception was when I was a boy. I
thought that God was a strict and solemn and
awful king who was very angry because men
had broken his law. He was just, and his justice
had no mercy in it. Christ, his Son, was much
better-natured and more compassionate, and he
came forth into our world to suffer upon the
cross that God's justice might relax a little, and
his heart be opened to forgive our race. I supposed that that was the teaching of the New
Testament, it certainly was the teaching of the
hymns in the hymn-book, if not of the preachers.
And when I became a young man, I supposed
that that was the teaching of the Christian
religion. My heart rebelled against it. I would
not accept it. I became an infidel. A man cannot accept an interpretation of God that does not
appeal to the best that is in him. No man can
accept a doctrine that darkens his moral sense,
or that confuses the distinction between right and

wrong. I would not accept the old interpretation because my soul rose in revolt against it. I shall never forget how, one evening in his study, a minister, who had outgrown the old traditions, explained to me the meaning of the reconciliation. He assured me that God is love, invisible, eternal. Christ, his Son, is also love. The Son becomes visible that we may see God. In becoming at one with the Son we become at one with the Father. This is the at-one-ment. And when that truth broke upon me, my heart began to sing : —

> " Just as I am — thy love unknown
> Hath broken every barrier down ;
> Now, to be thine, yea, thine alone,
> O Lamb of God, I come ! "

I wonder in telling this if I have not spoken the experience of many of you this morning. It is impossible to love God if we feel that he is stern and despotic, and must be appeased by the suffer-ings of an innocent man. The New Testament nowhere lends any support to that idea. Every-where the New Testament assures us that God is a lover of men, that he initiates the movement for man's redemption. "God so loved the world that he gave his only be-gotten Son. . . . " "Herein is love : not that we loved God, but that he loved us." "God com-mendeth his love toward us, in that, while we were yet sinners, Christ died for us." "The Father spared not his own Son, but delivered him up for us all." "He that hath seen me hath

seen the Father." "I and my Father are one."
These are only a few of the passages in which we
are told that God is our Saviour. When an old
Scotchman once heard the text announced, "God
so loved the world that he gave his only begotten
Son," he exclaimed, "Oh, that was love indeed!
I could have given myself, but I never could have
given my boy." This, then, is the very highest
love of which it is possible for the human mind
to think: the love of a father that surrenders his
son to sufferings and death.

And this brings us to the second great truth
which is growing increasingly clear in the consciousness of the church. The death of Jesus is
the revelation of an experience in the heart of
God. God is the sin-bearer of the world. He
bears our sins on his mind and heart. There are
three conceptions of God: the savage, the pagan,
and the Christian. God, according to the savage
conception, is vengeful, and capricious, and vindictive. He is a great savage hidden in the sky.
We have all outgrown that. According to the
pagan idea, he is indifferent to the wants and
woes of men. He does not care for men. He is
not interested in them. He does not sympathize
with them. He does not suffer over their griefs.
He does not feel pain or sorrow. I am afraid that
many of us have never gotten beyond the pagan
conception of the Almighty. But according to
the Christian conception, God suffers. He feels,
and because he feels, he sympathizes, and because
he sympathizes, he suffers. He feels both pain

and grief. He carries a wound in his heart. We men and women sometimes feel burdened because of the sin we see around us; shall not the Heavenly Father be as sensitive and responsive as we men? But somebody says that God cannot be happy then. Of course he cannot be happy. Happiness is not an adjective to apply to God. Happy is a word that belongs to children. Children are happy, grown people never are. One can be happy when the birds are singing and the dew is on the grass, and there is no cloud in all the sky, and the crape has not yet hung at the door. But after we have passed over the days of childhood, there is happiness no longer. Some of us have lived too long and borne too much ever to be happy any more. But it is possible for us to be blessed. We may pass into the very blessedness of God. The highest form of blessedness is suffering for those we love, and shall not the Father of all men have in his own eternal heart that experience which we confess to be the highest form of blessedness? This is the truth which is dawning like a new revelation on the church: the humanity of God. It is revealed in the New Testament, but as yet we have only begun to take it in. God is like us men. We are like him. We are made in his image. We are his children, and he is our Father. If we are his children, then we are his heirs, and joint heirs with Christ. Not only our joys, but our sorrows also, are intimations and suggestions of experiences in the infinite heart of the Eternal.

THE HOLY SPIRIT

THE HOLY SPIRIT

" Receive ye the Holy Spirit." — John xx. 22.

I WANT to think with you this morning about the doctrine of the Holy Ghost. I imagine I hear some one say: " I am sorry you did not select a more interesting subject. When there are so many urgent problems and so many practical duties to be done, what is the use of taking the time of a busy, hard-worked congregation in discussing anything so theological and ethereal as the doctrine of the Holy Ghost? " My answer to that is, that that is the very reason why I have selected this theme. It is because the age is so practical, and because there are so many complicated problems, and because there are so many things waiting to be done, that I have decided to call your attention to the Holy Ghost. For the fact is that there is nothing so practical and so helpful to the fundamental doctrines of the Christian faith. The problems will never get solved, and the duties will never get done, until we believe in the Holy Ghost.

The Holy Ghost! There is something repellent in the name "ghost." What is ghost? There is something uncanny and mysterious in the sound

of it. One thinks immediately of a spook or
spectre, an imaginary something that flits through
graveyards at the midnight hour, and that fright-
ens superstitious people into hysterics. What is
the meaning of this word ghost? How did such
a word ever get into the Gospels? It came about
in this way. In the language of old England
there was a word *gast;* the meaning of that
word was breath or spirit. When the translators
of the New Testament in the 15th and 16th centuries went to work to put the Greek Gospels
into English, they found in the Greek a word,
" pneuma," the meaning of which is breath or
spirit, and whenever they found this Greek word
meaning spirit, they translated it by the old An-
glo-Saxon word *gast* or *ghost*. But within the
last three hundred years the word has taken on
new associations and has gathered unto itself new
meanings, so that now it would be better not to
say Holy *Ghost,* but Holy *Spirit.*

What are we to think about this Holy Spirit?
How difficult it is to think of him at all! The
pictorial faculty is strong within us, and we do
not like to think of anything that we cannot picture to our minds. It is easy to think so long as
we can form pictures. That is one of the reasons
why it is so easy for us to think of Jesus of Nazareth. He has a body, outlines, boundaries. He is
tangible and real to our imagination. We have
seen the pictures which the artists have painted,
and they help us in our thinking of him. Even

to this day it is impossible for us to get away from
the pictures of him which we saw in the books in
the nursery. To be sure none of these pictures
are any more than guesses. No one of them is
an authentic likeness of our Lord. It is impossible for us to know what were the physical char-
acteristics of Jesus as he appeared in Galilee
nineteen centuries ago. Nevertheless these old
pictures help us, and we will not, cannot, let them
go. The Roman Catholic Church appeals constantly to this pictorial power of our human nature. She educates her devotees by giving them
statues and pictures. She holds the crucifix constantly before their eyes, and at every service she
displays her pictures of the Saviour and his apostles. By means of these pictures the Roman Catholics are assisted in all their thinking and their
devotions. But how are we going to picture the
Holy Spirit? He has no body, no outlines, no
boundaries, no figure. He has never been painted,
he never can be painted. The imagination can
conceive no image of him. That undoubtedly is
one of the reasons why we so seldom think of
him, he refuses to be pictured to the mind. The
pictoral faculty is baffled, and whenever we begin
to think about him, we find ourselves lost in vague
abstractions and dreary mists of speculation. We
can make some progress when we think of God,
and also when we think of Christ, but whenever
we think of the Holy Spirit we move with difficulty and misgivings. " The wind bloweth where

it listeth, and thou hearest the sound thereof, but canst not tell whence it cometh, and whither it goeth " — so is the movement of the Spirit.

Neverthless Jesus wants us to think of the Holy Spirit. He tells his disciples that it is expedient for them that he should go away. So long as Jesus was in the body, his body was a stumbling-block to all the people who came in contact with him. If a man is to live in this world at all, he must live in some locality, and the locality in which Jesus lived was a rock of offence to all the leaders of the Jewish church. He lived in Nazareth, and Nazareth was an insignificant little vulgar country village. " Can any good thing come out of Nazareth? " That was a question which would not down. If a man is living in this world at all, he must be a member of some household. Jesus was a member of Joseph's household. He had brothers and sisters, and this was a great offence to a people who were looking for a Messiah. Joseph's family was not a family from which a Redeemer could possibly come. Men said in great disgust, " We know his mother and we know his sisters," as much as to say, " We are acquainted with all his folks, there is no education or culture in any of them. We know the disposition and limitations of the whole set." And so men could not believe in Jesus because of his family relationships. If a man is going to earn a living in this world, he must do some kind of work. Jesus had to work at the trade of a car-

penter. But this was also offensive to the Jews.
A carpenter! they said, and turned their backs
upon him. Could rabbis and doctors of the law
sit at the feet of a carpenter? If a man is to be a
man he must have a certain age. Jesus' age was a
stumbling-block to the Jewish people. He said to
them one day " Before Abraham was I am," and
the people immediately cried out, " Why, you are
not fifty years of age yet!" And so Jesus was
continually causing men to stumble because of the
accidents of his physical condition. Even after
his resurrection Paul found that men persistently
went back to the facts and conditions of his earthly life, and out of these created difficulties which
kept them from accepting the grace of God. That
is why in his second letter to the Corinthians
he writes with such passionate earnestness that,
" Henceforth know we no man after the flesh;
even though we have known Christ after the
flesh, yet now we know him so no more." It was
the spirit of Christ moving on humanity from the
throne of God, embodying himself by spiritual
processes in the life of man and society, which
thrilled the heart of the apostle and gave him impulse for his mighty work. " It is advantageous
for you that I go away, for if I go I will send you
another comforter." So even the Revised Version reads, but that is not the best translation of
the Greek. When John Wycliffe in the 14th century translated St. John's Gospel, he translated the
Greek word *paraclete* by *comforter*. In doing

this he did correctly, for "comforter" was a good translation in the 14th century of the Greek word which St. John had used. If you boys and girls will take down the big dictionary as soon as you go home and turn to the word *comforter,* you will find that it is made up of two Latin words *" con "* and *" fortis."* Fortis means strong, and comforter is one who supplies strength. And so, if we are to translate the Greek properly to-day, we are not going to say comforter, but helper, strengthener, advocate, defender. Jesus had been one who had stood at the side of his apostles in their difficulties and dangers. He had answered hard questions thrown at them. He had protected them from the assaults of the mob. He is now going away, he says to them : " I will send you another helper, another person who will stand by your side and protect you from the assaults of the evil one. It is advantageous that I should go away, embodied in flesh as now I am, and that you should have for your defender one who is not limited or weighted down with flesh or hampered by the limitations of humanity. I will send you a helper who will abide with you forever." And saying this he ascended. By this it is not meant that he passed somewhere out into distant space, he passed from visibility to invisibility. He passed from the limitations of humanity to the freedom and glory of the divine life. He passed to the higher level of existence, from which he works incessantly on the hearts of men.

If it was expedient for his disciples that he should go away, of course it is expedient for us that he be hidden from our eyes. It is a great blessing that a cloud has received him out of our sight. "It is advantageous for you," so he says to all of us. What a rebuke that is to these foolish dreamers who are always imagining what a blessing it would be to the world if Jesus were upon the earth to-day living in Jerusalem. "What pilgrimages we could make! How eagerly we should sit at his feet! How comforting it would be to receive his ideas on all the great problems and questions!" How foolish all that is. Suppose he were in Palestine to-day, what a squabble his appearance there would cause. It would be infinitely harder for us to believe in him than it is. A thousand new questions would be brought up. There would be a thousand obstacles to faith. Suppose that he should give a decision on all the questions that harass and torment the minds and hearts of men. What a hubbub the whole Christian world would be thrown into. It is infinitely to our advantage that he should be received out of our sight. It is only a childish imagination that pictures a better state of things if Jesus were still in the flesh. Some of us possibly have been tempted to think sometimes that the apostles had a great advantage over us; the fact is we have the advantage over them. We have an advantage over the men who went with Jesus up the Mount of Transfiguration, and who followed him to the

Garden of Gethsemane. We have the advantage of Mary, Martha, and Lazarus, and all the people at whose table Jesus sat. He says " It is expedient for you that I go away." And by means of the Holy Spirit it is possible for us to know him in his mind and heart, in his greatness and his goodness, as it was not possible for any man to know him in the days of his humiliation.

This brings me to my text, " Receive ye the Holy Ghost." Whenever we repeat the Apostles' Creed, we say, " I believe in the Holy Ghost " — but do you? Is that a phrase without meaning? Is that a piece of religious cant? Do you believe really in the Holy Ghost? Paul in one of his journeys came to Ephesus and found there a dozen men who were trying to live the Christian life, and who became interested at once in his preaching. There was a dulness and deadness about their conversation and their conduct which immediately excited Paul's suspicion. Finally he said to them, " Have you received the Holy Ghost since you believed? " They scarcely knew what to say. Finally they confessed that they did not know that there was such a being as the Holy Spirit. In amazement the apostle Paul asked them into what they had been baptized. They replied that they had been baptized into the baptism of John. In other words, they had forsaken their sins, and were trying to do the will of God, but farther than that they had not gone. The apostle went on to tell them that they had not tasted the sweetness of the Christian life, that they did not understand what it is to be a Christian, that they were living yet under the old dispensation, and had not come out into the liberty and joy of the sons of God. It is not enough to forsake one's sins and to try to do the will of God; he must receive the baptism of the Holy Spirit, else all his life is dead. Those Ephesians are to be found everywhere. They are the men and women who are trying to forsake their sins and endeavoring to do the will of God, but who do not know that there is a helper into whose joy and peace it is possible for them at once to pass. Probably there is no doctrine that needs to be set forth more emphatically and more urgently to-day than just this doctrine about which we are thinking here this morning. There is a widespread restlessness and hunger which indicate that the Ephesians realize there is something lacking in their spiritual experience. Why is it that so many thousands of Englishmen go every year to Keswick? Why do so many thousands go every summer to Northfield? It is because they are hungering for an experience which they have not yet attained unto, and are longing to enter more deeply into that life which is hid with Christ in God. This, then, is the doctrine which this practical age is most of all in need of. Jesus did not say much about the Holy Spirit until he neared the end of his life. It was not until he came into the upper chamber, at the very end of his career, that he brought out in all its fulness the great doctrine which was to give courage and life. The disciples sat around him broken-hearted. It seemed as though all the stars had fallen from the sky. In every soul there was anxiety and forebodings and fears. It was then that Jesus began to speak to them about the other helper that would abide with them forever. And as he spoke all the room became light again, and the chill in the air, which had been put there by doubt and by fear, melted away in the glow of the summer which his new teaching created. We are living in dark and troubled times, one cannot pick up a paper or a book without reading something about the horrible materialism, the greedy, grasping commercialism of our age. Men everywhere are in dismay because of the complexity and multitude of our social and religious problems. There is no message so helpful and so strengthening which the church can possibly give to the people as just this message which lies embodied in our text, " Receive ye the Holy Spirit."

See what he does. Jesus told his disciples that the other helper would do these four things, and for nineteen centuries he has been doing them, even as Jesus said. " He shall teach you all things." Does he teach you? The teacher in the school stands behind the desk at which sits the little boy puzzling his head over a sum which is difficult to do, and the teacher leads him along step by step, correcting his blunders and making

luminous the way. Do you believe that there is
a teacher standing by your side teaching you
day by day how to do the things that are difficult
to do? " He shall guide you into all truth." We
cannot get into truth at a bound, we must be led
into it a step at a time. There is one who goes before us pointing out the way, throwing light upon
the path where our next step shall fall. Does he
guide you? " He shall glorify me. He shall
take the things of mine and show them unto you."
When we are most under the influence of the
Holy Spirit we see no man but Jesus only. In
our lower moods the various characters of history
seem attractive to us, but in our highest moods
there is but one who is altogether lovely, and that
is the man of Galilee. Saints in their dying hours,
when the old earth falls away, and the loved faces
are lost in the mist, see what our eyes are not permitted to behold, the King in his beauty. Does
the Holy Spirit glorify our Lord for you?
Through the last ten years, for instance, has his
character seemed increasingly majestic? Has his
face to you grown more tender and beautiful?
Have you received the Holy Spirit? " He dwelleth with you, and shall be in you." That is the
greatest promise of them all. He is not only the
teacher by our side, and the guide who goes before, and the revealer of spiritual things, but he
is the guest of the heart. He gives a peace that
the world cannot give. He breathes into the soul
a joy which the world cannot take away. He

creates a blessedness that cannot be expressed. Does he dwell in you? Would it be so difficult to forgive and to forget if you had received the Holy Spirit? Would it not be easier to be patient, courageous, and true, to turn away from everything that is mean and contemptible and low, if you had opened your heart to this other helper? Alas for you if the Holy Spirit is not your teacher, not your guide, not your revealer, not a guest in the soul.

Who then is the Holy Spirit? A distinguished theologian has recently answered the question thus, " The Holy Spirit is God in the heart of man." How shall we think of the Holy Spirit? Think of him as the manifestation of God in the soul. Who is the Son of God? God manifesting himself in Jesus of Nazareth. Who is the Heavenly Father? God manifesting himself in creation. Who is the Holy Spirit? God manifesting himself in humanity. These are the three manifestations of the Almighty. They are the manifestations of the one God. The name of our God, therefore, is a long name. Jesus taught men how to pronounce it. " Baptize the nations," he said, not into the names, but " into the name of the Father, and of the Son, and of the Holy Spirit." There are distinctive glories in the divine nature. There is a manifoldness in the infinite life, and this manifoldness is declared in the triune name, Father, Son, and Holy Spirit.

When we bring ourselves face to face with

these great truths we feel like saying, with Paul, " Great is the mystery of godliness." What a mystery it is that the infinite God, whom the heaven of heavens cannot contain, is willing to dwell in the heart of man. "Behold, I stand at the door and knock; if any man hear my voice and open the door, I will come in to him, and will sup with him, and he with me." "Know you not that you are the temple of God, and that the spirit of God dwelleth in you?" But the God in the heart is a God that hides himself. He hides himself in human nature just as he does in the external creation. Our experience is the experience of Job: " I go forward," said Job, " and he is not there, backward, and he is not there. I turn to the right and I do not find him, I turn to the left and I do not behold him. But he knoweth the way that I take." That is our experience. We cannot lay our finger upon a single form of life or matter, and say, that is God. God is everywhere, but he hides himself. He hides himself in the human heart. He is in us, but we cannot find him there. That is a remarkable saying of Jesus', " He shall not speak of himself." That is the literal truth. The Holy Spirit never speaks of himself. He carries self-abnegation to perfection. He effaces himself so completely that we cannot say, Lo here or Lo there! The Holy Spirit is in prayer, but what part of the prayer is his? and what part is ours? St. Paul says that we know not how to pray as we ought, but the

Spirit himself maketh intercession for us with groanings that cannot be uttered. The Holy Spirit and our spirit unite in the act of prayer, but which is human, which divine, we cannot say. So it is in every act of benevolence. We decide to assist some worthy cause. The Holy Spirit is working in us, but how much of the impulse came from him and how much from our own heart we do not know. We decide to engage in a good work. God works in us to do it, and yet who can say how much of the energy is his and how much of the energy is ours?

> " Who shall draw the mystic line
> Severing rightly his from thine,
> Which is human, which divine? "

We only know that he is the fire of our fire, the energy of our energy, the life of our life, the love of our love. Two flames have united to produce the candle of the Lord.

But though the method of his operation is mysterious, we know he is incessantly working. By the fruits we are convinced of his presence, and assured of his redeeming power. He is working in the world, giving convictions to men, of sin and righteousness and judgment. He is working in the church, leading men into larger knowledge, wider sympathy, and deeper love. He has been with the church through all the ages. He will abide with it forever. This, then, is the Gospel for us this morning, " Receive ye the Holy

Spirit." We may have God in us, in our heart, in our home, in our church. " Unless you eat my flesh and drink my blood," so Jesus said, " you have no life abiding in you." " I am the vine, ye are the branches. Abide in me and I in you " — so he said and says. Let us refresh our hearts and renew our faith in the great truth that God is in us, by taking again the sacrament of the bread and the wine.

GRADED PENALTIES

GRADED PENALTIES

"But I say unto you, That whosoever is angry with his brother
without a cause shall be in danger of the judgment: and whosoever
shall say to his brother, Raca, shall be in danger of the council :
but whosoever shall say, Thou fool, shall be in danger of hell fire."
— Matt. v. 22.

I HAVE taken this for my text this morning
because it has such an ugly and savage sound.
It grates upon the ear. Such a sentence does not
seem to have any rightful place in the New Testament, a book of gentleness and love. Certainly
we ought to investigate the sentence and find out
what it means. It is only one of many sentences
of the same sort. If we can once get light through
this sentence other sentences will become luminous too. It offends not only the ears, but the
reason also. It seems to say something that
is not fair. It threatens a punishment that is not
just. We have no objection to punishment, but
we want it to be fair. The penalty must fit the
sin. If the penalty is out of all proportion to the
transgression, our soul rebels against it. Is it
reasonable to believe that a man will be cast into
hell for so slight a sin as saying "fool"?

What does the sentence mean? In the first
place we must get rid of that word "hell." It

has no right any longer in the New Testament.
It has kept bad company for so many centuries it
is hopelessly degraded. It has been on the lips of
every cut-throat and rogue and blackleg and
blasphemer and drunkard and libertine and scoundrel for the last eighteen centuries. So much vul-
garity and passion and vindictive hate and animal vengeance and poison have been breathed into
that word that it is impossible to speak it or to
hear anybody else speak it without having it suggest to us meanings which the word that Jesus
used never had. It is impossible to express anything which Jesus had in his mind by such a poisoned and degraded word. It has no right to any
place whatsoever in the message of our Lord.
We must go back to the Greek word, or better
still to the Hebrew word, " Gehinnom," which
means " the valley of Hinnom." Our sentence
now will read: " Whosoever shall say, Thou fool,
shall be in danger of the valley of Hinnom." And
what does that mean?

We must remember that Jesus in this Sermon
on the Mount is talking about character. He
says that character is an interior and spiritual
thing. He reminds men that they have not done
their full duty when they have obeyed the requirements of the civil law. Civil law takes account of
external actions only, but the law of God takes
into account the movements of the spirit. There
are actions within us as well as actions without,
and both the interior and exterior must be taken

together in order to determine what a man really
is. And then he goes on to give an illustration.
He says: You men have been taught that you shall
not kill, and you think you have obeyed that law
because there has never been any blood on your
hands, but I want you to look deeper into the
meaning of that law. You have never committed
murder by an open act, but the root of murder is
in the heart. Hate is the essence of murder, and
you have all nourished hatred in your souls. You
have been told that you shall not get blood upon
your hands, but I say unto you that whosoever is
angry with his brother shall be in danger of the
judgment. Whosoever nourishes hateful feelings in his heart is guilty of a sin. He shall be
in danger of the judgment — which means the
judges. There were in Palestine courts of various grades. There was in every little village a
local court presided over by seven justices or
judges. This local court had limited powers. It
could inflict penalties, but not the severest penalties. It could condemn a man to death, but it
was death by the sword. Jesus goes on to say,
" Whosoever shall say, Raca, shall be in danger
of the council." What does he mean by " Raca? "
We cannot say with absolute confidence. That
is a word which it is difficult to translate. It is a
Chaldaic word. When Matthew's Gospel was
translated into Greek whoever did the translating
could not do anything with this Chaldaic word,
Raca. He simply wrote down the Chaldaic word

in Greek letters. In the 16th century, when William Tyndale and other English scholars put the Greek Testament into English, they were conquered when they reached this word " Raca." They could not translate it, and so they spelled it in English letters. Twenty years ago when the leading scholars of the world got together to make a revised version of the New Testament they were unable to translate this word. And so through all the centuries it has remained what it has been from the beginning — a Chaldaic word whose meaning it is difficult for us to ascertain. Fifteen hundred years ago a Jew told St. Augustine that really it was not a word at all. It was a sort of *sound* — an interjection — ahem? — a snort of disgust — a groan of contempt. Jesus says that to nourish a hateful feeling in the heart is bad, but to allow it to explode is worse. We are guilty of a sin whenever we nourish hatred in our heart, but our sin becomes still greater when we allow our hatred to leap into the air and hurt a brother man. Whosoever shall utter a sound indicative of contempt shall be in danger of the council. The council was the Sanhedrin. The Sanhedrin was the supreme court of the Jewish nation. It sat in the city of Jerusalem. It had a larger jurisdiction than that which the local courts enjoyed. It could condemn a man to death by stoning. Jesus says that a man who allows his bad temper to vent itself in expression is liable to a severer punishment than

is the man who keeps his bad feelings to himself. He then goes on to say that whosoever shall
say, Thou fool, — here again we come to a word
which is difficult to translate. *Fool* in the Hebrew
language meant one thing, *fool* in our language
means another. To us a fool is a blockhead or a
dunce, to the Hebrew he was more than that; he
was a man whose head was light and whose heart
was bad. He was a blockhead and a scoundrel
combined. Fool, therefore, upon Hebrew lips
was one of the bitterest words of scorn. Jesus
says that a man who coins his language into vituperative speech shall be in danger of the fire in
the valley of Hinnom. This valley of Hinnom
was south of Jerusalem. In the early times it
was one of the loveliest valleys in all Palestine,
but in the days of Solomon shrines were erected
there to the pagan gods and later on the most
abominable rites were celebrated there. When
Josiah came to the throne he pronounced a curse
upon the valley, and from that time onward it
was a polluted place. It was converted into a
vast sewer into which the rubbish of the city was
dumped. Into this valley was thrown the car-
casses of animals and the corpses of the worst of
criminals. Fires were kept burning all the time
in order to cleanse the polluted air. To have one's
body thrown into the fires of Gehenna was the
worst punishment of which the Hebrew mind
could possibly conceive. Jesus says that a man
who runs bitter and scornful words through the

heart of his brother man is liable to a punishment still greater than that which will come to the man to whom he has already referred. Here then in this sentence we have a picturesque statement of the great principle that different degrees of guilt bring different grades of punishment. If a man nourishes bitter feeling in his heart he is a sinner, he must pay the penalty. If he allows his bitter feeling to express itself in hateful and contemptuous sounds he is guilty of a greater sin, and his punishment will be more severe. But if he deliberately coins his bitter feeling into vituperative and scornful language, he will be overtaken by a still more fearful retribution. And so the old savage sentence is not so savage after all. As soon as we strip it of its Oriental dress and robe it in American clothes, we recognize in it the old familiar principle which we have known from the beginning, namely, that the punishment must fit the crime, and that the worse the crime the greater must be the penalty. There is nothing unreasonable about that. It is the doctrine which Nature is always teaching. Nature says that if you sin a little you will be punished little; if you sin more you will be punished more; if you sin a great deal you will be punished a great deal. If you hold your finger for two seconds on a red-hot stove you suffer; if you hold it there for ten seconds you suffer more; if you hold it there for sixty seconds your suffering will be greater still. We never find fault with Nature because she insists upon that fundamental principle. The same principle is recognized by all civil jurisprudence throughout human history. The civil law has always endeavored to make the punishment commensurate with the crime. It has said that if you commit a certain crime you must pay a fine; if you commit a greater crime you must go to prison; if you commit a crime greater still you must be hanged or electrocuted — and we all say that this is just. There is nothing unreasonable in grading penalties in order to meet the different degrees of sin.

It is wonderful how the difficulties of the Bible disappear when we once come to understand its language. How many of us, I wonder, puzzled over this sentence when we were children. We could make nothing of it. Later on our reason rebelled against it. But when we come to understand its meaning, it states nothing to which we can possibly object. It is hard for us to get away from the imaginations of our early days. When we were children there were only two places in the other world — heaven and hell. Heaven was a vast and lovely place through whose shining doors all good people went, and all who were so fortunate as to find entrance there were equally happy. Hell was a deep and awful pit into which bad people were hurled, and all people who were doomed to that frightful place were equally wretched. That was what our childish minds imagined, but that is not the teaching of the New

Testament. You cannot lump people together in
any such fashion as that. In a certain sense
there will be as many heavens as there are souls
fixed in virtue, and there will be as many Gehen-
nas as there are souls fixed in incorrigible sin.
Every soul will go to its own place just as Judas
went to his place, and every soul makes its own
place by its choices and the life which it leads.
There will be different degrees of blessedness and
different degrees of wretchedness, and the degree
of blessedness will be determined by the degree
of virtue and the degree of woe will be determined
by the grade of sin. This is the plain teaching of
the Gospel. In the parable recorded in the 12th
chapter of St. Luke Jesus explicitly declares that
the servant who knows his lord's will and refuses
to do it shall be beaten with many stripes, whereas
the servant who does not know his lord's will,
although he may do things worthy of stripes, shall
be beaten with only a few stripes. And then he
lays down the general principle which is true
throughout the entire universe of God: " To
whomsoever much is given from him shall much
be required." In this parable Jesus asserts that
ignorance is to be taken into account in determining what a soul's punishment shall be. A man
who knows more and sins is to receive a greater
punishment than the man who knows less and
sins. If ignorance is one of the mitigating circumstances in determining what punishment
ought to be, we can easily think of a hundred

others. Heredity must be taken into account, and so must environment, and so also must deliberation — a score of considerations must come in. A hundred complex influences are at work to determine the extent of the retribution which a sinner must be called upon to suffer. So mysterious and so complex is the whole affair that God, and God alone, knows what each soul ought to suffer. We can only be sure that the punishment will be fair, and that the great principle will never be departed from: to whomsoever much has been given from him shall much be required.

Probably no other doctrine of the Christian faith has been so persistently misrepresented and misunderstood as is its doctrine of the punishment of sin. Probably no other doctrine has driven so many people away from the Christian church, and has so tormented so many sensitive and faithful people inside the church, as just this doctrine with which we are dealing here this morning. Notwithstanding the teaching of so many centuries, it is a doctrine constantly misunderstood and persistently perverted. If a man wants to say something derogatory of the Christian church, he is almost certain to make some assertion in regard to what the church has to say of hell. Only the other day you may have read a letter in one of our daily papers in which a writer made this assertion: "The Roman Catholic Church dooms to perdition all who are not members of that church." What an outrageously false thing that was for

any man to say, and yet thousands of people have
said it — thousands of people are saying it still.
A man ought to be ashamed of himself who says
it. It is not true! It never has been true! The
Roman Catholic church does not teach that all
outside her communion are going to destruction.
Does anybody for a moment believe that Leo XIII
or Cardinal Gibbons or Archbishop Corrigan or
Bishop Ireland, or any other leader in the Roman
Catholic church believes that William E. Gladstone or Queen Victoria or Benjamin Harrison is
lost? The Roman Catholic church teaches that
all good people who believe in Christ are saved,
whether they are in the Catholic church or not.
Indeed she says that all these people are in reality
members of the Catholic church, although because
of false education and erroneous conceptions they
have been kept away from her sacraments. It is
a sin therefore to malign the Catholic church by
accusing her of a form of bigotry of which she is
not guilty.

A similar accusation is often hurled against
Protestants. Now and then we hear some ignorant person say that each denomination has its
little creed and insists upon it that all who do not
accept that creed are going to destruction. Could
anything be more ignorant or unfair? Does the
Episcopalian believe that the Congregationalist is
lost? or does the Baptist believe that the Meth-
odist is lost? Do we not believe and teach that if
a man has the spirit of Christ he belongs to Christ,

no matter by what name he calls himself? Do we not believe and teach that if a man has not the spirit of Christ he is none of his, no matter how faithful he is in church attendance or how high up he is in church influence and authority? Do not the churches teach precisely what the New Testament has taught for eighteen hundred years: that it is possible to serve God in this world and not realize the full significance of our actions? Has not the Christian church always recognized the fact that many at the last great day will be greatly surprised to find that they had the spirit of Christ and were serving him who were not willing to admit that fact upon the earth. The Protestant churches are by no means so narrow as many uninformed people would try to have you think.

How frequently it has been asserted that the Christian church proclaims the awful fact that the majority of the human race are doomed. Even to-day the church is accused of being pessimistic and teaching a dismal and depressing doctrine because she is always asking men to believe that the vast majority of all the people that have ever lived are suffering in the other world. That is not the teaching of the Christian church. What does the Christian church know about that subject? Absolutely nothing. When did Christ ever give the Christian church authority to speak concerning the proportion of the lost and saved? On one occasion a man said to him, "Master, are

there few that be saved?" and he pushed the
man aside with an answer which as much as told
him that he was dabbling in things that did not
concern him. A man must pay attention to his
own salvation, and not squander time in speculat-
ing about the number that will be lost. Jesus
was silent in regard to that matter, and so must
the Christian church always be. It is a matter of
pure speculation, — what a man's speculation is
will depend largely on his temperament. Whenever you hear anybody asserting that it is the
teaching of the Christian church that the majority of human beings are lost, you may say
with confidence that they are asserting what is
not a fact.

But somebody says at this point, " Surely the
Christian church has taught that sinners are
doomed to everlasting torment; surely the Christian church teaches that those who refuse to believe in Christ are tortured forever and forever."
If there is any one here this morning who is making that assertion, I want to say with the greatest
emphasis that that assertion is not true. I do not
deny that individuals here and there have taught
that awful doctrine, but they were not commis-
sioned to do so by the Son of God. They were
drawing upon their imagination, or upon the imagination of John Milton, or upon the imagination
of Dante, or upon the imagination of Virgil, rather
than upon the plain teaching of our Lord. The
New Testament does not teach that sinners are

doomed to everlasting torment. In studying the
language of Jesus concerning punishment we
must bear in mind that he always taught in such
a way as to produce a profound impression.
What is the use of any one teaching unless he produces an impression by the words he speaks? In
order to produce an impression a speaker must
make use of language familiar to the men to
whom he speaks. He must use the images
and figures which have been domesticated in their
minds, else otherwise he cannot find access to
them. It was necessary that Jesus should impress
his generation in order that the generation that
followed it should be impressed. Had he not
stirred and thrilled the first century, the twentieth
century would have received no benefit from his
teaching. In all that Jesus had to say, therefore,
concerning punishment, we find him speaking
words that had clear and definite meanings to the
people to whom he spoke. He spoke frequently to
farmers, and farmers were familiar with the use
of fire. That is one of the reasons why he used
the word fire so frequently in speaking of the
penalty of sin. A farmer cannot farm without the
use of fire. Dry twigs must be consumed, un-
fruitful branches must be cut off and burnt up,
blasted trees must be cut down and cast into the
flames. At a certain season of the year a smoke is
always going up from a fire, which gets rid of
rubbish which the farmer does not want. Jesus,
in speaking to these farmers, said, " Men, there

is a fire by means of which the spiritual universe is cleansed; there is an agency by means of which the evil is gotten rid of." Sometimes he spoke to fishermen, and then he spoke in different terms. He said: "You men draw your net up on the shore and then sit down to make a division of your fishes; the good ones you throw into one pile, and the bad ones you throw into another. God has ways of separating the evil from the good." But what is the nature of the fire? Jesus did not declare. What is the nature of the separation? Jesus never told. There is nothing in the New Testament that throws any light upon the nature of the penalty which the soul suffers after death. He made large uses of images and illustrations taken from civil government. He did this because such images were impressive to the minds of the men who listened to him. Oriental government in those days was arbitrary and cruel. It scourged men and scourged them unmercifully. It employed tormentors. It would torment prisoners to extort confession. It would saw men in two. It would cut men into pieces. All this language Jesus carries over into the body of his parables, not in order to illustrate the nature of the punishment which God inflicts, but in order to make it clear that punishment is not simply a whim or caprice of earthly government, but is an eternal feature in the government of God. The simple fact then is that we do not know what punishment in the next world is going to be.

The Christian church has no revelation upon that point. We can only guess and dream and speculate. We do not know. We only know what punishment in this world is, and we know that punishment does not always involve pain. There may be punishment without pain. Physical death in its various stages does not always involve suffering. Some diseases bring torture but others bring none. In many diseases there is simply an ebbing of the life currents, a shrivelling and dying until at last life is totally extinct. We observe the same phenomenon in spiritual death as it goes on before our eyes. Many sins in this world bring great suffering, other sins bring none. There is only a failing of the spiritual vision, a dulling of the spiritual hearing, a deadening of the spiritual sensibilities, a shrivelling up of the spiritual affections, until at last the poor hardened heart makes no response whatever to an external appeal, having lost apparently all capacity for feeling. It may be that punishment in the other world will follow processes with which we are already familiar. It may be that the stages of spiritual death will be, at least for many sinners, altogether without pain. It is this gradual dying and deadening of the sensibilities in this world which has helped to lead thousands of Christians within the last quarter of a century to believe that in all probability in the next world not only will sensibility die, but intellectual activity will also fail, until at last the very substance of the soul shall be dissolved, and the incorrigible sinner shall become extinct. That may be the end, but nobody knows.

This brings us face to face with the question that is always sure to arise whenever we discuss the penalty of sin, namely, How long will penalty endure? It is a question that disturbs us very much in our earlier years. It is a question which may be disturbing to some of you even yet. But as a rule I think, as Christians go on in the Christian life, deepening their knowledge and coming into fuller communion with God, they care less and less for all these speculative questions. We are willing to leave them all with him. If any one should ask, how long will penalty endure, the answer is, so long as sin endures. But how long will sin endure? So long as the soul makes wrong choices. How long will the soul continue to make wrong choices? The answer to that question lies deep buried in the mystery of human freedom. The human will is an insoluble mystery. What are its powers of resistance, it is impossible to say. We only know that in this world it is capable of resisting every appeal that can be brought to bear upon it. It can resist the love of mother, the love of wife, the love of children, the love of Christ, — the four highest manifestations of divine love which are known to our world. If God can manifest himself in still higher forms, we do not know what they are. Some Bible students seize upon such expressions of Jesus as, "I, if I be lifted up, will draw all men unto me "; and such expressions as this of Paul, " As in Adam all die, so in Christ shall all be made alive "; and upon these expressions they build an argument by which they prove that every rebel will at last surrender and every soul attain supreme blessedness; but the argument is exceedingly precarious and one not to be depended on. Other Bible students seize upon expressions which are found in Jesus' parables, such as: "The door was shut "; " the gulf is fixed "; " eternal sin "; " eternal punishment "; and upon these they build an argument to show that doom is final. But the argument is not altogether conclusive; for the reason that the language is figurative and capable of two different interpretations. It is impossible for us to say what shall be the final destiny of any human soul. We do not know what the future body is going to be. We do not know what the spirit is going to be. " It doth not yet appear what we shall be." What shall a world be like in which " time shall be no more "? It is impossible to say. All that we know is that the punishment of sin is certain, inevitable, awful, deserved, graded, just.

Probably no other doctrine of the Christian church has received greater confirmation at the hands of science than just this doctrine of punishment. The scientists of the last century have brought manifold reënforcements with which to drive upon men's consciences the teaching of our

Lord concerning sin. One of the ruling ideas of the modern scientific world is the law of cause and effect. Every cause has its effect, so says the man of science — and upon that law he builds his theories and pursues his investigations with absolute assurance. The law is universal, the law is inexorable. It has never yet been known to fail. If you have your cause, you will also have your effect. The world of matter has that law written large across its face. The New Testament says that that law runs through the spiritual creation. Sin is a cause, retribution is an effect. If you sin, you suffer. Law is universal, it is inexorable, it is inescapable. Another of the great conceptions of the modern scientific world is the law of seed growth. Everything grows! It grows according to fixed and unchanging law. Whatsoever we sow we reap. If we sow oats, we reap oats; if we sow wheat, we reap wheat; if we sow corn, we reap corn; if we sow acorns, we reap oaks; if we sow little, we reap little; if we sow much, we reap much. Every particle of matter is obedient to that great law. We do not find any fault with it in Nature. We simply accept the teaching and guide our conduct accordingly. The New Testament says that this is the great law that runs through God's great universe from top to bottom. Whatsoever you sow you reap. If you sow to the flesh, you shall of the flesh reap corruption. If you sow to the spirit, you shall of the spirit reap life eternal. There is nothing harsh or arbitrary or unreasonable in it at all. The Christian church simply teaches therefore a principle which is illustrated in a thousand ways by the revelation which has come to us through the discoveries of modern science.

We are never, therefore, to be ashamed of Christ's teaching concerning the punishment of sin. It is altogether reasonable, fair, and beautiful. It is one of the glorious features of the Christian revelation. There is a tendency nowadays for us to shrink from things that are disagreeable and painful. We have formed the habit of shutting our eyes and refusing to look at things which are not altogether pleasing. Men almost resent sometimes the teaching of the doctrine of penalty as though they had no right to be imposed upon by so dismal a doctrine as the doctrine of the punishment of sin. The result is we are in danger of becoming effeminate, enervated. We ought to act like men and face the universe as it is. The universe is not altogether a lovely thing, as anybody knows who looks at it. It is not all sunbeams, there are thunderbolts which smite and kill. It is not all velvet lawns and gardens of flowers, there are thickets and briers and countless square miles of snow. It is not all musical and foaming mountain brooks, there are running streams of molten lava. Nature has her hideous and her horrible aspects, and these have a ministry to the soul of man. Wondrously beautiful she is in many of her phases, but at times she is terri-

ble and terrifying, and we hide our face in fear.
But these contracts exist in Nature for a purpose,
and a man who would study Nature and understand her must study not only roses and June sun-
sets, but earthquakes and volcanoes belching fire.
The same contrasts are stamped upon all human
history. What has the history of this world been?
Surely not a long-drawn banquet! The nations
have not gone on a great holiday excursion with
bands of music and dinner baskets filled! There
have, to be sure, been grand processions and festal
days and nights, and the air has rung with ho-
sannas and songs and glad rejoicings, but between
these times of loveliness there have been agonies
— Golgothas — and streams of flowing blood.
There have been falls of Babylon, sieges of Jerusalem, French reigns of terror, and American
civil wars by which the king of heaven has uttered
his purposes to the world. If a man wants to understand the history of the world, he must not
shut his eyes when he comes to the dark and dismal pages. What is true of history is true also
of all high literature. Literature at its best is
always faithful to human life, and therefore in all
great poetry and in all great prose we find the
beautiful and terrible, the lovely and the awful,
the joyous and the painful, lying side by side.
What shall we say of a man who never wants to
read a book unless it deals with pleasant things?
What must you think of a woman who will
never read a volume that does not contain a

beautiful story with a lovely chapter at the end? Such people are not fit to add to the moral standard and stamina and worth of the world. When we go into literature we must prepare ourselves, not only for sunlight, but for gloom. We must walk among the roses and also among the thorns; we will laugh with the happy and we will cry with the broken-hearted. By all means give us "Pickwick Papers," but we must also have "The Scarlet Letter," for that also is a part of life. Give us "Merry Wives of Windsor," and "Much Ado About Nothing," but we must also listen to the agonizing cry of Lear and follow Macbeth to his awful doom, — for this also is a part of life! The world of literature is like the universe, there are changing scenes of joy and sadness. There are summer mornings and long nights wild with storm. And when we come to the Bible we find that it is true to history and to life; it is a book of contrasts. The sweet and bitter, the glad and sorrowful, the beautiful and the hideous, lie side by side through all its immortal pages. At the very beginning of the book we find a lovely picture of a lovely garden, and outside the garden a man is killing his brother man, prophetic of all that is to follow through a thousand pages descriptive of human life. We see Jacob and Rachel, two lovers, walking across the fields at evening-tide, the glory of the setting sun resting on their faces — a little later a broken-hearted, aged man sits looking at the bloody coat which tells him that his son is dead. We see Esther climbing the golden stairs that lead upward to the throne, and on the next page we see Job coming down from his high estate to sit disconsolate and forsaken on an ash heap. We see David, ruddy-faced and glad of heart, coming from the sheepfold to the throne, amidst the acclamations of his joyous people — a little later under a sky that is sullen we hear an agonizing father crying, " O Absalom, my son, my son! " We see King Solomon, wisest of all the kings of earth sitting in royal magnificence at the head of a united and prosperous people — a little later we see sad-eyed and silent captives sitting beneath the cypress trees of Babylon. We open our New Testament and the tragic story is continued. At the very threshold there is a burst of angelic music. We stand entranced as we hear the angels singing, " Peace on earth, good will to men." But the heavenly strain is soon drowned by the angry shout of hateful voices, " Crucify him! Crucify him! " We turn to the last book in the Bible, and there at the very close we find a city with walls of jasper and gates of pearl, and close by its shining walls the lake of fire. The old Book is true to the universe as God made it, and to human history as we know it. And indeed the world all around us thrusts upon us this everlasting contrast. It is not altogether a lovely world in which we live, sweet and bitter are still mingled in every cup. The two roads run out before our eyes : one to life and one to death. We build our prisons close to our schoolhouses; not far from the happy home the walls of the penitentiary rise; near the parlor of the mansion is the home for the insane; near the banquet chamber is the chamber of death; behind the marriage procession the funeral procession marches; in the great city there is laughter, but beneath the laughter there is a continuous wail of woe.

It is foolish, therefore, for us to come to the Christian church, saying, " Please give us something soft and sweet," when God persists in giving us things which are hard and bitter. We are not in this world to be babied and coddled, but to stand up like men and take the consequences of our deeds. We are responsible for every dollar that comes into our possession, we are responsible for every hour that God gives us, we are responsible for every talent which he intrusts to our keeping. For everything which he gives us we must answer at the judgment bar. I do not wonder that Daniel Webster used to say that the greatest thought that had ever entered his mind was the thought of his personal accountability to Almighty God. Dr. Samuel Johnson, as he approached the end of life, frequently became despondent. In one of his despondent moods a friend came upon him, and in order to cheer him up said to him, " Dr. Johnson, you seem to forget the merits of our Redeemer ! " The old philosopher looked up out of eyes unutterably sad, and made this reply, " I do not forget the merits of my Redeemer, but my Redeemer has said that he will set some on his right hand and others on his left." I believe that we should all be better and more faithful Christians, and I am sure the world would be a happier and nobler world if the Christian church would teach with greater earnestness and fidelity the message which has been given to her by her Lord, and would obey the injunction which came to the Hebrew prophets, " Say to the righteous it shall be well with him; woe to the wicked, it shall be ill with him."

THE CROSS

THE CROSS

" For I determined not to know anything among you, save Jesus Christ, and him crucified."— 1 Cor. ii. 2.

LET us think about the cross. And when I say "cross" I mean the cross set up on Golgotha. We are in the habit of using the word nowadays with many significations. The cross — what is the cross? It is an architectural decoration, a pretty way of ending a spire. It is a piece of jewellery dangling from a man's watchchain, or hanging from a woman's neck. It is a figure of speech. Do we not talk about our "little crosses," and smile over them through our tears? But the cross about which I wish to speak is a piece of rough timber with a dying man nailed to it. That hideous spectacle lies at the very centre of our religion.

It is a misfortune of our age that Christianity is surrounded by a golden haze. When seen through this golden haze the religion of the Son of God seems to be a beautiful and ethereal thing. It is a poem whose rhythmic cadences soothe the imagination and satisfy our æsthetic nature. It is a lovely song, to be handed over to the lips of expert singers, and to be interpreted by the great masters of tone. It is a picture, tragic and pathetic, before which we can sit down in our hours of meditation and wonder or cry. It is a philosophy, to be studied and discussed, a learned thing, to be expounded in essays and eloquent orations. It is a dream, beautiful and luminous as the Syrian sky under which it had its birth. And when we speak about " the cross," we mean a certain line in the poem, a verse in the anthem, a color in the picture, an enigma in the philosophy, the central glory of the dream.

But that is not the religion of the Son of God. The Christian life as Jesus lived it was a simple, prosaic, practical thing. "Wist ye not that I must be about my Father's business?" "I must work the works of him that sent me while it is day, for the night cometh when no man can work." "My meat is to do the will of him that sent me, and to finish his work." So he said as he labored through the years. He went into society, where men and women were tied round and round with foolish customs and ridiculous fashions, and he defied these fashions by acting as a Son of God ought to act. He stepped over dividing chasms and walked through estranging walls as though they did not exist, to the consternation of all the sticklers in the land. He went into the church, where men were bound hand and foot by the traditions of the fathers, and he swept these traditions away as though they were so many cobwebs. He went into the temple, and drove

out the men who were desecrating God's worship,
even though his action stirred the leading citizens
to murderous rage. He went into politics, and
condemned the men who were seated on thrones
because those men were not doing the will of God.
Of course it was not pleasant, it was exceedingly
disagreeable. He stirred up all sorts of hatreds
and oppositions. It was not only unpleasant, but
it was also dangerous and fatal. The world
would not endure his interference and his condemnation. It snarled at him, and began to show
its teeth. Jesus saw that he could not go on in
the way in which he had started without suffering
martyrdom, and he decided to drink the cup, no
matter how bitter it might be. It was at Cesarea
Philippi that he began to tell his disciples about
his coming death. He must go to Jerusalem, he
said, and suffer many things. Peter was filled
with consternation, and began to protest. " Never
can such a thing happen." Jesus said: " Get thee
behind me, Satan. You are full of the thoughts
of men. You do not understand the ways of
God." After the marvellous experience on the
Mount of Transfiguration, he repeated this dismal
prophecy. "I am going to Jerusalem, and there
they are going to kill me." While travelling
through Galilee he stopped them one day by the
road and said, " Let these words sink into your
hearts: I am going to Jerusalem, and there I am
going to die." A little later, in Perea, with his
face steadfastly set toward Jerusalem, he painted

the picture in more detail. He had now come close enough to the cross to see how the tragedy was going to end. " They are going to mock me, and spit upon me, and scourge me, and then they will kill me." When James and John wished to sit on the highest thrones of his kingdom, his reply was, " Are you able to drink the cup that I shall drink of, and be baptized with the baptism which I shall be baptized with? "

Not only was it certain to him that he must move steadily toward the cross, but it was equally clear that every man who would do the work which he was engaged in must also move toward a cross. His experience was not to be exceptional, but it was to be the established rule. He never attempted to conceal from his disciples the fact that they would suffer persecution. Repeatedly he reminded them that to be his follower meant to be a sufferer, and that unless they were willing to endure afflictions they need not attempt to come after him. Read the 10th chapter of St. Matthew's Gospel and see what he says to the twelve when he sends them out to preach the Gospel: " I send you forth as sheep in the midst of wolves. Beware of men: they will deliver you up to the councils, and they will scourge you in their synagogues and ye shall be brought before governors and kings for my sake. Ye shall be hated of all men for my name's sake. The disciple is not above his master, nor the servant above his lord. It is enough for the disciple that he be as his master and the servant as his lord. Do not be afraid of them which kill the body, but rather fear him who is able to destroy both soul and body in Gehenna." It was with those direful words ringing in their ears that the disciples went out to do their work. Read the 10th chapter of St. Luke, and see what he said to the seventy when he sent them out before his face into every city into which he himself would come. He said to them substantially what he said to the twelve. There was nothing else to say. " Behold, I send you forth as lambs in the midst of wolves." This world is a wolf to a man who would live a Christ-like life. It is impossible to modify the marching orders.

It was in this tone that he spoke to his disciples to the very end. Read the 16th chapter of St. John's Gospel. He is in the upper chamber. He is saying the last things to them that he will ever be permitted to say. He is repeating the things which he wishes them to remember. " They shall put you out of the synagogues. Yea, the time cometh that whosoever killeth you will think that he doeth God service." " These things have I told you that when the time shall come, you may remember that I told you of them." " In the world you have tribulation, but be of good cheer, I have overcome the world."

He would not allow men to follow him unless he was first assured that they understood the condition on which discipleship became possible.

Read the 9th chapter of St. Luke and see how he turns away man after man because he sees they are not made of the stuff of which heroes are made. One man comes saying, " Master, I will follow thee whithersoever thou goest." There is something in the man's face or tone which reveals a cowardly attitude of spirit, and Jesus says to him, " Foxes have holes, and the birds of the air have nests, but the Son of Man hath not where to lay his head." Another man comes saying, " I will follow thee, but suffer me first to go and bury my father." The only reply is, " Let the dead bury their dead, but go thou and preach the kingdom of God." A third man comes saying, " Lord, I will follow thee; but let me first bid them farewell which are at home at my house." Jesus says, " No man, having put his hand to the plough, and looking back, is fit for the kingdom of God."

And what he said to one he said to all. When he spoke to the multitude he held before them the picture of crucifixion. Read the 14th chapter of St. Luke and see how clear and how severe are his words, " Whosoever doth not bear his cross and come after me, cannot be my disciple." It costs something to be a Christian. Count the cost before you make the start. " Which of you intending to build a tower sitteth not down first and counteth the cost, whether he have sufficient to finish it? Lest haply after he has laid the foundation, and is not able to finish it, all that behold it begin to mock him, saying, This man began to build, and was not able to finish." " Or what king, going to make war against another king, sitteth not down first, and consulteth whether he be able with ten thousand to meet him that cometh against him with twenty thousand." " Whosoever he be of you that forsaketh not all that he hath, he cannot be my disciple."

So he spoke before the crucifixion and resurrection, so also did he speak after his ascension. Read the 9th chapter of Acts. See what he says to Ananias. " Go, Ananias, and tell Saul of Tarsus how great things he must suffer for my name's sake." The call to follow Jesus is a call to suffering, so the New Testament represents it from the first page to the last. You read the Scriptures with your eyes shut if you fail to see that.

It certainly seems reckless to be so frank in stating the conditions of discipleship. Certainly Jesus by such talk as this will chill men's blood and reduce the number of his followers! Will it not retard progress and postpone the coming of the Golden Age? Why not conceal the worst things from men's eyes? What is the use of talking about suffering? Why not keep the cross in the background?

Jesus made the cross conspicuous because he knows what is in man. We know what is on the surface, and we know some of the things which lie immediately below the surface: coiled serpents

which hiss and bite; we have heard them hiss and
felt them bite; and knowing these things we
should never dare to speak to men as he spoke to
them. We should not venture to make such tremendous demands on them, nor to subject the
human spirit to so great a strain. Jesus comes to
men talking about the cross because he knows
what is in human nature down deep in the silence
and darkness of the soul. He knows that down
in the abysmal depths of the heart there is that
which responds to high demands, and which is
capable of daring and enduring all things. This
is the glory of the Christian religion, that it
appeals to the deepest that is in us. Whenever we
get sick of our frivolous and superficial living,
Christianity offers us rest by calling us to a life
that is serious and high. We always make a mistake when we represent the Christian life as
something that may be luxurious and easy, commonplace and prudent. How many times Christians have urged others to become followers of
Jesus, in order that they might be happy. " Oh,
be a Christian! You do not know how happy you
will become!" How different that sounds from
anything to be found in the New Testament.
When did Jesus say to any human being, " Follow me, and through all the days you are certain
to be happy." Again and again Christians have
urged young people to be followers of the Lord
in order to please their parents or their friends.
" Why not be a Christian? it will please your

mother. All your friends are Christians, why not join them and be a Christian too?" How far below the level of the New Testament such an exhortation is! How many times we have heard it: "Oh, be a Christian! Save your soul! Do you not want to be saved? Think what an awful thing it is to be lost! If you will only become a Christian, then you will save your soul from hell." How foreign all that is from the tone of the New Testament! That appeals to a man's selfishness. The New Testament talks in a different tone and speaks with a grander accent. *"Be a Christian in order that you may help save a world!"* When Jesus met those young men on the shore of the Sea of Galilee, he did not say to Peter and Andrew and James and John: "Follow me, young men, and I will make you happy. Or, follow me, and I will save you from destruction." He spoke in a manlier tone than that. "Follow me and I will make you fishers of men." Get off of your snug little Sea of Galilee and venture out upon the ocean, where storms are tremendous and vast interests are in danger. And whenever throughout his life he succeeded in getting men to come to him, he immediately said: "Go preach the gospel. I send you like so many sheep into the midst of wolves." That is what it is to be a Christian: to throw one's self into the hard, rough work of bringing this world back to God. That is the appeal, and the only appeal that goes deep into a man's soul. That is the appeal which Christianity brings to the young men of America. Young men, be Christians, not in order to be happy, not in order to please your friends, not in order to save your soul; but in order to redeem your city, strengthen your nation; in order to bring a world back to God.

Whenever Christianity is preached in its simplicity and truth, it develops heroism and produces a company of heroes. Within the last few months we have seen it written, in many a magazine and paper, that wars are necessary in order to develop heroic virtues. Without war, it is said, humanity sinks back into effeminacy and sloth and cowardice. Unless several times in a century a nation is called to fight upon a battle field, the young men become luxurious and lose the highest qualities of robust manhood. There is no doubt that war gives opportunity for the display of heroic qualities, but war is not necessary so long as there is in the world the Christian church. Military heroism is only one form of courage, and not the highest form. The courage demanded in times of war is the courage that is common even among savage nations. It is the lowest form of heroism. It was developed thousands of years ago to a perfection beyond which it is impossible for human nature to go. Barbarians can be as brave as the most highly civilized on the battle field, and America does not have a man to-day braver than many an Indian who roamed through the Manhattan forests. How is it possible to secure a bravery passing the bravery of the Indian? If a man is willing to endure the most excruciating sufferings without a whine or a groan, if he will face death with contempt and meet it with a laugh, if he will allow his body to be burned without a cry, and will allow his heart to be cut out without showing a trace of suffering, — how is it possible for human nature to go beyond the heroism of the savage? There is not a general nor a private in any of the world's armies to-day who has a whit more courage than was possessed by the fighting barbarians of five thousand years ago. In *physical courage* the world has made no progress since the dawn of human history. This physical courage is a good thing, and it must be perpetuated, and it is worthy of our admiration. The world could not progress without it. But there is another form of courage which is even higher, and that is moral courage — the courage that dares to do one's duty in the times of peace. Christianity introduces us to a state of war. According to the Christian religion, the whole world is a battle field, and we are all called upon to be soldiers. St. Paul, in writing his letters to the Christians of the first century, constantly used the metaphors and imageries of war. He was always urging men to put on the whole armor of God, in order that they might stand. He called them to a tremendous conflict, but he reminded them that the weapons of their warfare were not carnal. We are not wrestling against flesh and

blood, but against the principalities, against the
powers, against the world rulers of this darkness,
against the spiritual hosts of wickedness in the
heavenly places.   It was Paul's proudest boast,
" I have fought the good fight."   To his beloved
son Timothy his exhortation was " Endure hard-
ness as a good soldier of Jesus Christ."   Unless
a man is willing to suffer he cannot be a soldier
of the cross.

Never since the world began has there been
a greater opportunity for heroism offered to
young men than is offered to the young men of
America to-day.   We have made marvellous
material progress, but moral progress has not
kept pace with our progress in material things.
Everywhere the world is crying out for men.   The
social world is full of frivolity and foolishness,
and the atmosphere needs cleansing by the spirit
of heroic souls.   The political world is sordid and
corrupt, and giant evils must be beaten down by
the strong arms of heroes.   The commercial world
is full of selfishness and dishonesty, rapacity and
cruelty, and the only men able to redeem it are
men who have the mind and heart of Jesus.   The
religious world is full of formalism and hypocrisy,
and the church's need to-day is, is always, high-
minded, stout-hearted men.

Here is the opportunity to work and suffer.
No man can be a Christian even in the 20th century without risk and loss.   We are not in danger
now of being cut to pieces by the knives of sav-

ages, but words are daggers and cause more suffering than drawn swords do. Bullets kill, but words lacerate and leave the heart bleeding. Popularity is as sweet to-day as it has ever been, but popularity is something we must be ready to part with at any hour. John Greenleaf Whittier once laid his hand on the head of a fifteen-year-old boy and said: " My lad, if you want to win success, identify yourself with some unpopular but noble cause." Whittier when a boy had done just that thing. He had identified himself with the antislavery cause. He had suffered many things because of his convictions, but in his old age he had the joy of seeing the world come round to where he stood. At the end of the day he wore a crown. Young men, never run away from an unpopular but noble cause, no matter what men around you are saying. Most men simply repeat what they read or what they hear. They do not think. They do not read the future. Identify yourself with a noble cause, and no matter what the world says to-day, by and by humanity will come round to where you stand. It may cause you suffering for a little while, but your light affliction is but for a moment. Without such suffering humanity cannot advance, nor can you be a worthy follower of the Son of God. " It is a faithful saying: For if we be dead with him, we shall also live with him: if we suffer, we shall also reign with him."

" Let this mind be in you which was also in

Christ Jesus: who, being in the form of God, counted it not a prize to be on an equality with God, but emptied himself, taking the form of a servant, being made in the likeness of men and being found in fashion as a man, he humbled himself, becoming obedient even unto death, yea, the death of the cross." Behold! Down, down, down! Up from the pit of his humiliation there comes the exhortation, " Follow me," and down from the heights of his glory there falls the great promise — " To him that overcometh will I grant to sit with me in my throne."

SEEKING TO SAVE

SEEKING TO SAVE

"For the Son of Man is come to seek and to save that which was lost." — Luke xix. 10.

THESE words were spoken by the world's Redeemer. He spoke them by way of explanation of an unprecedented act. He had looked into a tree and had seen a man there. The man was reputed to be the greatest scamp in the town. To this man he said, "Make haste and come down, for to-day I must abide at thy house." A look of mingled disgust and indignation swept across the faces of the crowd, and in answer to this look of horror and amazement Jesus said, "The Son of Man is come to seek and save that which was lost." It is one of the greatest sentences in the New Testament. In it we have sketched for us Jesus' conception of his mission. It is therefore worthy of our closest scrutiny and most careful consideration.

The distinguishing characteristic of a religion is its conception of God. Find out what a religion thinks of Deity, and you will know what it must think of man. It is in their conceptions of God that the great religions of the world differ from one another. Christianity has much in common with the religions of the East, but if you would appreciate the difference between the religion of Jesus and those of other religious leaders, compare Jesus' conception of God with the conception of God expounded and presented by others.

Christianity represents God as a seeking God. It is remarkable how early that note is struck in the development of the Hebrew people. In the very first story recorded in the book of Genesis, God is represented as walking in the garden looking for the man whom he has just created, and unable to see him he calls out, " Where art thou?" It is a bold conception, but the Bible never recedes from it. From the lips of a long line of poets, orators, and prophets, we receive the same message expressed in different forms and spoken with varying accents. God is seeking man. In the last book of the Bible God is still seeking: " Behold I stand at the door and knock. If any man will hear my voice and open the door, I will come in and sup with him and he with me."

I know of nothing more beautiful in the Old Testament than the fashion of its writers of speaking of God as a God who comes down to see what man is doing. What a story is the story of the Tower of Babel. A company of men come together intending to build a tower which shall reach to heaven. And while they are engaged in their ambitious undertaking, God comes down to see what they are about, and blasts their audacious undertaking with confusion. God came

down! Certain fastidious men of our time have
been scandalized by all such expressions. They
call that manner of speech " anthropomorphism."
It is a terrible word to look at, but not so dangerous as it looks. Call it anthropomorphism or
what you will, it is a striking and telling way of
expressing a profound spiritual fact; that God
descends to man and does not compel man to
climb to him. It is this conception of a descending God which lies at the base of our civilization.
What makes the difference between the Orient and
the Occident? The differences upon the surface
are vast because there is a vast difference in the
conceptions of God which lie at the roots of the
Eastern and Western worlds. The East has always attempted the Tower of Babel method of
reaching God. It has pictured God as lofty and
passive, and man in order to reach him has attempted to climb on rising steps of dream and
hope and speculation. But poor man is frail and
soon grows weary. He cannot climb to heaven.
He climbs a little way and then falls back into
hopelessness and despair. The Orient is fatalistic
and hopeless. It has tried to climb to heaven, and
God has blasted the undertaking with confusion.
But here in the West we have always believed that
God seeks man. He comes down. And so long
as we believe that we cannot lose hope. Who
knows what may happen if God comes down?
We have our disappointments and discouragements and defeats, but who knows what victories

may be won and what glorious days may dawn when God comes down? It is this conception of a descending and a seeking God which keeps all the future vast, and rims all the horizon with celestial fire.

When we open our New Testament we are in the presence of one who came down. "I came down from heaven." So spoke Jesus of Nazareth, and men did not understand what he said. "Is not this the carpenter? Do we not know his mother and his sisters? What is this that he saith: I came down from heaven?" Men hated him for saying it, but he never retracted a syllable, and when they listened for his explanation of his coming they heard him saying: "The Son of Man is come to seek and to save that which was lost."

The evangelists portray for us the figure of a seeking Christ. What eyes he had! No other man ever saw as he did. There was a searching and sifting fire in his glance. He called the scribes and Pharisees blind, and blind they were compared with him. He saw things that for ages had passed unnoticed, and observed people whom nobody had ever seen. He saw a blind beggar in an alley. He had been blind from his birth. It was a case of hopeless blindness. And Jesus saw him. He saw an invalid at the Pool of Bethesda whom no one had seen for thirty-eight years. He was at the rear end of the procession of cripples and Jesus saw him! He saw a

man in a tree. The man was so little and so mean
that nobody would look at him. He saw a man
under a tree. And when later this man in surprise
asked, " How did you know me? " Jesus replied,
" When you were under the fig tree I saw you."
He saw a man in a crowd to which he was speaking in Capernaum. He saw the lights and shadows chase one another over the man's face. He
saw in his eyes the darkness of a great struggle,
and saw later on the glory of a deep peace. And
the very next time he met that man he said,
" Come on, Matthew, follow me." He was always seeking and saving the lost. In his search
he went anywhere and everywhere. He shocked
all the polite people and all the people to whom
propriety was a religion, and he antagonized all
the best people of the country by his reckless enthusiasm in searching for that which was lost.
Some thought he was crazy and others thought
he had a devil, but he kept right on seeking. He
made himself of no reputation. He took his reputation and deliberately tore it into shreds and
went without a reputation, so eager was he to
find men who were lost.

He said he was doing simply what God is doing. What man of you having a hundred sheep, if
he loses one, does not leave the ninety and nine
and go after the one that is lost, and when he has
found it he lays it on his shoulders and comes rejoicing home, saying, " Rejoice with me, for I
have found the sheep that was lost." That is a

picture of God! What woman, if she has ten
pieces of silver and loses one piece, will not light
the candle and get out her broom and peer into
every nook and corner of her little hut, and brush
into every crack and crevice of the walls and floors
until she finds it, and when she has found it how
glad she is. That is a picture of God! A man
has two sons and one of them goes away. He
wastes his substance in riotous living. At last
he decides to come home. And while yet a great
way off his father sees him. The father's eyes
have been on the horizon all the time, and the
moment the boy's face appears in the distance the
father's eyes take him in and his heart beats with
joy. He does not wait till the boy arrives. He
himself goes out to meet him. He does not walk,
he runs. He is so happy that he cannot speak.
He falls on his neck and kisses him. That is a
picture of God!

A man makes a great supper and sends out invitations to his friends, but they are preoccupied
and cannot come. One has bought a farm, another has bought five yoke of oxen, and still another has married a wife. The invitations are all
refused. The man says to his servant, " Go out
into the streets and lanes of the city and bring in
the maimed and the halt and the blind." But these
were not sufficient to fill the banquet hall. " Go
out," says the host, " into the highways and narrow footpaths that run along the hedges, and
constrain them to come in, that my house may be
filled." That is a picture of God!

And if this is God, this is what man must do.
Man must be like God in disposition and in purpose. One of Jesus' great words was Go! He
called the twelve to him, filled them with his truth,
and then said "Go!" He called the seventy to
him, instructed them in their work, and then dis-
missed them with the command, "Go!" To the
six hundred on the hill in Galilee just before his
ascension he repeated the word once more —
"Go!" And if we have ears to hear, even now
we can hear it spoken from the heavens into which
he has ascended: "Go! Go seek and save that
which is lost."

Has not the church lost this note too largely
out of its thought and life? Would you call the
Christian church to-day a seeking church? If it is
not seeking to save the lost, then we have an explanation why its life is bound in shallows and in
miseries. Ever since the church statistics of 1899
were published thoughtful men have been asking
what is the matter with the church. In 1899
forty-nine religious denominations in this country
made an annual gain of one per cent. Considering the millions of dollars invested, and the millions of professing Christians in the field, such a
rate of increase is little short of appalling. The
statisticians say that only about thirty per cent
of the people of this country go to church with
anything approaching regularity. About twenty
per cent attend church occasionally, while fifty
per cent never go to church at all. Mr. Dwight

L. Moody was not a pessimist. If there was a silver lining to a cloud he was sure to see it. He had one of the keenest pair of eyes God ever put into a human skull, and knew the religious condition of this country as few men have ever known it. For years he kept saying, " The gulf between the church and the masses grows wider and deeper and darker every day." Men who are best informed know that Dwight L. Moody spoke nothing worse than the truth. What is the matter?

There are two answers. One set of doctors say the trouble lies with the church. But they are not agreed as to what feature of the church is most in need of overhauling. One man is sure that all the trouble is due to the wretched preaching. If preachers only knew how to preach, and were willing to preach the simple gospel, all the difficulties would vanish. Another man thinks the trouble lies with the music. We have our choirs filled with unconverted singers, and they sing operatic and fantastic music, and if we only had music full of spirit and the gospel, the churches would be so crowded it would be necessary to hang out placards saying, " No room! " Another thinks the church lacks commercial common sense. It should have more business enterprise. It should adopt commercial measures and keep its services constantly before the eyes of men. Another thinks the church is too stiff. Preachers ought to follow the example of Jesus, and get out of church buildings. Let them go into a tent or into a theatre, or on the street corner where men are. If the church were not so prim, all its problems would soon be solved.

But there is another interpretation, say another set of doctors. The trouble is not with the church at all, but with the world. The world is sordid and materialistic, and has not sense enough to appreciate the good things which the church provides. Men are tired on Sunday and do not care for religious things. Men are interested in their Sunday newspaper, their bicycle, or their golf, and what can the church do with people given over soul and body to secular interests and worldly amusements? The church is all right. The preaching is good, and so is the music. The feast is prepared, but the invited guests are too stupid to accept the invitation.

Now this is largely superficial. Men who talk after that fashion do not grasp the situation and do not know how do deal with it. We shall never get out of our difficulties by making little changes on the surface. The man who says, change this little thing or that little thing, and all will be well, is not a man safe to follow. The trouble does not lie in the advertising or in the music or in the preaching. The trouble lies deep in the life of our age, and it is not to be reached by any cheap remedies applied to the surface. The secret of the present crisis is the fact that certain forces which have been operative in the past have al-

ready been exhausted or have ceased to exercise
their former power.   For a thousand years our
ancestors were drilled to go to church.   State and
church were united, and church attendance was a
part of the duty of a respectable citizen.   If a man
did not go to church, he was suspected as a traitor.
Protestantism inherited that idea from Rome, and
all through the 16th and the 17th centuries
Englishmen were expected to go to church.   Our
fathers would not go to the church which the
state had provided, and hence were thrown into
prison or driven across the sea.   In Massachusetts
and in Virginia in the early days men were expected to go to church, and to assist them in this
direction the state used the pressure of civil law.
After a thousand years of training such as that
it became an ingrained habit for Englishmen to
go to church.   But the pressure of civil law has
long since been removed, and the force of the ancient habit has been weakened by the atmosphere
of democracy and liberty.

After the pressure of civil law had been removed the pressure of the terrors of the divine
law remained.   Throughout the Middle Ages the
Church of Rome made prominent her doctrine of
purgatory and hell.   The punishments of the
wicked were pictured in vivid language which
frightened men into obedience to the laws of the
church.   That teaching in part was carried over
into Protestantism, and far down into the present
century the wrath of God was in many pulpits

the supreme topic of discussion. I am speaking
to men and women old enough to remember the
days when men trembled under the awful descrip-
tions of the sufferings of the damned. But this
pressure has been removed. If you attempt nowadays to frighten people into church by telling
them of hell, they will laugh at you for your pains.

For many years men were driven to church by
the pressure of intellectual hunger. The minister
had the largest library in the town. He was the
best read man in all the country. He could bring
out of his treasury things new and old to his hearers, and men who were not interested in spiritual
things went to church for intellectual stimulus
and for information not to be so easily obtained
anywhere else. But the printing press has
changed all that. Men have the daily papers and
weekly papers and monthly papers and pamphlets
and magazines and books, and if a man is hungry
for information on any subject he can easily get it
at home. Men may come to church for impulse
and uplift and outlook, but not for information.

There is a power in social custom which is not
easily dissipated. After communities have formed
the church-going habit they will continue to go
long after the motives which first prompted them
to go have ceased to act. The practice of church-
going is more general in smaller cities than in
larger ones, not because town people are more
spiritual than city people, but because they are
more completely dominated by prevailing fash-

ions. In a town if a man does not go to church some one is likely to ask him the next morning, " Where were you yesterday? " In a city social customs are speedily dissolved in the strong acid of cosmopolitan life. City people as a rule no longer go to church because it is fashionable. The ancient forces have lost their grip, and what are we to do?

We may do either one of three things. We may carp and criticise and find fault. We may say if this were fixed or that were changed, then all would be well. We have worked ourselves into the false notion that if the church makes out a good programme, people will flock to the worship of God. Where did you get that idea? There is nothing to support it in revelation or reason or experience. Men say the people are hungry for the Gospel. It is not true. It never has been true. The people have never been hungry for the Gospel. They were not hungry for the Gospel in Jesus' day. He said to the biggest crowd he ever faced, " You are hungry to have your stomachs filled, but you do not care anything for spiritual things." That was true of the crowd then, and it is true of the crowd now. Men say if a preacher knows how to preach people will flock to hear him. It is not true. Paul knew men. He said that the natural man does not understand the things of God, and indeed he cannot understand them, because they are spiritually discerned. The average man does not want to come to church on

Sunday. What does he want to come to church for? He would rather have a paper or a magazine or novel, or a bicycle or a horse, or a yacht, or a big dinner, than hear a sermon, no matter who preaches it, or listen to an anthem no matter who sing it. This idea that if you make a religious feast and send out invitations, people will come flocking in, is unscriptural. It is sheer nonsense. The New Testament assures us that men are pre-occupied and they will not accept the invitation, and that if the house is to be filled men must be constrained to come in.

Or we may whine about the materialistic age and the sordid-hearted world. It is not a good business for Christians to be in. It is high time that we stop our whimpering about the worldli-ness of the world. It has always been worldly. It is no more worldly now than it has always been. Paul did not cry because Corinth was worldly. John did not moan because Ephesus was materialistic. The saints in Cæsar's house-hold kept alive the flame of Christian faith, though all around them was an atmosphere filled with dust and poison. Jesus did not sit down and succumb because Jerusalem was sordid through and through. Who are we that we should sigh and murmur because we live in a worldly-hearted age? Our business is not to grumble over bicycles and golf clubs, but to over-come the world in the strength of Christ.

If we cannot carp and cannot whine, what shall

we do? Let us be Christians. The source of all our troubles is that we do not live the Christian life with sufficient energy and self-abnegation. Does not that tell the whole story? If we were Christians!

What is it to be a Christian? It is to be a missionary. A missionary is one sent. We are all sent to seek and to save that which is lost. Are you seeking? Whom have you brought within six months?

A Christian is a saviour. We hear much about the submerged tenth. A tenth of our people are sunken. I never hear the expression without thinking of the awful picture which Dante paints in the twelfth canto of his " Inferno," of the river of blood in which human beings are immersed, some up to the chest, others to their chin, and still others to their eyebrows. God in Christ has taken us by the hand. Clinging to him with one hand, with the other we ought to clasp the hand of some man that is submerged. Do you?

A Christian is a servant. Our Master has made a great feast and we are to fill the banquet hall. We are to go into the streets and alleys, into the highways and hedges, which being interpreted means that we are to go out into the stores and shops, the offices and warerooms, the clubs and the parlors, and constrain men to come in. They will never come unless pressure is applied. We must overcome their incredulity, inertia, reluctance, and prejudice. In the Gospels we are told of one man who was carried to Jesus by four men. There are men in New York so weak in spiritual strength that it would take twenty men to induce them to come to church. But the twenty men are here and that is what they are for. That is our business in this world, constraining men to come to God.

A Christian is a man who believes in the brotherhood of man, and lives it. Christ says, "If you are about to offer a sacrifice and remember that your brother has aught against you, leave your gift and go and be reconciled to your brother." Your brother has something against you. He has something against you and your church and your religion. He thinks you are a hypocrite, professing to believe one thing and living another. He thinks your church is aristocratic and exclusive and cold. He thinks that religion is a fake and a sham, and has no confidence in you and your fellow-members. You say, he is mistaken. Yes. He is prejudiced. Of course he is. He is unjust and ignorant and unreasonable. No doubt! But he has something against you, and it is your duty to go to him. You say he does not understand you. That is true. It is also true that you do not understand him. If you should talk it all over with him, it might be that his prejudice would vanish and his opinions would change. It is your duty to be reconciled to your brother.

What will you do? Oh, for five hundred Chris-

tian men and women to live a week completely
dominated by the law and love of Christ! This
congregation touches ten thousand people every
week. Suppose that each one of us were seeking
always for that which is lost. Suppose we should
catch the New Testament idea that men must be
constrained to come to the Gospel feast, and then
set out to exercise this constraint. The old press-
ures have been removed. Never again will men
be driven to church by civil law. Never will they
be frightened into church by telling them about
hell. Fear is a legitimate motive, and was used
by Jesus and all his apostles, but it should never
be made the supreme motive as it was made in
former times. Never again will men go to church
because of intellectual hunger, or because it is the
fashion. There is only one pressure left, and that
is the pressure of love. And this is the mightiest
of all. If there be laws they shall fail; if there be
fears they shall cease; if there be customs they
shall vanish away. But love never faileth. It
beareth all things, believeth all things, hopeth all
things, endureth all things. Love shall win the
victory at last. Why not constrain people by the
voice and by the pen? Why not write a letter
each morning to a non-church goer? Let that be
your morning prayer. Offer it as a morning
sacrifice and look up.

A wealthy man once talked with me about a
distinguished college president who has a genius
for raising money. He raises money largely

through the exertions of a little circle of personal friends. One of these friends one day went to the man with whom I was talking, saying: "President —— wants to buy a collection of fossils, and I want five hundred dollars from you." He got the money. The man, in telling me the story, said: "I didn't care anything for the old bird tracks, but I gave him the money because he was so interested in those fossils." That is just like a man. Men are always doing things for their acquaintances and friends. Their love constrains them. The Son of God wants a company of saints who shall stand as pillars in the temple of God. He is gathering the company through us. If we were Christians, if we were really willing to live the Christian life, we should be glad to go anywhere and make any sacrifice, if only we might save some of the men for whom our Master died.

THE IMPOSSIBLE COMMAND-
MENT

THE IMPOSSIBLE COMMAND-
MENT

"Love your enemies." — Matt. v. 44.

THIS is a commandment of our Lord. It ex-
presses the climax of Christian duty. It places
before us the distinguishing characteristic of
Christian morality. It has been called, The Impossible Commandment. Let us study it this
morning.

Love your enemies! It falls upon us with a
shock. It is not a shock of surprise, for the words
have been familiar to us from the days of childhood, but the commandment comes to us even
now with a shock of bewilderment and almost
consternation. Our first impulse is to say, What
does he mean? What does he mean by that word
"love"? Love is a word of many meanings. With
what significance does he use the word in this
commandment? Enemies! What is an enemy?
Who are one's enemies? Which enemies are we
to forgive? Our first inclination is to quibble
about the meaning of Jesus' words. He knew that
we would do that, and so he defines the meaning
of this commandment with greater care than he
ever defined the meaning of any other sentence

that he ever spoke. He says, " Love your enemies! By that I mean, bless those that curse you";
but here again we are likely to stop and ask for
further definition. What is it to bless? What
does he mean by curse? Our enemies do not curse
us. For the most part they are not cursing
people. What does he mean by "bless" and
"curse"? and the answer comes immediately, "I
mean this: do good to them that hate you." Ah,
now we have come down to the fundamental
forms of speech. There is room now for no
further quibbling. "Do good," we know what
that means. "Hate," we know what that is.
We have gotten into the heart of that bad word.
We have hated, and we have been hated. And
when he tells us to love our enemies, or, in other
words, to do good to them that hate us, we have
no further opportunity to say we do not understand the meaning of his words. But suppose
our enemies will not let us do them good; suppose they keep out of our way, and we cannot
come near them, then certainly this commandment
will let us go free. He anticipated all that, for
he never closed his sentence until he said, " Pray
for them which despitefully use you and persecute you."

O this severe, and pitiless, and relentless, and
unescapable Jesus of Nazareth! When he once
gets on our track, there is no getting away from
him. He cuts off every avenue of escape. He
pursues us to the end of the road. When he has

gotten us with our back to the wall, there is nothing to do but look into his face and listen to what he says. If he had only given me a chance, I could have explained that commandment to my entire satisfaction. I have dictionaries and encyclopædias and all sorts of learned books, and I could have seized that word "love" and toned it down and given it a meaning which would have made the commandment easy for me to keep. I could have taken that word "enemies" and bent it in such a way as to give my natural disposition a chance to act. But he knows the trickiness of my nature, and so he locks every door and will not let me out. He tells me that love is not a sentimental thing to be buried deep in the recesses of the heart; it is a disposition which must express itself in language. My good will must pour itself into speech. When my enemies throw at me words which blast and cut, I must throw at them words which caress and heal. And even this is not enough: I must not only speak my good will, but I must also live it. My kindly disposition must be poured into forms of conduct. I must not only bless, but also do good. But even this is not enough. If he had given me the opportunity, I could have evaded the law even here: I could have spoken sugared words and poured honey upon the sentences so that it would drop from every syllable. I could have done all sorts of gracious deeds, and at the same time carried the dagger in my heart. But he says that there must be no shamming, that my speech must be genuine, and my conduct must be honest. I must love my neighbor in the deepest recesses of my soul, and carry him to the throne of grace, and ask from the great good God the same blessings upon him which I would ask for myself. And in order to make his meaning clear beyond all question, he says, "If you forgive not men their trespasses, neither will your Heavenly Father forgive you your trespasses." He shuts the door of heaven and writes above the door, "No soul shall enter here who has an unforgiving disposition." If this is the law of the kingdom of God, who can be saved?

This is a familiar question, we have heard it before. It is a question that always leaps to the lips of men whenever the Gospel of Jesus is squarely preached. When Jesus talked to men in Jerusalem and in Capernaum, men listened to him dumfounded and amazed. "Are there many that be saved?" they cried out, as he made the conditions high and hard; "who, then, can be saved?" "This is a hard saying, who can hear it?" "How can these things be?" "Lord, increase our faith!" These were the ejaculations that sprang spontaneously to the lips of the men who drank in his severe and lofty words. But never did he apologize for anything he ever said, and never did he go to men with any suggestions of a compromise. He pushed up his standards higher and higher, and left them shining there.

He took his position on certain principles, and all
the learned men of his day could not budge him
from the spot on which he stood. He laid down
the law of love and never modified it in a single
syllable. He had a strange way of repeating his
hardest sayings. In that he imitated nature.
Nature often seems unreasonable and cruel. We
cry out against her. " Do not do that, nature!"
And nature goes right on and does the unreasonable thing again. We ask nature to give us a
reason for her conduct. We say, " Tell us why,
O nature, why you persist in doing that," and
the only answer that comes back is, " Verily, I
say unto you, I am going to do it again." So it
was with Jesus. He said to Nicodemus, " You
must be born again." When Nicodemus asked
for the reason, his answer was, " You must be
born again." To the men in Capernaum he said,
" You must eat my flesh and drink my blood,"
and when they asked for an explanation, his
answer was, " You must eat my flesh and drink
my blood." There were certain facts which he
would never allow his hearers to get away from.
He never would allow them to escape from the
fact that to enter the kingdom of God they must be
changed. The change must extend to the roots
of their being. They must be built up anew from
the very foundation. This change could be
wrought by God, and God only.

Because God is almighty, and human nature
can be changed, the Christian religion does not

hesitate to put at the very forefront of all her teaching this impossible commandment, " Love your enemies." That high doctrine was not spoken in a corner and is not hidden away in some footnote in the New Testament, it is written large on the very forehead of our faith. All the enemies of Christianity have known that it is the command of Jesus that his followers shall love their enemies. This has been in every age a stumbling-block and a rock of offence. Men have derided Christianity because of this high teaching. They have said it teaches a grovelling and cowardly disposition, it commands a man to abdicate his manhood. It takes out of him a virile and noble spirit. So men have always said, and so they are saying still. Others have found in the law of love something beautiful to think about, but impossible to live. They have said Christianity is a lovely dream, but it is absolutely unworkable in a world like this. But no enemy of Christianity has ever ventured to suggest that the carpenter of Nazareth does not teach the doctrine of love to enemies. We know it is the teaching of our religion, and we measure Christians always by this law of love. Whenever we find a man or woman who is spiteful and revengeful, ugly and unforgiving, we say he is not much of a Christian. Instinctively we condemn him if he does not live up to this law of love. We measure ourselves by the same high standard. Whenever we allow hateful feelings to take possession of our

hearts, whenever we breathe revenge, or keep
alive the fire of hatred, we feel so out of sorts, so
wretched, and so unworthy that we know we
have parted company with the Lord, and there is
no peace for us again until we have allowed him
to take all the bitterness away. We may say
sometimes that our religion is unpracticable, but
we are not honest when we speak so. It is not
true that Christianity cannot be lived upon this
earth. It has been lived here once, and it can be
lived here by every man who is willing to give
himself to God. Did not Jesus live the doctrine
which he preached? What other man in all
human history has ever been so misrepresented
and maligned, so hooted and hated and hounded?
What man ever had greater exasperations and
more numerous provocations to retaliate and
strike back, and yet it is impossible for us to conceive of Jesus of Nazareth entertaining a malicious feeling. On one occasion, two of his
disciples, disgusted by the boorish action of some
Samaritan peasants, wanted to burn them up.
They rushed to Jesus for the permission to do
this. His only reply was, " You do not know my
spirit. I am not come to destroy men's lives, but
to save them. No matter what they do to me, it
is my mission to do good to them." What an
illustration of self-control we have in his treatment of Judas! The despicable wretch steps out
in the moonlight and imprints a kiss on Jesus'
cheek. Certainly any man with any spirit in him

will hurl the traitor off as he would spurn a viper.
No, his only rebuke is, " Judas, betrayest thou the
Son of Man with a kiss? " He would not strike
him with a sword; he struck him only with a
glance of his loving eyes. " Father, forgive
them, for they know not what they do," so he kept
repeating as the Roman soldiers drove the nails
through his quivering hands. Never allow any
man to tell you that Christianity is not practicable,
that it cannot be lived upon this earth. That
assertion is a lie. Christianity has been lived
here, else our New Testament does not speak the
truth. But some one says, Jesus was unique, he
was different from all the men who have ever
been or ever shall be. There was that in him
which has never been in any other man, and
therefore conduct, which to him was possible, is
beyond the reach of ordinary men. It is true that
Jesus was different from all the other members of
our race, but it is not true that ordinary men cannot follow him in obeying this law of love. The
New Testament tells us that other men besides our
Lord were able to love their enemies. Within a
short time after Jesus' death one of his followers
was stoned. As the stones came crashing into his
flesh, he fell upon his knees and prayed, " Lay not
this sin to their charge." What Jesus did upon
the cross, Stephen did upon the ground. Nor is
Stephen the only man who did that. St. Paul
was able to forgive his enemies as Jesus forgave
the men that hated him. Wherever Paul went, he

was misrepresented and misunderstood. He was made the offscouring of the world; but harsh treatment never soured him, and injustice never made him vindictive. In one of his letters he sets forth the manner of his living, "Being reviled, we bless; being persecuted, we suffer it." Not only did he suffer all sorts of abuse at the hands of the pagan world, but he suffered still greater insults at the hands of his Christian converts. Never did a minister have a more cantankerous and unreasonable and ungrateful church than St. Paul had in the church of Corinth. But he treasured up no malice against these quarrelsome people in the Grecian city. After they had done their worst, he says, "I will gladly spend and be spent for you, though the more abundantly I love you, the less I be loved." The apostles were all able to live up to this golden law of love. But some one says, That was nineteen hundred years ago, that was in the age of the apostles, after the descent of the Holy Spirit; but you cannot expect such dispositions in these later and colder times. Do not say that. Do you mean to say that forgiveness is such a delicate plant that it blossomed once upon our earth, to blossom no more forever! Has there been only one tropical age when this plant could put forth its bloom, and have the petals been scattered on the icy winds of this chill world? No, forgiveness is a plant that grows and blossoms in every time where human hearts are willing to give access to God's eternal spirit.

There are men and women living now, and they
are numbered by the thousands, who obey this
law of love. You have known some of them, and
so have I. I think of one just now, Dr. John G.
Paton. Who that has ever known that man
would hesitate to say that there is at least one
man upon this earth who cannot think a malicious
thought or nourish a resentful feeling. His
heart is as sweet and tender as the heart of the
beloved disciple. We have had in this country at
least one president who was near and dear to the
heart of Christ. We have had others; but I am
sure of this one, for in his life there was a marvellous manifestation of the spirit of the Gospel.
It was our president who said, " With malice
toward none, and with charity for all." Abraham Lincoln was great in many ways; but the
crowning proof of his transcendent greatness was
his Christ-like freedom from resentment.

But while the law is practicable, there are various questions which are certain to arise in every
thoughtful mind. Is there a limit to this forgiveness? Can we set boundaries to love? How
many times may a person do me a wrong and
still have a claim upon me for forgiveness? It is
a living question in our day; it was a living question in the time of Christ. For hundreds of years
the rabbis had been arguing about that question
in their various schools, and in the time of Jesus
they had reached the conclusion that after a man
has forgiven his enemy three times, forbearance

ceases to be a virtue. One day when Jesus was talking about offences he spoke in such a tone as to arouse the curiosity of his disciples. Peter restrained himself for a little while, and then broke out, " Master, how many times must my brother offend against me and I forgive him, until seven times?" That question of Peter is full of meaning. It gives us a revelation, not only of Jesus, but also of the man who asked it. The rabbis had decided that three forgivenesses were sufficient; Peter knows that three will never satisfy the heart of Jesus, and so he suggests the figure seven. He knows that Jesus is unlike all the other religious teachers of the land; his mercy outruns their mercy, their forgiveness is no match for his, and so Peter runs far beyond the rabbinical law — goes more than twice as far as any rabbi has ever gone, and sets the stake down at what seems to him the farthest limit of the demand of God, and then says to Jesus, Shall I forgive a man seven times? The question of the disciple shows what a profound impression the Master had made upon the men that were nearest to him. The question also gives a revelation of the heart of Peter. Peter knew that vengeance is sweet, and he did not like the idea of having every possibility of retaliation taken from him. His natural disposition was like a tiger. He was willing to hold it in once, twice, thrice, even seven times, but he could not allow himself to think that the natural disposition

must be held in forever. Master, he said, shall
I hold the tiger in seven times, and then let him
spring? Jesus' reply was, "Forgive thy brother
seventy times seven." O Peter, you do not
know what spirit you are of, you have not yet
gotten out of the sphere of law into the sphere of
love. Love never counts, you must quit your
counting. So long as you count, you are not in
the world of affection. Forgive your brother
seventy times seven. This interpreted into our
modern speech means, Forgive your brother a
million times. When we say we have done a thing
a million times, we do not mean we have done it
nine hundred and ninety-nine thousand nine hundred and ninety-nine times, plus one. Nobody
ever counted up to a million — that expression
is simply a figure of speech. It means always.
When we say we have done a thing a million
times, we mean to say we have always done it, it
is our habit to do it, we would not think of doing
anything else. And so when Jesus says forgive
your brother seventy times seven, he says you
must always forgive him. There must never be
in your heart any malice or vengeance. You must
always and everywhere maintain the spirit of
love.

Are we, then, to say that we must take no
notice of any wrong whatsoever? Are we to submit to injustice without rebuke? May people
injure us with no remonstrance from our lips?
Are we to be blind and deaf to every unkind

word and every unjust deed? Are we to allow
people to walk over us as though we were a
worm? Certainly not. We are to do our enemy
good. In order to do him good it may be necessary to rebuke him. Jesus gives his disciples
instruction on this point. Read what he says in
the seventeenth chapter according to St. Luke:
" If your brother offend you, rebuke him, but do
it in a brotherly way; do not make a fuss about it
in public, but go and have a quiet talk with him
in private. Tell him that he has done you a
wrong. Try to show him the sin which he has
committed. By being brotherly you may bring
about a reconciliation. But if he will not listen
to you alone, then take a friend along. Possibly
two or three of you together may accomplish what
one cannot do alone. If he will not listen to you
and your intimate friends, then make the matter
public, bring it to the attention of the Christian
brotherhood. If the man is still unrepentant and
goes on in his evil way, then have no more to do
with him; separate yourself from him. Let all
the world know that the man has been guilty of
unchristian conduct, and that your disapproba-
tion rests upon him." All this, of course, must
be done, not for vengeance, but in love. We
must treat our enemies in such a way as to do
them good and bring them, if possible, to repentance. And so there are occasions when it is
necessary and Christian to hand evil-doers over
into the custody of the civil law. It is not right

for any man to allow himself or his family to be abused with impunity. If a man breaks my windows or cuts down my trees or insults my wife or beats my children, it is my duty to bring him to punishment. He is not only my enemy, but he is the enemy of society, and I owe it to society to bring that man, if it is possible, to a better frame of mind. I must do everything in my power to do him good. I must call upon the state to help me in my efforts to do him good. To arrest him may be to him a means of grace. A few months in jail may bring him to repentance. Love does not always caress. Love may sometimes strike. Blows may be necessary to redeem. God loves us, but he rebukes us. He rebukes us because he loves us. He chastens us because he has compassion on us. He hands us over to the tortures of our conscience because he is not willing that any should be lost, but wishes that all men should come to repentance. Love may seize upon painful measures in order to bring the transgressor to himself again. Jesus was not teaching unmanly conduct when he told men to love their enemies. We always do him wrong when we interpret his language in such a way as to take out of human life the elements essential for its preservation. No flimsy, sickly sentimentalist was he, but the manliest, bravest, sanest man that ever lived.

Another question is, Can we forgive an injury? We sometimes hear people say, I will forgive, but I cannot forget. It is often said in a very

significant tone. When people say that it is pretty
certain there is no forgiveness in their hearts.
When a man has really forgiven, he never makes
any such speech as that. Forgiveness puts on no
qualifying phrases, does not add an appendix in
which to state that the wrong will never be forgotten. In a superficial sense it is true that nothing that ever happens to us can be forgotten. The
intellect holds on to it and will recall it as long as
the soul endures, but in a deeper and truer sense
we do forget. The Bible everywhere assures us
that God Almighty forgets. "As far as the east
is from the west, so far does he remove our transgressions from us." He casts our sins behind
his back so that he cannot see them. He casts
them into the depths of the sea, covers them so
that they are hidden forever. He blots them out.
He remembers our iniquities no more. When he
forgives, the old estrangement is done away with
and the reconciliation is complete. He not only
forgives, but he forgets. The heart has mysteries
which the head knows nothing at all about. This
forgetfulness is not a trick of the brain, but an
art of the heart. A mother knows what it is to
forget. Her boy some evening speaks to her an
insolent or contemptuous remark. It hurts her,
and for a day or two her heart bleeds, and then it
is all forgotten. She forgets it, but the boy does
not. He remembers it. He does not think of it
much at the time, but by and by it comes back to
him — ten, fifteen, twenty years later he begins

to realize what a sin he has committed. Finally he determines to speak about it. He says, " Mother, do you remember the evening when I said that hateful thing to you? " She replies, " Why, I had forgotten all about it." Mothers know how both to forgive and to forget — so does everybody who knows the meaning of love.

Can we feel the same toward our enemies and friends? Certainly not. But that is not essential. God does not expect this. No two kinds of love are alike. One cannot feel the same toward his parents as he feels toward his wife, or toward his wife as he feels toward his children, or toward his children as he feels toward his brother, or toward his brother as he feels toward his friend. Those are five different types of love, and one love differs from another love in glory. They are all genuine and they are all sweet, but no two of them are alike. So is it with the love toward our enemies and the love toward our friends. They are different, but they are both genuine. Any one who has lived close enough to God to be able to forgive his enemies, and who has taken his enemy to the throne of grace again and again, and prayed for his soul as he has prayed for his own, knows that there is no love any finer or higher or sweeter than the love which the soul can feel for its enemies. Jesus did not use the wrong word in this commandment. He used the word " love," and love it must always remain.

Let us consider the motives which Jesus puts behind this great act of the soul. He never urges us to great duties without laying mighty motives before us.

He tells us to love our enemies because this is the condition of God's forgiveness. One day he gave his disciples a sketch of what true prayer ought to be. He told them the manner of it and the spirit of it, suggested the direction in which the petitions ought to move. Right in the middle of the prayer he put this strange petition, "Forgive us our debts as we forgive our debtors." As soon as he had completed the prayer, he went back to give a word of explanation on that strange petition. He said, "I have put that in because unless you forgive those who trespass against you, your Heavenly Father will not forgive you your trespasses." The gates of the kingdom of heaven are closed to the unforgiving heart.

We ought to love our enemies as a recognition of God's forgiveness of us. No man has done us as large a wrong as we have done God. No man owes us so much as we owe God. If he is willing to forgive us our trespasses, we ought out of sheer gratitude to forgive the transgressions of our enemies. In order to make this plain, Jesus one day told the parable of the unforgiving servant. A certain king came to make a reckoning with his servant. One man owed him ten million dollars. He could not pay his debt. The king ordered him and his wife and his children to be sold. And the poor debtor in great distress throws himself on the ground and says, " Have patience with me and I will pay you all." The king's heart is moved with compassion, and the man is forgiven. But no sooner is he loosed than he goes out and finds a man who owes him twenty-five dollars. He takes him by the throat and says, " Pay me what you owe me." And although the man begs to be released and promises to pay all, his petition is spurned, and the man is cast into prison. The word is immediately carried to the king, who orders his debtor to be handed over to the tormentors, to be kept by them until he has paid the entire debt. Jesus ends the parable with these awful words, " Even so shall my Heavenly Father do unto you, if ye from your hearts forgive not every one his brother their trespasses."

Love your enemies, says Jesus, in order that you may be children of God. This is the aim of the Christian religion — to make men godlike. It will stop at nothing short of that. We must reproduce his disposition and temper. We must be like him in order to be with him where he is, and behold his glory.

Is not this a gospel for us all? How hard it is to live in a world like this without offending and without being offended. We have such different temperaments and dispositions, and we live so close together that there is friction somewhere all the time. If God should strip us naked this morning and lay open the secret recesses of the heart, I wonder how many alienations and estrangements, how many enmities and hatreds, how many grudges and un-made-up quarrels are hidden in this single congregation! — how many unforgiving spirits have come up to worship in the temple of our God! Let me bring to you the command of Jesus, "Forgive your enemies." Some of you are brooding over wrongs that have been done to you; quit it! Quit it immediately! You are never so completely in the devil's power as when you are thinking of the things your enemies have done. Some of you are nursing your resentments — do not do it! Resentment is a fire that burns up the very tissues of the soul. If you have misunderstandings, make them up! If you have quarrels, get rid of them! Do it all before Easter. Do not say that you will go half the way — go all the way. Be like God. Christ did not come half way to earth, he came all the way. He did not descend half the way into the depths of humiliation. He descended even to the death on the cross. Unless you die with him, how can you ever expect to reign with him?

Let me give you six reasons why you ought to forgive your enemies. In the first place, the offences are trivial. The sins which men commit against us are not great sins. They do not burn down our houses, or kidnap our children, or slap us in the face. All the offences are only penny debts. Somebody insults us or snubs or misrepresents us on some insignificant matter, or somebody does not agree with us in art or music or politics or religion, and we are mortally offended. Or somebody lies about us because he does not know us. If he only knew us, he would quit his lying. But because he has lied about us, we are burning with the fire of vengeance. What are these but penny debts? Little boys and girls occasionally keep banks in which they drop their pennies from day to day, and now and then they shake the bank to see how the pennies are increasing. Grown men and women sometimes act like children: they keep a bank in which they drop from day to day the slights and insults and misunderstandings and disagreements and cruel words and unkind deeds, and every now and then they shake the bank to remind themselves how fearfully the old world is abusing them. The next time you go to your little bank remember God's great bank; when you count up your penny debts, calculate your great debt to God. If you expect his forgiveness, how mean it is in you not to forgive your offending brother!

Love your enemy! Forgive him now, for he may die. He may die before Easter. In Ian Maclaren's recent story the hero, on approaching Communion Sunday, thinks of a misunderstanding he had had with a college friend years before. That misunderstanding lies like lead upon his heart. One night he does not go to bed, and

after midnight he walks a long distance to the
telegraph station and sends a message to the man
to whom he has not spoken for many years. It
so chances the man is on his death-bed, but before
he dies he regains consciousness long enough to
send a message in reply. That is the way it
happened in the story, but that is not the way it
generally happens in the world. Usually we wait
too long. We wait until our enemy is dead, and
then we say, " If he were only back, I would not
be so proud. I would put out my hand. I would
take the first step forward. I would work to
bring about a reconciliation."

Love your enemy! Forgive him, and do it
now, for you may die before Easter. What
would you say if you should go into the presence
of God and admit that the preacher had made it
all plain; that he had read to you the parable of
the unmerciful servant with its great words of
warning at the close? Would it not be an awful
confession to make, " I had my attention called
to it — I wanted to do it — I was half inclined
to do it — but I would not do it. I did not do it,
and here, O God, I am ! "

Love your enemy, because you may live. God
may give you many years yet upon the earth, but
no matter how long you stay here, you will never
know what life is so long as you hate a single
human being. Life is not life when there is hatred
in the heart. Those of you who have ever had a
misunderstanding or a quarrel and have made it

up, know that after your pride had been crucified, and you had done the disagreeable and long-postponed duty, a flood of joy came into the heart that could not be expressed in words. It is after such experiences as that that one comes to know the meaning of the phrase, " The peace that passes understanding."

Love your enemy! Forgive him because God has forgiven you. Do not be ungrateful. Do not be mean. If God will wipe out a debt of ten million dollars, shame on you if you will not wipe out a debt of twenty-five dollars.

Love your enemy, and by so doing become a child of God. He causes the sun to rise on the evil and on the good. He sends his rain on the just and on the unjust. Be like him. Reproduce his disposition, and by and by you will behold him in his beauty.

It sometimes happens that men who have been harsh and hard all their lives become strangely sweet and mellow on their death-beds. A man who has not known the meaning of forgiveness will sometimes, in the closing hours, manifest the sweetest graces of the spirit. " Wife, bring to me the writing-pad, there is a man out west — we had a misunderstanding years ago — I have been proud and so has he, and neither one of us has ever been willing to take the first step toward an explanation, but I am going to write to him. I am going to ask him that it all may be forgotten and forgiven. And there is a man down town to whom I have not spoken for a dozen years. He did a mean thing to me. I felt very hateful at the time. I wonder if he would come to see me if I should write to him. I think after we have shaken hands it will not be so hard to die." Why do men so often act thus? Undoubtedly it is due to the work of the Holy Spirit. When the world begins to recede, its noises grow distant and faint, its hub-bub and thunder die out of the air, and in the awful silence that precedes the hour of dissolution the soul can hear as it could not hear in the noisier days the voice of Jesus saying, " Verily, I say unto you, love your enemies."

THE PRINCIPLE OF GIVING

THE PRINCIPLE OF GIVING

"Give to him that asketh thee, and from him that would borrow of thee turn not thou away." — Matt. v. 42.

THERE is evidently some mistake. How can a man do that? If a man should do that he would be a pauper in less than a month. There must be a mistake.

Possibly it is a wrong translation. The King James Version was made nearly three hundred years ago, and the translators did not always succeed in catching the meaning of the Greek. They possibly slipped in translating this sentence. But a few years ago a company of the keenest scholars in this country and in England made a new translation of the New Testament, and brought to their work the assistance of modern scholarship. We can therefore trust them to give us the correct translation. Here it is: "Give to him that asketh thee, and from him that would borrow of thee turn not thou away." They did not change a syllable.

Possibly Matthew wrote it wrong. What do the other Gospel writers have to say? Luke has the same idea, and here are his words (vi. 30) : "Give to every man that asketh of thee; and of

him that taketh away thy goods ask them not
again!" That is worse yet. There is no relief in
that direction. Possibly the context will throw
light on the sentence. It is evidently only a part
of a large sentence, the beginning or the end of it,
and after we have read what goes before and
what comes after, the mystery will be made clear.
But the sentence that goes before has no connection with this one. It ends a paragraph. The
sentence that follows has no connection with this
one. It begins a new paragraph. This text of
ours is a complete sentence. It ends with a period.
The context affords us no relief.

What shall we do? The easiest, laziest thing
to do is to say that it is figurative, that is, it
means nothing. If a thing is figurative it does
not amount to anything. Jesus was simply talking to entertain and astonish. It is an easy way
to get rid of the New Testament simply to say it
is figurative. But this will not answer. If it is
figurative it means something, and if it means
something we must find out what the meaning is.

What shall we do with it? The question is an
important one, because there are many sentences
like this scattered through the New Testament,
and if we learn how to deal with this sentence, we
shall know how to deal with all sentences that
belong to its class. This is a sentence which seems
to be impracticable, and the charge made against
Christianity just now is that it is not practicable
for men living under present conditions. It is

beautiful but theoretical, lovely but incapable of being reduced to practice. Now, if Jesus was visionary, and laid down rules which cannot be obeyed, then he is not the world's Redeemer, and we must look for another. We men are obliged to live upon this earth, and the only teaching that helps us is teaching that can be translated into conduct. If Christianity is beautiful to think about on Sunday, and impracticable on Monday, we cannot afford to think about it even on Sunday. The religion which we need is not a beautiful dream, but a solid reality which we can make use of along the dusty and difficult way. It is well worth our while, therefore, to find out if this sentence is the command of a visionary, or the exhortation of a man who knows the practical and indispensable principles of everyday life.

To understand the sentence we must first study the art of Jesus in public speech. He had a fashion of speech founded on certain principles, and it is by grasping these principles that we become able to interpret his sentences.

First of all, Jesus invariably spoke in such a way as to secure the attention of his audience. This was his first aim. This is the first aim of every man who knows how to speak. Unless he gets attention there is no use of him speaking at all. If he gets and holds attention he is a good speaker; if he cannot get attention he is a poor speaker, no matter how many good things may be said about him. Physical presence has nothing to

do with it. Men with the physique of Daniel
Webster have not been able to hold an audience
ten minutes, and little hunchbacks with thin
voices have chained audiences by their unique
and irresistible eloquence. Learning has nothing
to do with it. Some of the most learned men
become great bores as soon as they try to address
an audience, whereas many a man with no
knowledge of books has thrilled audiences with
his compelling and passionate speech. Rhetoric
has nothing to do with it. Men with a style as
polished as that of Apollos have proved tedious
and tiresome, while men with a style ragged and
unkempt have charmed audiences unable to escape their power. Grammar has nothing to do
with it. A man may be faultless and dull, and a
man may murder the Queen's English and succeed. Dwight L. Moody was one of the greatest
speakers this country has ever produced. He
could carry ten thousand people with him through
an hour, leaving them unconscious of the lapse of
time, even though he tripped in his grammar every
tenth sentence. What does an audience care for
grammar when held in the grip of a man who
knows how to talk? The first thing a speaker
must do is to get attention. Jesus always got it.
To get it he made use of various verbal devices.
It is not easy to get attention, and it is harder still
to hold it. Men are preoccupied. Their heads
are filled with their own ideas and schemes, and
only a strong man can compel them to listen.

The door is shut, and he who would enter must knock loud and long. Jesus knew how to knock. He used pictures. All men like pictures. We all have the child in us, and the child in us likes pictures. Jesus used pictures constantly in his preaching. The parables are so many stereopticon views of spiritual truth. The peasants of Palestine stood with open eyes looking at the verbal pictures which this genius from Nazareth painted. He used something stronger than pictures — paradoxes. He said things which on the face of them were contradictory, leaving it for the audience to wrestle with his contradictions and find out if they could how they could be reconciled. " Do you want to be great, be little." " Do you want to be chief, be least." " Do you want to be first, be last." " Do you want to rule, be a servant." " Do you want to save your life, lose it." These are a few illustrations of his paradoxical method. Men could not help listening. A paradox takes a man by both ears. He used something stronger still, hyperboles. " It is easier for a camel to go through the eye of a needle than for a rich man to enter into the kingdom of God." And at the end of the sentence the audience groaned. " Impossible! Impossible for anybody to be saved," was the cry. Jesus said, " You are mistaken. I did not say that. With God all things are possible." Again: " If you have faith and believe, you can say to this mountain, be ye removed and be cast into the sea, and it shall be done." Such language as that was sure to arrest attention. We can almost see the faces of the men as they listened. They listened so intently they could not keep still. They murmured. Time and again when he spoke an ugly buzz ran through the audience. The ideas, like cold water on fire, hissed as they fell into the hot hearts of men. Now and then a man would begin talking to himself, "Who is he? How did he learn that? I know his sisters. Isn't he a carpenter?" And occasionally men in the audience would enter into a great controversy even while he spoke. One man would say, "He is a good man." Another would say, "He is a bad man, he is deceiving the people." That is the best of all proofs of attention: mental activity in the audience. Jesus spoke with such power that his words entered into the very blood and marrow of men.

A second principle. He dealt with but one truth at a time. He always spoke to create an impression. He knew that the human mind is not capable of taking in two ideas at once. He singled out one truth which he wished to stamp upon men's hearts, and then drove that truth home with all the energy of his great nature. There was a theory once current among our theological wise men which had it been universally accepted would have wrecked the entire church. According to this theory Christianity is a system of truth, and the entire system must be presented in every sermon. Jesus is the Son of God. He is divine.

His divinity must be proclaimed therefore every Sunday. No matter what the text or what the subject, a sermon is incomplete unless it holds up Christ as a divine being. But that is only one truth. Christ died for men. He who knew no sin was made sin for us. By his blood we are redeemed. This is essential. The doctrine of atonement must have a place in every sermon. Man is a sinner. He must be born again. God calls on all men to repent. Every sermon, therefore, must have an appeal to the unconverted. Life is uncertain. A man may never hear but one sermon. It ought to be arranged, therefore, that no human being should ever enter a church without being told that he is a sinner, that Christ is divine, and that atonement has been made for his sins. The theory is quite plausible, but mischievous and fatal. It wrecks the pulpit and wears out the congregation. If a preacher is going to say the same things every Sunday, his sermon soon loses its power. People may come out one hundred times, but not five hundred times, to hear the same thing. Under preaching modelled after that pattern it became a proverb, "Dull as a sermon," dull because threadbare and worn out by constant repetitions.

The example of Jesus is a flat contradiction to this theory. He never presented truth as a system. He often spoke without referring to his divinity or his death or to the sin of man. There are many truths that man needs to know and these must be presented one at a time. This was the method of Jesus. He dealt with one truth as though there were none other in the entire universe of God. He carried his principle to extremes which seem to us reckless. Take, for example, his parable of the Unjust Judge. That parable fits at only one point. If you do not catch that one point you miss the lesson altogether. Or take even a stronger illustration, the parable of the Dishonest Steward. How easily misunderstood that is. Unless you grasp the one idea he is endeavoring to inculcate, you will be misled. I do not know of any public speaker so reckless as Jesus was in his allegiance to this principle of speech — " one idea at a time."

Jesus trusted his audience. Some men are always afraid of being misunderstood. They say, " Now, please do not misunderstand me, I did not mean to say " — and then they spend three minutes in explaining what they did not mean to say, and then they squander five minutes in making plain what they had intended to say, and the result is that half the people do not know when they get through what it is that they are expected to believe. Jesus trusted the people. He tossed his sentences into the air with great boldness, saying, " He that hath ears to hear let him hear." Some speakers weary an audience by running things out into their finest details. Jesus allowed men to do their own thinking. He simply started them, gave them a hint, a mental push, and then

said, " Now think it out for yourself." Second-
rate speakers wear the audience out by a foolish
striving for mathematical accuracy. They load
their sentences with parentheses and tack on
amendments and qualifying clauses. They in-
ject here an adjective which subtracts and there
an adverb which supplements, and the mind is
exhausted in trying to carry the great load. Some
speakers seem to speak an hour when they speak
thirty minutes, and others seem to speak thirty
minutes although they have spoken for two hours.
The difference lies in the difference in style. Why
is a German book harder to read than a French
book? The Frenchman has a finer literary style.
As Carlyle used to say, " The German does not
know how to drop the rubbish out of his sentences." The Frenchman knows how to do this.
The German sentence is long and involved, and
as Mark Twain says, you can travel all day in it
without changing cars; whereas the French sentence is clean cut, and transparent as crystal.
Some speakers are insufferably tedious because
they load down their sentences with rubbish.
Jesus never did. His sentences are like jewels.
He introduced no parentheses, tacked on no
amendments. He threw his ideas into the air
unencumbered and unentangled, and men were
left to make the necessary modifications and ad-
justments.

And now we are ready for our sentence, " Give
to him that asketh thee, and from him that would

borrow of thee turn not thou away." That is a
principle of life. Every man ought to give it
place in his heart. Without that principle life
would be a wreck, a failure. But this is not the
only principle. There are others just as important. There is one other far more important. No
principle lives to itself, and no principle dies to
itself. They are all united in the Lord. Love is
the central principle of human life. Jesus announced that first of all. Love was the heaven he
arched above men's heads before he began to
preach. Love was the foundation he spread beneath their feet before he attempted to teach them
the way of life. Love was the sun which he
hurled out into space, and all other principles were
planets to revolve around this central sun. All
that he said must be read in the light of the sun.
All that he commanded must be interpreted by
bringing it into relation with the chief of the
commandments.

"Give!" That is a planet. Its orbit is determined by the sun. It is limited by love. But
Jesus would not encumber his sentences by modi-
fying clauses. He wanted his idea to stand out
clear and sharp, so that every man would feel it.
He was talking to Jews. They all had itching
palms. Their ambition in life was to get. They
counted themselves happy in proportion to their
success in adding to their accumulations. The
whole nation was moving in that direction. Men
passed before him in an endless procession, and

they were all in pursuit of money. The Pharisees and the Sadducees and the scribes and the
publicans and the sinners, good and bad, pious
and wicked, — they all alike loved to get rather
than to give. And he threw at them this great
principle, "Give! Turn round. You are moving
in the wrong direction. You are missing the
glory of life. You have the wrong attitude; take
a new one. You live to get; live hereafter to
give! Give to the man who asks thee — from
him that would borrow of thee turn not thou
away." He burned that idea into the substance
of their brain. They never got away from it.

But suppose he had gone at it in a petty and
punctilious way. Suppose he had said: "Now
you ought to give under certain circumstances
and on certain conditions. If you can give in
justice to yourself and your wife and your children and your dependent relations, you ought to
give, providing you have first investigated the
needs of the person asking assistance, and convinced yourself he would not be injured by the
acceptance of your bounty." How tame and
commonplace all that would have been. It would
have made no impression. Nobody would have
remembered it. Matthew would not have caught
it, he could not have written it in his book. We
might never have known that Jesus said it. But
he said it in his own unique and magnificent way,
and those men never forgot it. To the day of
their death they talked about the carpenter of

Nazareth, marvelled at the passionate way in which he had told them that men ought to live to give.

But the principle has limitations. Love sets limits to all giving. We are never allowed to give unless our giving is a service. We have learned that in our homes. "Mamma, I want that," says the little child, with his big eyes glued upon the match box. To a child a match box is a mysterious institution. No other sticks are quite so fascinating, and those queer painted ends have wondrous possibilities. "Mamma, I want that," and the mother says, "No, my child." "Mamma, I want that," and this time he has his eyes on a bottle with a pictured label, and the mother says, "No, my child." Again the voice comes, "I want that," and this time the child is looking at his favorite dish. He has eaten much and he wants more. And again the answer is, "No, my child." But does not Jesus say — "Give to him that asketh thee"? Yes, but he also says, Love — and a mother cannot give unless her gift is a blessing to her child. Many a mother breaks Christ's commandment by giving when she ought to withhold her hand. "Mother, I want that!" "You cannot have it." "But I am going to have it." "No, you cannot have it." "But I am going to have it." "No, you cannot have it." And thereupon Johnnie cries and sobs and threatens to go into a fit of hysterics, and the mother says, "Now, Johnnie, I will let you have it this time,

but remember you can never have it again!" You
say, — that is mother love! Do not call it that.
Call things by their right names. Do not dese-
crate a noble word by throwing it on the shoulders
of a mischievous sin. That is not love. It is
weakness. One reason why there are so many
spoiled men and women in the world is because
there have been so many weak-willed and foolish
mothers. All giving is wrong that violates the
law of love.

We are under the same great law wherever we
go. We meet a man on the corner. He has been
in six saloons and wants to go into another. He
wants a dime to get him something to eat. We
refuse. Do we break the law of Christ? We
keep it. We must not give to any man unless our
giving will do him good. All Christian giving
must be a service. When we hurt by giving we
wound the heart of Christ.

The shiftless and lazy man comes to us for another loan. We know him, for he has been to us
before. He makes his plea, and we say, No. But
does not Christ say, " From him that would borrow of thee turn not thou away?" Yes, but he
also says that we are to love our brother and never
do him wrong. And we do a man wrong when
we encourage him in his shiftlessness and abet
him in his improvident courses.

It is exceedingly difficult to help men with
money without hurting them. " Charity is a terrible evil," said Edward Denison from the slums

of London. And that is what Christian workers in the slums of New York are saying all the time. It is a terrible evil, this indiscriminate, reckless giving, scattering money with a thoughtless hand, and demoralizing the very people we are trying to help. Andrew Carnegie is putting nearly all his gifts into libraries and art galleries and schools, because he has learned by bitter experience how difficult it is to help men without hurting them. Give to the man who asks you if you can in justice to him and yourself, and from him that would borrow do not turn away unless you must do so in loyalty to the law of love.

But we want no modifications this morning. Let us look at it in its naked simplicity — this great principle of life. " Give! " That is a Christian word. That is not a word of this world. The world never spoke that. Jesus uttered it. The world inscribes upon its banners, " Get." That is the ambition of all great cities. The struggle in a city is tremendous, and all things conspire to develop in us the acquisitive powers of our nature. Does a man want bread, he must struggle for it; does he want money, he must wrestle for it; fame, he must work for it. What is a city but a few hundred thousand human beings huddled together in a few square acres of land, every one of them striving to get!

But getting is not the great thing in human life. I hear men say with a twinkle in their eye — ah, he is a money-getter—as though that were a great

eulogy. But what does it mean? A money-getter? He may be a mean, narrow, contemptible
wretch. A Mexican bandit is a money-getter, so
is an Italian brigand, so is a prize fighter. Ralph
Nickleby was a money-getter, but every reader
of Dickens hates him. " Put money in thy purse,
put money in thy purse, put money in thy purse!"
Do you recognize the words? They are those of
Iago — Shakespeare's devil.

We are animals so long as we live to get. We
came into the world with our fists tightly clinched,
and some men need an entire lifetime to get their
hands opened. The shut hand is the symbol of
animalism; the open hand is the emblem of the
new man in Christ. Animals live to get. The
lion goes forth to seek his prey. Some men are
like the lion. The city is a forest in which they
search for victims. The dog snatches the biggest
bone and runs. His ambition is to get. The hog
steps into the trough with all four feet because a
hog lives to get. Man alone is capable of giving.
He can stand erect with open hand, his face
toward his brother's face, and can imitate the example of Almighty God and be a dispenser of
benefactions. You do not live unless you live to
give.

The commandment is for all. It is addressed
to no one class or circle. It is for the poor as well
as for the rich. There is a feeling prevalent to-
day among the poorer classes that their poverty
releases them from the obligation of giving.

They have a fashion of saying: "Let the rich people do this and let the rich people do that. They are able to do it, why not let them do it?" We sometimes hear such talk even inside the Christian church. Where do you find such doctrine anywhere set forth in the Scripture? By what word of apostle or Lord has the poor man been released from the obligation of giving? The Lord is the friend of the poor and so he urges them to give. He does not want them to be dogs under the rich man's table. He wants them to take their places among the hosts of the redeemed. It is only by giving that we enter into the life of God. A poor man can give much, but a rich man cannot. If the latter is worth a hundred millions and gives half of it away, he does not give much. He has given out his superfluity. But the poor man who gives out of his pittance gives much — and great shall be his reward.

Give! The word comes to those who are in moderate circumstances. Give, and do not delay. Giving is one of the duties we like to postpone. We say, "When my income is larger, when times are better, then how generous I shall be." The man who waits to give until he can give largely is in danger of never giving at all. Now is the accepted time, now is the day of salvation. The other evening the richest man in New York gave an address to a company of young men. In the course of his remarks he took from his pocket a little book, the most precious book to him, he

said, in the world, and read out of it certain figures. It was an account book in which he had
recorded his expenditures in the first years of his
business life, when he was earning from four to
six dollars a week. One cent a week went to the
Sunday-school. There was a contribution of ten
cents to foreign missions. There was a gift of
twelve cents to the Mite Society. They were all
small contributions, but they did a great work.
They kept alive in that man's soul the spirit of
generosity. And the reason he now gives away
a million at a time is because when he was poor
he gave a cent every week to the Sunday-school.
His advice to those young men was, " Give now.
It is a mistake for a man who wishes for happiness and to help others, to think that he will wait
until he has made a fortune before giving away
money to deserving objects."

Give! The commandment comes with special
emphasis to the rich. For to whom much has
been given from them shall much be required. A
man with wealth in a world like this has weighty
responsibilities. His temptation is to dress in
fine linen and fare sumptuously every day, and
forget that needy humanity lies sick at his door.
As a man prospers in this world's goods he naturally adds to the number of his luxuries, and
these luxuries in time become necessities, swallow-
ing up his income, and leaving him little opportunity to obey Christ's command to give. The
stewardship of wealth as taught by the Redeemer

of the world fastens upon a rich man's soul a weight of responsibility for whose discharge he must answer at the judgment day.

Give! That is the attitude for every soul to take. That is the disposition for every soul to cultivate. Let the poor man say, " I will give out of my poverty." Let the rich man say, " I will give out of my abundance." Let every man say, " I will make it a principle of my life to give, and nothing shall set limits to my giving but the golden law of love."

MORE THAN OTHERS

MORE THAN OTHERS

" What do ye more than others ? " — Matt. v. 47.

My text is a question — a question of Jesus.
He is preaching to a crowd in Galilee. He is telling men how to live. He is putting up the standards. The people of Palestine in the first century
were in a very complacent mood. They were so
self-satisfied that many of them were self-conceited. They had divided all the world into two
great sections, and between the two sections they
had run a gulf broad and deep; on the one side
were the Jews and on the other side were the Gentiles; the Jews were saved, the Gentiles were lost.
The Jewish world they had divided into two sections, and as a dividing line they had run a chasm
broad and deep; on one side were the religious
people, on the other side were the publicans and
sinners. It was to the self-complacent people that
Jesus was speaking. " It was said to them of old
time, do this and do that; that was all well
enough for people two thousand years ago, but I
say unto you, you must live on higher levels than
did the people who lived in the morning of the
world. It was said to people in the olden times,
you must not do this or that, but I say unto you,

you must do more than was ever commanded your fathers." When he saw the look of astonishment and opposition on their faces, he said, " If you love those that love you, what reward have you? do not even the publicans the same?" Mark that word "publicans" — oh, what a dagger thrust was that! Do not even the publicans the same? He stepped across the chasm and picked up a man that was regarded as lower than the dogs. He said, " O you religious people, if you love those only who love you, you are on a moral level in that respect with the lowest of the sinners, and if you do *good* to those who do good to you, what reward have you? do not even sinners the same? And if you lend only to those from whom you expect to ask the same favor, do not even sinners as much? And if you salute your brethren only, what do ye more than others? do not the Gentiles the same? I say unto you, Love your enemies. Do them good. Lend, never despairing, and your reward shall be great. You shall be sons of the Most High, for he is kind toward the unthankful and the evil."

We are all creatures of imitation. We come into the world with a strong disposition to mimic the actions of those about us. Every child is born with this tendency strong within him. It is marvellous how readily a little child picks up the oddities and mannerisms of his parents, and reproduces them in his own face and conduct. As soon as the child goes out into the street he begins to conform his life to the life with which he comes in contact there. " Mother, why can't I do that? all the other boys do it." That is the sort of logic which grows up naturally in a boy's brain and heart. " Mother, won't you buy me that? all the other girls have one." That is the argument which every girl makes use of. We smile at children, and yet we do the same things ourselves. We measure ourselves by the standard of society, we ape the manners of those with whom we live. We count ourselves happy or unhappy in proportion as we possess, or do not possess, the things which our neighbors are enjoying. We are good if we are not worse than our neighbors. In the first century in Palestine the Jews imitated one another in all the services of religion. They fasted and they feasted; they went to church in obedience to fixed rules; they watched the fringes on one another's garments, and were satisfied with the praise of men. Into this complacent and self-conceited circle, with its petty standards and arbitrary and fantastic etiquette, the Son of God walked. " How can you believe," he said, " who receive honor one of another and seek not the honor that comes from God only? "

That is what he says to us to-day. Society is divided into sets; each man is satisfied if he lives up to the requirements of the set in which he moves. The thieves and murderers have a standard to which they willingly conform, and all the way from the bottom upward there are codes of morals for the various grades of people. The average man is always satisfied if he is doing no worse than his neighbors. We need to be called away again and again from the little circle in which we live, that our minds may be pressed hard against the standards of the Son of God. This is the question which he keeps putting to us, " What do ye more than others? "

What is your attitude toward your enemies? Do you hate them? Do you hold a grudge against them? those people who have lied about you, and who deserted you when you needed them; and who pretended to be true and were your enemy behind your back; what is your attitude toward them? Do you say, if they will come and apologize to me and say they are sorry for what they did, then I will forgive them — if you say that, what do you more than others? Do not even prize fighters so? Lives there a man or woman who, if his enemy gets down in the dust before him, will refuse to grant forgiveness?

On what principle do you live your social life? If you salute your brethren only, what reward have you? On what principle do you give your dinners and your suppers? Jesus said, " When you make a dinner or a supper, do not invite simply your friends and brethren and kinsmen and rich neighbors in order that they may in turn ask you to take a meal with them, but when you make a feast invite the poor and the maimed and the lame and the blind. Let people sit at your table who can make you no return, and you shall receive a reward in the resurrection of the just." On what principle do you give your dinners? Jesus did not condemn the practice of inviting friends and brethren and kinsmen and rich neighbors, he was not opposed to the courtesies and civilities of life, but do you stop there? Have you learned Christian hospitality? If a man is a Christian, he must go beyond the common civilities of polite society. Social position is a sacred trust to be used in the world's redemption. Have you ever asked the poor to take a meal with you? Have you ever opened your door to the friendless and the lonely? In this great city, where there are thousands of young men away from home, working hard all day and going home at night to dreary lodging houses, have you ever asked any of these young men to sit for an hour at your table? In this city, where so many thousands of young women have come bravely to fight their way against obstacles innumerable, have you ever asked any of them to step inside your door? You know what the city is, and how the houses stretch away through dreary miles of wood and stone and iron, in the midst of which human hearts grow sick and faint, and have you ever in your life asked a lonely-hearted woman to sit one hour at your table? The Son of God says that social position is to be used, not simply for personal enjoyment, but for the consolation of those to whom our ministry may be sweet. If you give all your dinners simply to those who will give you dinners in return, what do ye more than the shallowest and giddiest so-called lady in the most godless society in the city?

What is your principle of action in the industrial world? How do you treat the people who work for you? The relations between employer and employee are strained the world over. The wage-earning classes are increasingly discontented and envious. What are you doing to sweeten the hearts of the people who earn their bread by the sweat of the brow? You men who have men working for you, what is your behavior toward them? Do you treat them like hands, slaves, machines? or do you treat them like brother men? When a man does well, do you praise him? When he is faithful do you reward him? Are you kind to him? Do you sympathize with him when his wife is sick or when the baby dies? Are you a brother to him? Mistresses, how do you treat your servants? What kind of a bed do they sleep on? What kind of a room do they live in? Do you ever commend them? Do you encourage them to read? Do you sympathize with them and endeavor to throw any sunlight into their lives? Do you ever give them a day of rest? or do you oblige them to work six days of the week, and then give them extra work on Sunday? If you do that you are lower than the people were under the Mosaic dispensation, for Moses said, " On the seventh day thou shalt not do any work, thou, nor thy son, nor thy daughter, nor thy man servant, nor thy maid servant." God's compassion is over the servants, and they as well as their mistresses need rest. It is an awful thing to compel any human being to work seven consecutive days out of every week straight through the year. Do you give your servants a day of rest? Do you say to them, " Drop your work and do to-day what you please? " or do you say, " Work on, and the minute you stop your work I will stop your wages." If you drive your servants straight through the month, giving them no opportunity for recuperation or enjoyment, then what do you do more than the Egyptian taskmasters that drove their helpless slaves to build the pyramids in the dark days of Pharaoh?

How much Christianity do you carry into your church? The church is the body and the bride of Christ. It is the instrument by means of which Christ is to subdue the world. No man can turn his back upon the church without turning his back on an open door of usefulness. The church must be supported by Christ's followers. Every Christian is under obligation to contribute to its support. If he is rich, he must give out of his riches; if he is poor, he must give out of his poverty. He must give whether he attends the services of the church or not. Attendance has nothing to do with his obligation to give. He may be so circumstanced that he cannot come at all. He may be an invalid, deprived of the privi-

lege of worshipping in God's house, but he is
under the same obligation to contribute to the support of the church as he would be were he in his
pew every Sunday in the year. On what principle
do you determine your contributions to the
church? Do you say: " I will give as much as my
neighbor gives. I have twice his income, but I
will not give a cent more than he does "? Do you
say, " I am not going to be present the entire
year, therefore I will pay in proportion to the
number of Sundays I attend "? Now, if a man
throws so many anthems and sermons into one
pan on the scales, and so many dollar bills into
the other pan, and endeavors to secure a fine
balance between them, pulling out a few dollars
in order that he may not pay for any sermon or
anthem which he does not get, — if a man does
that, what is he doing more than a pagan merchant in Canton who buys and sells goods at a
bargain? If you pay for only the sermons which
you hear, what do ye more than others? Does
not the most godless theatre-goer in the town do
the same? for he pays when he goes and when he
does not go he does not pay.

What is your attitude toward national problems? There is no greater problem before
America to-day than the liquor problem. This
nation is spending more for drink than it is spending for clothing and meat, and for missions and
schools all together. The saloon is an alarming
danger and an intolerable curse. Its demoraliza-

tion is widespread. The horror of it cannot be expressed in speech. The havoc of it extends from the great city down to the smallest country hamlet, for even there men and boys are drinking themselves to death. Out of the saloon door come most of our criminals, most of our paupers, most of our lunatics. What is your attitude toward the saloon? We have over 7500 of them here in Manhattan, many of them dirty, stinking holes, where the air is heavy with profanity and where criminals congregate to hatch their nefarious plots, — all of them open doors through which human beings are passing in unbroken procession down to the chambers of death. What is your attitude toward the saloon? Are you indifferent? Do you say it does not touch you, that your family is all right? Suppose it does not touch you, do you never see in your dreams the great host of people that it does touch? Do you never see the thousand little children with faces white as chalk because there are no red corpuscles in the blood, owing to the fact that their fathers, instead of buying meat, have poured their weekly wages into the rumseller's till? Do you never see the thousand wives with haggard faces and broken hearts, afraid of the men who stood at the altar promising to love them until death? Do you never see the thousand mothers, dear, broken-hearted women, lying awake at night waiting until their boy comes home, praying to God to keep him, and not knowing whether he will come in his right mind or with reason all dethroned? Can you see all these and then talk about the saloon not touching you? What is your attitude toward the saloon? Do you ask sarcastically, what can be done? If you say that, what say you more than others? Do not even the cutthroats and the thugs say the same? The curse of our city life is that it takes the fire out of men. We are in danger of degenerating into a lot of dainty, fastidious dabblers in music, art, literature, incapable of feeling the burning indignation which Christian men and women ought to feel against gigantic wrongs. We are in danger of becoming a lot of industrious chatterers, chattering on all sorts of insignificant questions, and leaving undone the weightier matters of the law. What is your attitude toward the saloon? Do you smile at temperance people as fanatics? Oh, for the fanaticism which Jesus had! which Garrison and Wesley and Wycliffe and Huss and Savonarola and Polycarp and James and John the Baptist and Paul had! There is a leech sucking the red blood from the veins of our republic. That leech is the liquor traffic. Do you say that nothing can be done? O pessimism, thou art born of the devil and of a lack of faith in the Son of God! If you Christian men and women are content to let the saloon quietly run on, wrecking homes and damning souls, what do ye more than others?

Let us come out into the wider arena of the world's thought. The great problem before the

nations of the world to-day is the problem of war
and peace. What is your attitude toward war?
Do you hate it? What is your attitude toward
peace? Do you love it? War has been the most
gigantic evil of our century. A large part of the
suffering and hatred existing in modern civilization can be traced directly to war. The century
was opened by the booming cannon of that colossal highwayman, Napoleon Bonaparte. Some of
you have stood by his tomb. As you looked down
upon his sarcophagus, with the angels and the
flags around it, did you see in your imagination
his accursed arm stretched out over Europe still
grinding the faces of the poor? Nearly every
peasant in Southern Europe has a heavier burden
on his back because Napoleon Bonaparte sold
himself to the devil. A large part of all the social
and industrial disturbances of the last fifty years
can be traced directly to the Napoleonic wars.
John Richard Greene, one of the keenest-eyed of
all English historians, says this: " The war enriched the landowner, the capitalist, the manufac-
turer, the farmer, but it impoverished the poor.
It is indeed from the fatal time which lies between
the peace of Amiens and Waterloo that we must
date that war of classes, that social severance between rich and poor, which still forms the great
problem of the world of politics." Professor Rog-
ers, in his calm and cool discussion of " Work and
Wages," asserts that the distress of the laboring
classes had its deeper cause in the ruinous wars

of the present century. Europe is groaning under a debt of twenty thousand million dollars. Nearly all of this has been spent in war. Spain is practically bankrupt, and so is Italy, and so is Turkey. Austria is on the way to bankruptcy. Russia would be bankrupt should she undertake a great war. And, saddest of all, the burden, instead of growing lighter, is growing heavier. The armaments are increasing year by year. The expenditures for army and navy have increased within thirty years almost a hundred per cent. There are to-day twenty-four thousand miles of soldiers in the armies of Europe. You who have travelled up and down Italy and out through Austria, and back through Germany, know how in all the fields, on every hillside and in every valley, the men and women and little children are constantly at work. On coming to the cities you have seen soldiers marching and countermarching and drilling and loafing, eating up the produce which the men and women and children have scratched out of the fertile soil. On the back of every peasant there is a soldier, and yet men wonder that the masses are embracing the socialism of Karl Marx and the anarchism of Prudhon. The wonder to me is, not that there should be a few thousand anarchists and nihilists, but that the whole continent of Europe has not been blown long ago into the air. It is amazing that the fabric of society has not been torn down and trampled under the frenzied feet of the blind Samson who has been kept grinding at the mill. William T. Stead has had a recent conference with the Czar, and the other day he thrilled an immense audience in St. James's Hall, London, by saying that if the Czar's reading of present-day history is true, the civilized world is progressing at an ever accelerating speed to hell. Not the hell of after-death, but the hell that will seize upon corrupt and demoralized society in this world. What is your attitude toward war? Are you cynical? and do you say things must remain as they are? If you say that, what say you more than the sleek and shallow blasphemers who loaf and group in the cafés of Paris and Berlin?

What is your attitude toward war? Do you hate it with all your mind and heart and soul? O Church of the Living God, read the newspapers less and the New Testament more. A recent traveller through Europe has said that every ruler and statesman in Europe whom he had met is convinced that since the world began no more efficient instrument of Satan has ever been forged in hell for creating trouble and turmoil and fomenting wars among the nations than the irresponsible newspaper press. Turn away from the newspaper, read the New Testament, look into the face of that man who, when the devil suggested war to him, said: " Get thee behind me, Satan," who was so gentle that the bruised reed he would not break, the smoking flax he would not quench, so tender and quiet that he would not

strive nor lift his voice in the streets, so wise and
good that he refused the defence of the sword,
saying, " Put up your sword, for all they that
take the sword shall perish with the sword "; who
hated war so intensely that when the day arrived
for his triumphal entry into Jerusalem, he rode
on the back of an ass, the animal of industry
and peace.   If you apologize for expanding armies
and growing navies, if you say that war after all
is not so bad for it brings great and lasting blessings, what do ye more than others?   Do not even
the Napoleons and the Bismarcks and all the
other red-handed robbers say the same?

" What do ye more than others?"   The reason
why the church has so little influence in the world
is because it is so little different from the world.
The distinction between the church and the world
is almost rubbed out; you can scarcely tell where
the church ends and the world begins.   " I never
knew he was a Christian," said a man of a friend
of his who had been his friend for twenty years.
What an awful condemnation of a man's Christianity that was!   A Christian man ought to have
a tone in his voice that cannot be mistaken.   His
conceptions ought to bear upon their face the
impress of the Son of God.   His attitude toward
all perplexing problems ought to be so majestic
and so true, that all the world can say without
misgiving, He is a Christian man.

CONCENTRATION

CONCENTRATION

"These twelve Jesus sent forth, and charged them, saying, Go not into any way of the Gentiles, and enter not into any city of the Samaritans." — Matt. x. 5.

DID you ever quarrel with a Bible sentence? Did you ever anywhere in Scripture find a statement which you felt compelled to contradict because it seemed foolish, mischievous, or false? Did you ever read an assertion in the Old Testament or in the New which you were sorry to find because you felt it was necessary to apologize for it, as exhibiting the prejudice, narrowness, or ignorance of the man from whom the assertion came? I in my time have quarrelled with many Bible sentences, with several of them I have had a tremendous tussle. Again and again I have discovered sentences in the Scriptures unworthy of revelation, and have drawn my pencil through them and have cast them as rubbish to the wind. And I am bound to confess that I have often gone out and picked up the discarded sentences and discovered in them more wisdom than I had first seen.

I have taken for my text a sentence with which I quarrelled twenty years ago. "Go not into the way of the Gentiles." Jesus is sending his twelve disciples out to preach the Gospel. He is instruct-

ing them concerning their work. The first word
of their marching order is, " Go not into any way
of the Gentiles." In other words, confine yourself to little Galilee and little Judea, and let all the
rest of the world alone. I did not like that. It
did not sound well. It sounded Jewish, bigoted,
and narrow. It had a tone which reminded me
of harsh and crabbed tones which I had heard
from the lips of narrow saints in the old dispensation. " Confine yourselves to Jews, and do not
go near the rest of mankind," was not becoming,
I thought, on the lips of the world's Redeemer.

But what are we going to do with such a sentence? We might say that it is an interpolation, a
gloss slipped in by some impertinent redactor, but
the same idea runs all through the Gospels. Not
only did Jesus command his disciples to give
themselves wholly to the Jews, but he acted on
that principle himself. He hedged himself in, and
would not so much as look over the hedge into
the great world which lay dying in its sins. An
illustration of his attitude to outside people is
furnished by the story of the woman of Canaan
narrated in the 15th chapter of Matthew's Gospel.
One day Jesus and his apostles, in order to get
away from the people, slipped over the boundary
of the promised land and journeyed northward
into the country of Phœnicia. While walking
along the road a woman of that country, who in
some way or other had heard of Jesus and his
power, came rushing toward him, crying, " Son

of David, have mercy upon me, for my daughter is
tormented by a demon." But he answered her
not a word. Have you ever pondered that sentence? Is it not a mysterious sentence to be
found in the Gospels? "He answered her not a
word!" Is this the man who has been going up
and down the land saying, "Come unto me all
ye that labor and are heavy laden, and I will give
you rest?" Here is a woman weighted with a
burden which crushes her almost to the earth.
She cries, "Have mercy on me! Have mercy on
me!" And "he answers her not a word." He
does worse than that. He turns his back on her
and walks on, just as you walked on the other
evening when the man asked you for a dime on
the street corner. But the woman is persistent.
She does not give up her appeal. She follows
him, crying, "Have mercy on me! Help me —
Have mercy!" Finally the disciples cannot stand
it any longer. Peter — I know it was Peter —
is so distressed by the woman's cries, that he says,
"I am going to ask the Master to send that
woman away." Along with several of the disciples he goes to Jesus, saying, "Send this woman
away, for she keeps bawling after us all the time."
Thereupon Jesus gives them this explanation of
his conduct. "I am not sent but unto the lost
sheep of the house of Israel!" Is this the man
who has been saying, "Him that cometh unto me
I will in no wise cast out?" Is it possible that
the Lord is not so tender-hearted as his disciples?

He finally yielded and granted this woman's prayer, but there were times when he did not yield. It was near the close of his life that a company of Greeks travelled to Jerusalem to have an interview with Jesus. They approached Philip and told him the object of their coming. But Philip did not dare to introduce them to Jesus. Philip knew the Master's rule, and he dared not break it. But these men had come so far and seemed so earnest, that Philip hesitated to turn them away. He went to Andrew and asked him what ought to be done. They thought it over and decided they would tell Jesus that these men had come. But Jesus did not see them. Instead of going out and talking with these visitors, he began to tell his disciples that unless a grain of wheat falls into the ground and dies, it abides alone, but if it dies it brings forth fruit. As much as to say, " I cannot do this now, but after I am dead the Gospel will reach these men and many nations in far-off lands."

Here we have, then, an interesting question. What interpretation shall we give to the command, " Go not into the way of the Gentiles." Is it Jewish prejudice and provincial narrowness and racial exclusiveness, or is it superior wisdom and unparalleled strength and the gracious movement of far-sighted love? Twenty years ago I saw in the sentence nothing but narrowness and bigotry; to-day I see nothing but divine wisdom and boundless love.

Jesus set limits to his activities. He had but a few years to live, and he knew it. None of us have many, he had fewer than most of us. His nervous energy was limited, and nervous energy is the force with which great teachers drive home great spiritual truths. He had a mighty work to accomplish, and the success of his undertaking depended upon the depth of the impression he could make in a limited time. He was planting a tree, and it was necessary to plant the tree in one place. He could not run hither and thither, sowing seed in all sorts of fields. He had a tree to plant, and it was necessary to plant the tree in the one spot where there was greatest depth of soil to receive it, for if the tree struck root and grew, its leaves would be for the healing of the nations. He had an impression to make, and it was necessary to make the impression deep, or else it would be washed away by the storms of a dozen seasons. And to make the impression deep he was compelled to do all his work within a narrow circle. For over a year he practically gave himself up to twelve men, holding them always in his presence that they might be drenched with his spirit and completely dominated by his ideas. He knew if he succeeded in getting his principles into the sinew and marrow of these men, so that his thoughts and feelings would run red in their blood, they would be able to turn the world upside down. It was the breadth of his ambition which compelled him to be narrow. He hedged himself in because he kept his eyes on the ends of the earth. It was because his purposes were so vast, and his wisdom so far-reaching, that he could not allow himself to go into the way of the Gentiles. He could have done good anywhere. Up and down the Nile there were myriads of sick people that needed the cooling touch of his redeeming hands. In Rome society was sick, and had he gone there he could have lifted many a soul out of the pit of sin and despair. All around Palestine there were nations sick with many sores, lying helpless in a darkness which had no relieving ray of light, and unto all these nations he might have carried peace and liberty and joy. But he stayed at home. His knowledge of the world's great need kept him at home. He did not forget the world. It was always in his thought. " God so loved the world that he gave his only begotten Son." " The field is the world." " They shall come from the east and the west and the north and the south, and shall sit down with Abraham and Isaac and Jacob in the kingdom of God." " And I if I be lifted up will draw all men unto me." It was his knowledge of the need of the world, and his determination to save all the nations, which compelled him to stay inside the borders of Palestine, and forbade him to go into the way of the Gentiles.

Occasionally he seemed to violate the policy of his life, but the exceptions are only in appearance. The Canaanitish woman, although at first refused, finally secured the blessing for which she appealed. How are we to explain this change of conduct on the part of Jesus? We have all been told, I imagine, that Jesus intended to heal the woman's daughter all the time, and that he met her with silence and rebuff at first, simply to test her faith. But does not your heart rise in rebellion against that explanation? My soul cries out against it. Never will I believe that the Son of God is capable of toying with a woman's grief, or experimenting with a heart tortured to the point of breaking. There is a better explanation for Jesus' action than that. Jesus did not at first answer the woman's prayer, because he could not. Supreme wisdom would not allow him to do it. He had no right to overstep the line which God had laid down as the limit of his activity. He was not at liberty to do anything which human impulse might urge or suggest. He was obliged to work under laws which he could not transgress. His brethren and friends often tried to induce him to do things which he could not do. He had a strange fashion of saying, " My hour has not yet come." He could not use his hours to satisfy the whims of his friends. His mission would not allow this. He said one day to his brethren, you can go to Jerusalem at any time. You can go in the morning, or in the afternoon or evening, on Monday or Tuesday or Wednesday. Your time is always ready, but my hour is not yet come. He was limited in the use of his time, and also in the use of his nervous energy. His energy was bread, and it belonged to the Jewish people. So he told the woman in the country of Phœnicia. But this woman turned out to be an extraordinary woman. She revealed to him a preparedness of heart which he had not expected to find there. As he looked into her pleading eyes he saw the faith of Abraham, and the tenacity of Jacob, and the devotion of David. This woman, though a Gentile in name and dress, was in reality a member of the chosen family, and the moment she climbed to the level of the Hebraic faith, the instant she threw herself within the circle of his ordained activity, he cried, " O woman, great is thy faith," and gave her the blessing which she sought. He blessed her as soon as it was possible for him to do it. Even the pleading cry of a wounded mother would not budge him from the narrow path in which his Father had commanded him to walk; it was her spiritual preparedness which obtained from him the blessing.

My subject is, " Concentration essential for the production of great works and lasting results." It is my purpose to indicate to you one of the causes of the weakness of the modern church. The church is weak. So says everybody. What is the matter with it? One says the trouble lies with the ministers. Just what is the matter with the ministers is not clear. President Hyde of Bowdoin College declared at the last International Council in Boston that the trouble lies in the seminaries. They are antiquated institutions cumbered with obsolete methods of instruction. The professors are on the whole fossils who persist in teaching all sorts of ologies which the world has long since outgrown, and in which men of to-day have no sort of interest, and if we are ever to have a new set of ministers capable of effective preaching, we must overhaul our seminaries and breathe into them a fresh breath of life. So said President Hyde in his own elegant and convincing way — and there are many who agree with him. Others think the trouble lies in the ministers themselves. They are not of sufficient caliber to fill the positions whose duties they attempt to perform. Some critics have been kind and gracious enough to assert that if a man is not good for anything else he usually goes into the ministry. Those who hold this view of the situation think that the seminaries do as well as they can, considering the poor material on which they are obliged to work. The professors are wise men, and the courses of study are superb, but no school can make first-class preachers out of third-rate men. I am inclined to think that neither explanation is the true one. Whether there has been the decay in pulpit power of which we hear so much, is, I think, a debatable question, but certainly there is no question concerning the fact that the pulpit of to-day is not as effective as it ought to be. One reason is that preachers have been obliged to go into the way of the Gentiles.

They are not allowed to concentrate their strength upon one specific form of work, and by a dissipation of their energies they give the world a chance to scoff. Within the last fifty years there has been an enormous expansion of church machinery, and this machinery has proved the ruin of many preachers. Every church has from six to twenty different organizations, and each one of these demands a portion of the minister's energy and a slice of his time. The minister belongs to a denomination, and his denomination has its meetings, councils, conferences, associations; and these meetings must be attended, and they all eat up strength and time. A minister belongs to the city in which he lives, and around him there are scores of philanthropic institutions which need assistance, and to which he is exhorted to give time and thought. There are missionary societies of many types and names, and these societies must have their official boards. There are colleges and hospitals and asylums, and all these must have their trustees or overseers. The minister is a man of education and of noble impulses, and as he seems to have more time than anybody else, he is crowded into these positions, until all his time and strength are consumed in the administration of the big machine of modern philanthropic and religious work.

But a minister is not ordained to do this work. He is a teacher, and if he is to teach he must study, and if he is to study he must have time.

In our larger universities the best professors are given four months' vacation every year, and one year out of seven for study in Europe, and when they are on duty they have but few recitations in a week, the policy being to give them as much time as possible for study. If a man is to teach, and to teach with vitality and force, he must be an indefatigable student, and be given an abundance of time. The educational world has learned that long ago. The church must learn it or we shall be wrecked. The decay of pulpit power is caused by decay of study, and the decay of study is necessitated by the pressure which has driven ministers into the way of the Gentiles. Have you ever considered what a minister ought to know? He ought to know the Bible, but he cannot know it without the hardest kind of work. It is the most difficult book in all the world to master. It has more sides than any other book. It has deeper depths. It has vaster mysteries. It requires more time than any other book. Its truths cannot be taken in at a glance, but only by patient and long-continued meditation. If a minister is to teach this book as it ought to be taught, he must sit down with it and think about and digest it, and dream about it and live with it. If he spends his week attending meetings he cannot study the book. But the man who knows nothing but the Bible cannot preach successfully to this generation. He must know theology. He must be versed in the learning of the great scholars of the Christian church. He cannot preach the Gospel in a form acceptable to his age unless he knows the forces which have worked together to mould the thought and temper of the people to whom he speaks. He must be a student of history. He ought to know history, for history is a Bible in which God's will and character are revealed. There are various pages of history which he ought to know with special thoroughness, English history, for instance, from the time of the Tudors, and American history from the landing of the Pilgrims to the last presidential campaign. It is a wide field, but he must know it. He must be a student of philosophy. He ought to know the course of philosophic thought from Thales to Kant and from Kant to Lotze. Philosophic ideas lie at the basis of our life. The man in the street is influenced by what the philosopher is thinking in his study. A preacher must know not only what is in the air, but also how it got there, and how it can be used for God's glory. He must be a student of science, not to teach science, but to preach the Gospel with the right emphasis and discrimination. How can a man preach the Gospel with freshness and vitality if he is not familiar with the ideas which are dominating the thought of his time. He must be a student of the vast changes which are taking place in the industrial world. We are in the midst of one of the mightiest upheavals of the human mind known to history. The preacher must know the forces which are at work and study the outcome of present tendencies and impulses. He ought to know the entire socialistic movement from Karl Marx to Bebel, from Robert Owen to William Morris. He must be a student of Biblical criticism. For the last century there has been a school of scholars in the field which has modified all the traditional conceptions of Scripture, and compelled a rewriting of the doctrines of revelation. Thinking men are not going to listen to-day to a man preach who is not perfectly familiar with the whole trend and scope of Biblical criticism from Eichhorn to Harnack. He must be a constant reader of poetry to keep his vocabulary simple and rich and warm. He must be a student of literature in its noblest forms to keep his style from becoming slipshod and tame. He must read current literature to know the world in which his people are living. He must be an indefatigable student or he is lost. If he spends his week in writing letters and seeing callers and holding meetings, and manipulating the machinery of a dozen different organizations, he cannot go into the pulpit on the Lord's day and speak with that fulness of information, and that maturity of judgment, and that preparedness of feeling, and that grace and accuracy of speech, which intelligent and cultivated men and women have a right to demand of those who lead them in the higher realms of thought and feeling and action. If he wears himself out in details of church activity, he will have for the pulpit nothing but stale platitudes and feeble exhortations. I talked once with a minister just after he had read his letter of resignation. He had started out with bright prospects, and for years all had gone well. But by and by the congregations began to dwindle, and everything went hard and people began to say, " He is a good man, but — ! " That to a minister is what electrocution is to a criminal. Things went from bad to worse, and finally he resigned. He talked with me about his life and told me how hard he had worked. He had been the president of this and the treasurer of that and the secretary of something else. He had been on this board of trustees, and on that board of overseers, and on this executive committee, and he named over a list of a dozen or fifteen societies and organizations to which he had given his time and his strength. I then understood why he had failed. He had thrown away his life by going into the way of the Gentiles! Many a minister has driven nails into his own coffin by squandering his strength on outside institutions and causes. There are theological students in this congregation this morning. Let me say to you, young men, write this sentence in letters of gold on the walls of your study, " Go not into the way of the Gentiles." It is the first commandment of our Lord for preachers. In sending out the twelve he drew a circle before their eyes, and said, Do all your work inside of that. He does the same for you. Set limits to your activity or you will never preach the Gospel with grace or power. I do not advise you to shut yourself up in your study and pay no attention to the outside world. You belong to your denomination and your city and the church universal, and you owe them duties which it is not right to shirk. But remember that your pulpit has the first claim upon you, and beware of going before your people with your nervous energy exhausted and all your fires extinguished.

What the preachers have been doing the laymen have done also. They have frittered away their powers on a multitude of causes, and neglected the church they have promised to serve. We are the most inventive of all nations, and our organizations for ministering to the wants of humanity cannot be numbered. A great city has more societies and clubs engaged in philanthropic and religious work than a rose bush has roses in the month of June. These societies and clubs pass before us, pleading with us to join them and we are so good-natured and so weak-willed that we consent. We say, " Yes, I will join, but please do not ask much of me, for I am too busy to do anything but give my name." And so we have formed the habit of joining things, just because somebody asks us to join, and because we have not the courage to refuse. Many carry the habit into the church. They give the church their names and think that by doing this they have joined the church. They take the most solemn vows upon them, and before the ink is dry upon the church book in which their names have been

written, we look up to see their forms vanishing
in the distance. Calling to them, we ask them if
they are not going to do some piece of work
which the church wishes to have done, and the
reply is, " Oh, don't ask me, I am too busy already to live." And then they hasten on to join
something else. What consummate foolishness!
What wickedness! Emerson was right when he
said, " The one prudence in life is concentration."
The Christian church is the greatest of all institutions, and has first claim on all our energies and
powers. What is the use of joining the church
unless you intend to throw your life into it?
Names are worth nothing in church work. I
had rather have ten workers than a thousand
names. The only reason for joining the church
is to organize activity around a common centre,
to unify effort, and to consolidate the aspirations
and labors and prayers of many disciples in the
accomplishment of a mighty work. If men and
women join the church and then go scampering
off through the city, helping this thing and the
other thing, while their own church work lies
undone at home, they not only bring disgrace
upon their church, but they wrong their own
souls. They dissipate their strength and throw
their life away. It is not enough to say, " Am I
not doing good?" Of course you are. It will
not do to say, " Ought this not to be done?" Of
course it ought to be done, but it does not follow
that you are the person who ought to do it. You

cannot afford to go through life doing good at the beck and suggestion of every good enterprise you chance to meet. We are children of the Highest, and we must make our life count for most. We must spend our energy where it will do the largest good, and work within the circle wherein we can produce an impression that will last. Jesus could have done good to a dozen nations, he would not touch but one. He could have healed and helped a multitude of poor forsaken invalids in the last twelve months of his earthly life, but he steadfastly turned his back upon them, and gave his time and energy to just twelve men. He was working on the future church. If you want your life to count for most you must work upon the church.

We not only dissipate nervous energy, but we also squander money by scattering it with a too thoughtless hand. No organization can exist without the expenditure of money, and hence there are as many appeals for money as there are organizations. A great city is a vast aggregation of beggars. You can scarcely meet a man who does not hold out his hand for a contribution. Beggars from the ends of the earth make their way to the metropolis, each one clamorous for financial help. And most of the causes are deserving and most of the beggars are worthy. Every business man has a procession of them passing in front of him constantly. Some of us can see even in our sleep visions of the outstretched palm. It takes a deal

of will power for some of us to say no to a beggar
who is persistent and plausible. We give five dollars here and ten there and a hundred somewhere
else, and at the end of the year scarcely know
whether we have accomplished any good or not.
Now the church has the first claim on the purses
of its members. No other cause should be permitted to come in between a man's money and his
church. The church is the instrument by means
of which the redemption of the world is to be
wrought out. And anything which cripples the
church retards the coming of the Kingdom of
God. The church would be immeasurably more
effective if church members were willing to concentrate their gifts. South of us in this city there
is a church which spends over a hundred thousand
dollars every year in parish work. That church
is a mighty heart whose throbbings are felt
through all the arteries and veins of the social and
religious life in that section of the city. If we
could spend fifty thousand dollars in our work,
what results might be obtained. This congregation gives away far more than fifty thousand
every year. If we could concentrate our money
more fully than we do, we should make a deeper
impression on the life of the city. One mighty
church splendidly equipped and endowed with
ample resources, can do more for the Kingdom
of God in a city than a thousand isolated and
sporadic organizations, each one in its own separate field endeavoring to make an impression

which at the best must be superficial, and is almost certain to be washed away by the stream of time. Give your money more largely to your own church. I do not ask you to confine your gifts to the church. Other causes have a legitimate demand upon you. But let the church stand first. Go not into the way of the Gentiles with energy or hours or gold, until you have done the work which the Lord has assigned you in the large and needy house of Israel.

THE SINFULNESS OF WORRY

THE SINFULNESS OF WORRY

"For your heavenly Father knoweth that ye have need of all these things." — Matt. vi. 32.

THE New Testament is the most difficult of all books to read. It is difficult because of the profundity of its thought and the variety and fulness of its emotions. To read it as it ought to be read, one ought to have, not only a mind keen to see spiritual distinctions, and swift to trace subtle relations, but he ought to have a voice of unusual compass and flexibility, exceedingly rich in tone color and capable of almost infinite modulations and inflections. There are some pages of the New Testament which no man can read correctly. One of these pages is the twenty-third chapter of Matthew. In that chapter Jesus passes judgment on the scribes and Pharisees. Every sentence is a thunderbolt. Every paragraph is heavy with doom. When a man comes to the sentence, "Ye serpents, ye generation of vipers, how can ye escape the damnation of hell," he feels as Isaiah felt in the temple, and wants to cry out, "Woe is me, for I am a man of unclean lips." How can I read that sentence without squeezing into my tones some of my own bad blood? I cannot read it as perfect innocence and perfect love must have spoken it. With what cadence and inflection did the words fall from the lips of the man who spoke as never man spake! Some of us have been offended at that chapter. It has seemed to us cruel and harsh and unworthy of the Son of God. But the fault lies not in the words of Jesus, but in ourselves. We cannot read them properly. No one can.

There are other passages which no one can read with satisfaction to his heart. Such a passage is the story of the crucifixion. Who has a voice that will express the pathos of an infinite tragedy! And who can read of Jesus' death without feeling that his tones slip back from the blackness and horror of the reality as it is conceived by the imagination and felt by the heart. The story is unreadable!

There are other pages in the New Testament which it is difficult to read, owing to the nature of the thought. By bearing down upon the wrong word, and introducing here and there a wrong accent, the meaning of the entire passage is changed, and we have an altogether erroneous interpretation. A passage often misread is the last ten verses of Matthew vi. There is no passage in the New Testament more familiar, and probably none which has had so little influence on the temper of our lives. It has the authority of the Decalogue, but we ignore it as though it did not exist. The passage begins, " Take no thought for your life," etc.

According to the ordinary reading, food and raiment are trifles. Eating and drinking and wearing clothes are of insignificant importance and should give human beings no concern what-ever. They are things in which Gentiles, pagans, heathen, may be interested, but in which Christians should have no concern. Christians should busy themselves about spiritual things, and if they do this the temporal things will take care of themselves.

That is the way the verses are frequently read, and the whole mischief is caused by the voice. Because the chapter is misinterpreted, it is re-jected. Men do not like to hear food and raiment berated as trifles. When they hear this passage read they say to themselves, if they say anything at all, that is very beautiful Sunday reading, but not worth anything on Monday. Jesus is still acknowledged to be a great teacher, but he is a visionary and dreamer, not a guide to be followed through seven days of the week. After listening to these words of Jesus, the average Christian has gone out and given himself with renewed energy to the problems of food and raiment.

But when the verses are read properly, we see that Jesus does not say that food and raiment are trifles, but just the opposite. He says they are essential: " Your heavenly Father knoweth that ye have need of all these things." Man knows this. God knows it. God made man's physical wants. They are not, therefore, to be treated lightly or ignored. But, says Jesus, do not worry about these essential things. To worry about them is to sin. Worry is peculiar to man. It has no rightful place in the universe of God. Look out into nature, and you find no anxiety there. Birds never worry and flowers never fret. Only man worries. Worry is a serpent which has crawled into the paradise of man. Kill it. Cast it out. It is an intruder, a disturber of the peace, a destroyer of the life of the soul. All nations have been harassed by worry, but Christians should not follow their example. They should never fret about things essential, because God knows they have need of these things. Man cannot live a single day in health and strength without eating. He must eat to live. If he worries about his food he will have a cause of worry injected into every day of every week of every month of every year of his earthly life. He will be worried all the time. He never can get away from it. For God has so created him that the food problem is always with him. And why worry about raiment? Man must be clothed. God made the sensitive human skin, and he makes the storms of snow and rain and icy wind. And it is his good pleasure that man shall clothe himself. Raiment is one of the essentials of earthly life. It cannot be dispensed with. Since it is indispensable do not worry about it, for if you do you will have something to worry about all the time. All the years will be filled with vexation, because your need of raiment is constant and unending. If you are going to worry over things that are indispensable and unescapable and inseparable from existence on earth, your whole life will be wretched and wrecked. What a new light that reading throws on the whole passage. Jesus does not say that worry is a sin because food and raiment are trifles, unworthy the anxious thought of a spiritual man; he says they are of vital importance, and it is because they are essential to human life that no man or woman should worry about them. Instead of saying, " Your heavenly Father knows that ye have need of all these things," he says, " Your heavenly Father knoweth that ye have *need* of *all these things.*"

My subject is : The habit of worry, the uselessness of it, and the wickedness of it. My first proposition is that worry is a sin. Jesus declares it to be so, and he proves that it is one of the deadliest and most awful of all sins. It must be grouped with licentiousness and drunkenness and all the vile and destructive vices, for its effects are precisely those which are wrought by sins which are counted dishonorable and disgraceful. It wrecks the nervous system, saps the springs of vitality, and throws into discord all the harmonies of our life. And the world never knew that worry is a sin until Jesus came. What a genius he had for laying his finger upon the weak points of human nature, and saying, " Right there you are most in danger of breaking down." And with what eyes he saw the future. He knew the sins which were going to follow men across the ages, and he spoke words as fresh and pat and applicable to the needs of us New Yorkers as though they had been spoken yesterday and appeared in this morning's paper.

Worry is one of the universal sins. It is a cosmopolitan sin. There are sins which are provincial in their nature. They fasten upon certain classes of the population, and infest certain strata of our national life. They flourish within certain zones, but outside of those zones they are seldom met with. But worry is a universal sin. It flourishes everywhere. It is common in every continent and blossoms under every sky. It is no respecter of persons or places. It will live with the poor man in his hut. It will travel up the marble stairway of the king and lie down with him in his bed. It will live with the poor woman in the garret, and it is at home in the mansion of the lady. It is fond of great cities, and has many a rendezvous in the metropolis. But it is also found in little country villages, and has a home in the smallest hamlet in the land. It is cosmopolitan in its disposition, and there is nowhere it will not go. Sins are like flowers in this: some are hardier than others. There are flowers which flourish at the base of the Alps, but they flourish nowhere else. They start to climb the mountain slope, but before they have climbed a thousand feet they are out of breath and die. Other flowers can travel farther. They can climb five thousand feet toward the stars. They are not discouraged at first by the decreasing soil, or daunted by the chilling air, but at last they succumb. Little by little they lose their robustness and their beauty, dwindle, and fade, and die. But there are others, braver and stouter still, who move right upward after their companions have succumbed. They will, in spite of all discouragements and every obstacle, breast the storms of the upper air, and never succumb until the stern old mountain draws down upon his freezing head his crown of ever-lasting snow. And so it is with sins. Some flourish at the mountain's base, and others go halfway to the top, and others still climb to the very summit, and are never more at home than when seated on the loftiest pinnacle that over-looks the world. Worry is a strong-limbed, deep-chested sin. It climbs up the steep grades of human society and sits down with men on their thrones. It mingles with the discouraged and unsuccessful and despairful, and it is the boon companion of the fortunate and prosperous and successful.

It is the most difficult to conquer of all sins. There are some sins which it is possible to con-quer. Humanity has left behind it certain sins too disgraceful to be tolerated in civilized society. There they lie, stretched out on the sand of the past, transfixed by the spear of the world's wrath, and they will never disgrace us again. But worry is a sin not so easily conquered. It seems rather to grow in strength with the advance of the world. It flourishes in proportion to the progress of civilization. The savage in his forest is acquainted with worry, but when man emerges from barbarism he does not leave it behind him. Cares multiply as he presses toward the goal, and at last become so numerous as to threaten to overwhelm him. There are certain sins which are peculiar to man's youth. When we are young there is in us that soil in which these sins can strike down their roots, but as we advance in years we outgrow these sins and we leave them behind with the games of youth. But worry is a sin which is never outgrown. It even grows with our years. It haunts the old man on his dying bed, and it torments the schoolgirl at her books. It is a sin that, beginning almost in the cradle, persists in following us to the edge of the grave. The man who can conquer it is a conqueror indeed.

It is one of the most inexcusable of sins. It is not only wicked, it is foolish. There are times when worry does not seem to be a sin at all. Who can blame the poor man out of work because he worries over the fact that he cannot give his children bread? By the introduction of new machinery he and a thousand other men have been thrown out of work. He travels from factory to factory and from mill to mill, begging for an opportunity to work, and every door is shut in his face. He goes home and throws himself down in a chair and broods. The perspiration stands out upon his forehead, and in an agony which almost turns his hair white, he says, " What shall we eat? What shall we eat?" And who will blame the woman who has scarcely enough work to keep her children from starving, if she says, as the winter days draw on, " Wherewithal shall we be clothed?" With the winter wind in her ears and her children's faces before her eyes, would you condemn her if she worried about raiment and food? But it is not among the poor that we find the greatest worry about these things. There is, of course, among the poorer classes, an enormous amount of anxiety in regard to getting enough to eat and wear, but among the very poorest there is often an absence of the very thing we would naturally expect. Instead of worry, there is reckless indifference, a brutish sort of stolidity, a flinty-hearted stoicism which seems to have passed beyond the power of feeling. If I were to preach before men and women in the slums I should never take the text, " Do not worry over what you are going to eat and wear." I should reserve that text for men and women whose larders are filled, and whose wardrobes are over-flowing. It is among the middle and upper classes, among the well-to-do and the rich, that the questions are most frequently asked, " What shall we eat? What shall we drink? Where-withal shall we be clothed?" There is more worry among the upper classes than among the lower.

The explanation of this lies in the fact that as the world advances civilization becomes increasingly complex. It is the complexity of our modern life which confuses us and wears out the nerves. What a simple thing eating is. It does not require much food to sustain a body for twenty-four hours, and this food can be quickly and easily prepared. A few simple dishes, served in a simple way, are all that is necessary for the maintenance of strength and health. But we do not like simplicity. We love to elaborate. We have developed the art of eating into a fine art. We have elaborated the dinner table until it has become a burden. We have multiplied the knives and the forks and the spoons and the goblets. We have added to the courses, and each course must have its frills and accompaniments, and the dinner table has become such a complicated thing that it threatens to become a menace to the health of the nation. What shall we eat? That is not the simple question which it once was. It is a question which wears out the nerves.

And raiment is as simple as food is. It does not require much material to keep a human body in comfort. The creation of machinery has so reduced the price of all dress stuffs that even poor people can dress more comfortably than the aristocrats of a preceding age. If we were willing to dress for comfort, the whole dress problem would be easy. But as John Fiske has reminded us, it is display rather than comfort which has been the prime consideration in the matter of dress since human history began, and in our desire for display, what shall we wear becomes an embarrassing and momentous question. We come under the dominion of the big shop window. It says, with the authority of a relentless Pharaoh, " Put this on," and we timidly object. We say, " It is not comfortable." But the shop window replies, " Put it on." We venture to say we cannot afford it, and the reply is, " Put it on." We argue, " It makes me look like a fright," but the shop window is unconquerable and calmly says, " Put it on." And we meekly submit. All our neighbors and friends fall under the authority of the great shop window, and put on things which are a surprise to them and a puzzle to us. In order to keep up with one another, the question, " What shall we wear," becomes to some of us the great and absorbing question of human life. We have developed the simple act of eating into an elaborate ceremonial, and we have converted the simple act of dressing into a vast and arduous enterprise, and instead of wearing our clothes out, they are just now threatening to wear us out. Things have come to a pretty pass when the two great questions of existence are, " What shall we eat, and what shall we wear? "

And so worry has become our national sin. If licentiousness is the sin of France, and drunkenness is the sin of England, surely anxiety is the sin of America. We carry it in our faces. Europeans say they can pick out Americans in the streets of Vienna, Berlin, or Paris, by the anxious and harassed look which they carry in their eyes. Stand on the street corner of any American city and watch the crowd as they pass, and you will be struck by the large proportion of men and women who have a distracted and worried air. It is only now and then that we see a fresh and happy face, indicating freedom from care. The trail of the serpent is over us all. Like Cain, we bear the punishment of our sin branded on our brow. And it is because worry is our national sin that we are able to account for the triumphs of Christian Science. People frequently say: "How do you account for the success of Christian Science? How can they build such splendid churches? How do they get hold of such cultured and intelligent people, and why is it that, whereas the prayer-meeting of the average church is a dull and cold and dwindling thing, the prayer-meeting of the Christian Scientists is filled with enthusiasm and gladness, reminding one of the Christian church in the days of the apostles?" I do not wonder that people ask such questions. And what are we going to say? It will not do to deny that Christian Science healers cure people, for their cures are numerous and genuine. We must never deny a fact, but face it and explain it if we can. It is not enough to say that Mrs. Eddy's book is a hodge-podge of commonplaces and vagaries and errors and half truths and ridiculous interpretations of the Scriptures. It is, I think, all that, but saying that is not going to keep people from becoming Christian Scientists. You cannot induce a Christian Scientist to give up his faith by saying hard things about Mrs. Eddy's book. A Christian Scientist is like the blind man mentioned in St. John's Gospel. Christ opened his eyes, and the Pharisees tried to convince him that he had never been blind. But they could not budge him an inch. The whole Sanhedrin of learned men could not drive him from his position. He did not care to argue about the character or authority of Jesus. " One thing," he said, " I know. Once I was blind, and now I see." And standing on his feet, all Jerusalem could not move him. And so it is with Christian Scientists. If they have been cured they know it, and they are not going to run from their position because somebody calls Mrs. Eddy names. What shall we do? Find the secret of the power of Christian Science. And that secret lies in the fact, I think, that Christian Science makes war upon the sin of worry. It pulls it up by the roots. It comes to a person, saying, " Don't talk about your diseases! " That is good advice. We ought to have known that without being told. Some of us have known it all our lives. Nothing is ever gained by talking about our ailments and distempers. Christian Science says: " Don't think about your disease. Cast it out of your mind. Quit your brooding." And that also is

good advice. Thousands of people have thought
themselves into their graves. It only aggravates
a disease of the body to hold the idea of it in the
mind. Then Christian Science goes on to say:
" Believe that God is all. Say it to yourself, and
keep on saying it — God is all! God is all! "
Now it is not true that God is all in the sense in
which Mrs. Eddy says he is, but it is true that
God ought to be " all " in our thought and in our
emotional life, and many an invalid, simply by
repeating that phrase, has found the old oppositions growing less, the old dissatisfactions dis-
appearing, the old discords melting out of the
air, and the body, relieved of the burden that has
been pressing down on the nerve centres, has
swung back into health again, and the liberated
soul, rejoicing in its freedom, is ready to believe
that Mrs. Eddy is the greatest servant of God
sent into the world since the days of the apostles.
A little anxiety pressing down on the centres of
nerve force retards all the chemical and physical
processes of the body, causing a disturbance in
the functional activities of the various organs;
but when once this weight is lifted, the body
bounds back into freedom and strength, and life
is no longer a burden, but a joy.

It must not be forgotten that Christian Science
has a truth in it. It has much error, but it has a
truth. Christian Science kills some people, but
it also saves others. It works mischief in various
ways, but it also works blessings, for which bless-

ings we must be grateful. It will probably never make progress outside of great cities. It must do its work in cities, because city people are most worried and most need the peculiar stimulus which Christian Science has to give. It is not likely it will ever make many converts among men. It will win women because women are most susceptible to worry, partly because of their nervous organization, and partly because they are obliged to grapple with the two great problems of feeding and clothing the household. But Christian Science has not a single truth not in the possession of the Christian church. And if our members are guilty of the sin of worrying, they sin in defiance of the express command of Christ, and in spite of the plain and emphatic teaching of the Christian pulpit.

I have taken this subject to-day because we are entering upon a new year of life and work. It is important that at the very outset we get into the Christian mood. Some people come back from their summer outings with a whine in their heart and a scowl on their face. They say, Oh, New York is a hard city to live in! I wonder how many thousand times we hear that said in the course of a year! It is a saying that ought to be banished at once and forever. It would not be a hard city in which to live if we did not make it hard. We make it hard with our whimperings and moanings and whinings. It would be a delightful city to live in if we were stronger men and women, and we should be stronger if we had a more disciplined and Christian spirit.

Some of us have gotten into the habit of making a great ado about nothing. We magnify molehills into mountains. We look at a little piece of work which any right-minded man or woman ought to pick up and run off with, and say: " Oh, this is awful! I do not think I can live through it." It is just that sort of despondency that sucks dry the fountains of the blood and leaves the nervous system at last a ruin. How much work there is in the home that could be done with ease if we only thought so. How much work there is in the church which could be done at once, if we had a nobler type of Christians. Some Christians never do anything for the church without whining as though they were being killed. They are afraid church work will break them down. Most of us could do ten times more than we have ever done, and grow stronger in the doing of it.

Let this, then, be a motto for the year: Do not fret over trifles. The next time a peculiarly exasperating thing happens — and exasperating things are always happening — do not explode. Most of us explode too easily. But simply say, " That is nothing! " Who are you, a child of God Almighty, heir of immortality, that you should make such a fuss over a passing trifle? Toss aside all your vexations as you would push aside so many troublesome gnats, throwing yourself into the arms of the hymn: —

" How firm a foundation, ye saints of the Lord,
    Is laid for your faith in his excellent word."

And whatever work God gives you to do, do it
without a murmur. Form the habit of saying,
" that is easy, that is very easy, I like that," and
you will travel over the months with the tread of
a conqueror, and the blessedness of an archangel.

"Children of the heavenly king,
    As we journey let us sing."

We cannot afford to squander nervous strength
on trifles, for there are heavy burdens to be borne.
Jesus did not close his discourse without adding,
" Sufficient unto the day is the evil thereof."
There are evils that cannot be escaped. Sickness
comes. We cannot keep it away. It strikes down
a member of our household, and rolls a burden on
the heart. Sickness is a great strain on the
centres of life. Death comes. Into many of our
homes it has come already, and into others it will
come soon. Bereavement saps the fountains of
life, and the finer the body and the sweeter the
affections, the heavier is the burden and the
severer the strain. We need all our strength
without squandering it uselessly. The solicitudes
of love we cannot escape. We would not escape
them if we could. The nearer we come to Christ
the more capacity we have to suffer. But these
solicitudes of love are angels from heaven. They
do not crush us, they refine us. They put a new
beauty in the face, and add a new glory to the

soul. But the anxieties concerning the dinner table and the wardrobe add nothing to us. They subtract from us. They render us hard and peevish and ugly. Do not worry, therefore, about raiment or food. Believe in God. Believe that God is over all, and under all, and in all. Believe that you are his child. Believe that he knows your needs, and is able and willing to satisfy them all. He is your Father, and " your heavenly Father knows that ye have need of all these things."

CHRISTIANITY AND WEALTH

CHRISTIANITY AND WEALTH

"It is required in stewards, that a man be found faithful." —
1 Cor. iv. 2.

THE New Testament has much to say about money; and properly so, for Christianity is a religion which deals with a man where he lives. Nothing to it is common or unclean which has been made an essential part of human life by the Creator of the world. Money is a factor in human development, it is a power in human history, it is a centre round which much of the thought and sentiment and ambition and activity of every generation has gathered, and for a religion to despise it or pass it by as though it did not exist, would be proof that that religion was unfit to control the thoughts and guide the lives of men. The accumulation of money is a natural and laudable occupation; but, like all other forms of power, money is capable of abuse, and when abused no form of strength is more despotic or more destructive. Wealth is a gift, and, like all other gifts, carries with it momentous responsibilities, and when these responsibilities are denied or evaded, humanity suffers and God's purposes are thwarted.

The love of money is as old as the race. The scramble to get it has always been widespread and furious. Society has always had its rich and its poor, and there has always been a chasm between them. We sometimes speak as though our age were the only age that had ever bowed to the god of gold. Even a little knowledge of history ought to save us from that delusion. Did not Juvenal say, " No temples have yet been erected to the goddess money, but her majesty is most sacred of all." And did not Horace lament that everybody about him was hankering after riches? " The young and old," he said, " alike recite the lesson: money must be sought first of all, virtue after money." And what Horace and Juvenal said has been said by the moralists and censors of every land and every time. When Carlyle says, " The hell of these days is the infinite terror of not making money," he is making a statement which will fit all days alike. But there are special reasons why the subject of wealth is just now engrossing public attention. We are living in a wealth-producing age. It was the estimate of Mr. Gladstone that in the first half of the 19th century as much wealth was produced as the preceding eighteen centuries had handed down, and that as much more was created between 1850 and 1870. More than that has been produced in the last thirty years. In 1820 our natural wealth was less than two thousand million dollars. In twenty years it doubled, and in forty years it increased eightfold. In the thirty years following 1860 we created and accumulated forty-nine thousand million dollars — a thousand million dollars more than the entire wealth of Great Britain. We have to-day one hundred billion dollars of natural wealth, and all but five per cent of this has been created since this church was organized, sixty years ago. We are now piling it up at the rate of seven millions a day. Who can read such a book as, for instance, Josiah Strong's "Our Country," or Carnegie's "Triumphant Democracy," with their fabulous figures, without rubbing his eyes to make sure he is awake? The fiction of the Arabian Nights is tame compared with the history of our day. No other nation is growing rich so rapidly as our own. And this wealth is flowing into the cities. Urban wealth is increasing four times faster than rural wealth. We are destined to be a nation of cities. The greater the city the more wealth it absorbs. As a magnet draws iron so does a city draw gold. The money chest of New York is to be the largest in the world. Already the assessed value of our wealth aggregates $3,650,000,000.

The wealth is flowing into the cities, and in the cities it is accumulating in the hands of the few. Three or four years ago a statistician published a table showing the wealth of the millionnaires of this country. According to his estimate there were : —

200 persons	with	20 millions
400 "	"	10 "
1000 "	"	5 "
2000 "	"	2½ "
6000 "	"	1 million

Over 1400 of these were citizens of our city. Less than 25,000 people possess more than half the wealth of this country. Charles B. Spahr a few years ago startled us by his figures showing that one per cent of the families of the United States own more than the remaining ninety-nine per cent. Ours is a land of enormous fortunes and alarming inequalities. Along with this process of accumulation has now come a disposition to consolidate the forces of the money kings. Every day the papers have some strange story to tell us of the formation of a new gigantic trust, and these trusts, vast as the huge monsters of prehistoric times, move majestically through the industrial and commercial worlds, exciting the terror of many and the astonishment of all. There are two men in this city who are said to have in their control two billion dollars. Whither are we tending? Who knows?

A striking proof of the rapid accumulation of wealth is seen in the size of the gifts which fall from the hands of our more generous millionnaires. The giving of this country is unparalleled in the history of the world. One cannot pick up a paper without reading an account of a new act of generosity. And the gifts are not small, ranging all the way from $100,000 to $5,000,000. One man likes to build colleges, another hospitals, another libraries. The gold flows in constant streams. Only the other day, when one of our citizens started for Europe, he signalized his departure by giving a Western city five millions, and our own city an equal amount. When somebody ventured to thank him for his generosity he remarked that what he had already done was nothing at all, and that he was just beginning to give. Only a few months ago he published a book entitled " The Gospel of Wealth," in which he argues with great earnestness and force that " he who dies rich, dies disgraced."

If Mr. Carnegie has reached the conclusion that to die rich is to die disgraced, there are other men who have reached the still more radical conviction that to *live* rich is to live disgraced. The rapid growth of fortunes has produced a ferment in the hearts of men everywhere. Everywhere men are thinking and talking and writing, and the conclusions they reach are often erroneous and dangerous. For while the daily press persists in publishing pictures of the palaces and yachts and horses and banquet halls of the rich, there are men like Walter Besant and Charles Booth in London, and Jacob Riis in this city, who keep right on spreading before the world the sufferings and hardships of the poor. Charles Booth, in his great book, " Life and Labor of the

People in London," says that there are in London two and a half millions of people who singly or in companies live in one room — sleeping, cooking, eating, bathing, within the same four walls. England is counted a prosperous country, but one in every ten of God's Englishmen is doomed to drudgery, destitution, and despair. Thomas Huxley knew East London, and said that over it might be written Dante's words, " Leave hope behind, all those who enter here." " In my experience of all kinds of savagery all over the world," he said, " I have found nothing worse, nothing more degraded, nothing more hopeless, nothing so intolerably dull and miserable, as the life I had left behind me in the East end of London. There is a state of things which, unless wise and benevolent men take it in hand, will tend to become worse and worse, and to create something worse than savagery — a great Serbonian bog — which in the long run will swallow up the surface crust of civilization." Visitors from across the sea tell us that there is nothing worse in London than we have right here at our doors. It is these awful contrasts in social condition which have given rise to an enormous literature which increases in volume every year. Any one who keeps his eyes on the books which appear from month to month knows what a large proportion of them deal with the tangled problems growing out of the accumulation of wealth. Some men are so badly frightened by the present outlook that they are hysterical, and cannot write except in feverish vehemence and with exaggerated phrases. We need pay but little attention to their shrieks. But all men who are acquainted with the situation are sobered by the phenomena which the world to-day presents, and have solemn words of warning for all who have ears to hear. When Mr. Abram S. Hewitt said in this city, the other day, that many of our rich men are blind and that a social cataclysm is coming, he said only what all informed men know to be the truth. "The air is charged with thunder, and the times that are coming," said Dr. Hatch, "may be times of storm." "There are voices of battle and famine," said Ruskin, "through all the earth, which must be heard some day, whoever keeps silence." "The zones of enormous wealth and degrading poverty, unless carefully considered," said the Bishop of Winchester, "will presently generate a tornado which, when the storm clears, may leave a good deal of wreckage behind." That is the tone of the best thought of England, and that is the feeling of many of the keenest-eyed observers here. Professor Sumner, of Yale, says that the real issue that men of the future have got to meet is the struggle between plutocracy and democracy. Professor Giddings, of Columbia, says, "We are witnessing to-day beyond question the decay of republican institutions." Professor Small, of Chicago University, says: "Whether we realize it or not, our vision of freedom is passing into the eclipse of universal corporate compulsion in the interest of capital. The march of human progress is getting reduced to marking time in the lockstep of capital's chain gang." Thus, according to many scholars and thinkers, money has become one of the colossal dangers of our time. The calm historian, W. H. E. Lecky, says that "an enormous thirst for riches is among the chief evils of our day." "No vice of our day," says Justin McCarthy, another English historian, "is more glaring and more self-assertive than the passion for money." "The octopus of wealth," says John Clifford, "threatens our peace and strength, and even the very existence of our spiritual aims and ideals." Mr. Gladstone, in his later years, bewailed and feared the growing love of money, and the artist, George Frederick Watts, as he reads English life to-day, does not see how the mighty tendency toward Mammonism can ever be overcome.

When artists, philosophers, scholars, and statesmen are all alarmed over the signs of the times, certainly the Christian pulpit has an urgent duty to perform. Its message has been given to it in plain and simple syllables by the Son of God, and no part of the message came from his lips with more passionate emphasis than that which deals with money.

Whether the pulpit has been recreant to its duty in proclaiming Jesus' message concerning wealth I do not know, but it is certain that the one charge most frequently brought against ministers and churches is that they are on the side of the rich. John Ruskin said, " After hearing two thousand sermons, I have not heard a single one in which the clear issue between God and Mammon was presented to his hearers by the preacher." If you should ask a thousand non-church-going wage-earners why they do not go to church, the majority of them would say that the church is no place for poor people, and takes no interest in securing poor people their rights. We may dispute the fairness of their accusation, but we cannot dispute the fact that that is the accusation which they make. Only the other day there appeared in a Chicago paper this letter from a critic of the churches: " The ministry is nearly always to be found on the side of wealth, and opposed to every great movement in behalf of the poor and oppressed. Why is it? Because Mammon is mightier than the Messiah." This is also the complaint which runs through the diary of the Earl of Shaftesbury, one of the greatest philanthropists England has ever produced. " The clergy here, as usual, are cowed by capital and power." That is a charge often made against the clergy of this city.

And so, because the churches are conceived by many to be the peculiar property of the rich, and the ministers are hated as the hirelings of the men of wealth, the cry has been taken up, " Back to Christ." " Away with the churches." " Let us listen to Jesus, the carpenter of Nazareth, he was poor, he is our friend; down with the clergy, and away with the churches!" And thus in many circles there is current the idea that true Christianity is opposed to wealth, that a rich man must of necessity be a social monster, that if a minister does his duty he will not have any rich men to listen to him, that in order to be a good Christian a man must renounce his wealth and go into the kingdom of God a poor man. This is an idea which is diffused in the air, and the arguments by which it is bolstered up are all drawn from the New Testament. By picking out isolated sentences here and there, a plausible argument can be constructed, and even well-informed Christians do not always know how such arguments can best be met. Nor should you imagine that such arguments are offered only by the ignorant and foolish. Tolstoi, in his book entitled, "My Religion," would make the possession of wealth inconsistent with an honest profession of Christian faith; and our own novelist, Mr. W. D. Howells, says, " It is a sorrowful comment upon our Christianity that Tolstoi's frank acceptance of the message of Christianity should make him seem to the world as eccentric or mad." Thousands of young men on both sides the sea are getting their interpretation of the Christian religion from the great Russian reformer. Renan, the distinguished French scholar, says that the doctrine of Jesus is that the poor alone shall be

saved, and therefore Jesus was a visionary fanatic.
The Belgian political economist, Laveleye, in his
" Primitive Property," says, " If Christianity
were taught and understood conformably to the
spirit of the Founder, the existing social organism
could not last a day." Mr. Leslie Stephen, in his
" Social Rights and Duties," says that " If a man
who best represents the ideas of early Christians
were to enter a respectable society to-day, would
it not be likely to send for the police?" The
idea runs through the writing of a large number
of influential writers that Christianity has retro-
graded, that it has renounced the principles of
its Founder, and that the modern church is tied
hands and feet by its devotion to wealth. Let us
study the New Testament then, this morning, and
find out precisely what that much-quoted book
has to say.

And surely, if we read it hurriedly, it does seem
that Jesus is partial to the poor. He seems to
place them above the rich at every opportunity.
When he opened his ministry in Nazareth he
chose for his text this sentence of Isaiah: " The
spirit of the Lord is upon me, because he hath
anointed me to preach the Gospel to the poor."
When John the Baptist sent from his prison cell
to ask if he were indeed the Messiah, Jesus told
the messengers to tell John that " The poor had
the Gospel preached to them," as though this
were of itself sufficient to prove that the Redeemer
of the world had come. Not one word was said

about preaching the Gospel to the rich. In St. Luke's version of the Sermon on the Mount, he makes Jesus say: " Blessed are ye poor, for yours is the kingdom of God." " But woe unto you that are rich, for ye have received your consolation." Mark tells us that Jesus watched the people as they cast their gifts into the treasury. He noticed the rich, but had no word of commendation for them. But when at last a poor woman came along and dropped in two tiny bits of copper, he eulogized her in words which will outlast the stars.

Not only does he seem to be partial to the poor, but he appears to have a grudge against the rich. He says, " Woe unto you rich!" When he paints a picture of Hades, it is a rich man he puts into it. When he pictures a fool, it is a rich fool he portrays. He seems to have no words of comfort for a rich man. This is the style of his teaching concerning him: " Verily, I say unto you that a rich man shall hardly enter into the kingdom of heaven. It is easier for a camel to go through the eye of a needle than for a rich man to enter into the kingdom of God." " How hardly shall they that have riches enter into the kingdom of God."

And there are sayings of our Lord which indicate that he counted poverty a virtue, and wealth a form of sin. Did he not say to his disciples, " Sell that ye have, and give alms "? Did he not say to the rich young ruler, " If thou wilt be perfect, go and sell that thou hast and give to the poor "? Did he not say, " Beware of covetousness : for a man's life consisteth not in the abundance of the things which he possesseth "; " Lay not up for yourselves treasures on earth "? Did he not say that good seed is often choked by the deceitfulness of riches, and that it is impossible to serve God and Mammon? It is not surprising that men who believe that wealth is an evil and that a rich man is a sinner, should find confirmation of their opinions in the New Testament.

But we should read the New Testament with both eyes. We do it wrong when we read only half of it. Jesus spoke in paradoxes and hyperboles to catch attention. He succeeded. The men of his day listened to him, and the world is listening still. He had sympathy with the poor. He made that so manifest that the world can never get away from it. He warned the rich in speech so vivid that it burns like fire through nineteen centuries. That camel walking in front of a rich man is a picture which is burned into the fibre of the world's imagination. That it is hard for a rich man to be a Christian is one of the axioms of human thought. But he made other things plain, as we shall see when we read the New Testament, not with our prejudices, but with our eyes. You say he put a rich man in hell — Dives — so he did. Why not go on and tell the whole truth? He put a rich man in paradise — Abraham. Abraham was as rich as Dives, probably richer, but he was in paradise and the other rich man was in torment. Dives was in hell, not because he was rich, but because he was inhuman. All inhuman rich men go to hell. There are different kinds of rich men, just as there are different kinds of poor men; some go one way and some go the other.

And as for Jesus painting the portrait of a rich fool who pulled down his big barns to build still bigger ones, he also painted the portrait of a poor fool who built his little mud hut in the bottom of a ravine on the sand, so that the first freshet washed it away. There are rich fools and also poor fools, and folly is disastrous no matter what may be the size of a man's purse.

If it is said he noticed the poor woman casting in two mites, and overlooked the line of rich merchants, it may be said he did not always overlook rich men. He noticed one once in a tree. This man in the tree was not only rich, but he had been mean, and yet Jesus singled him out for special attention and honored him by dining at his house, although the leading people of Jericho were scandalized beyond measure. Let Zacchæus always stand in your imagination by the side of the poor woman who cast in her two mites. The one is rich, the other poor. Christ's benediction covers both.

But what shall we say of the young man who was commanded to sell all his property and give it to the poor? Surely if this man could find perfection only in the renunciation of wealth, the rich of to-day, to win God's favor, must follow the directions which the Lord then laid down. Not necessarily. Jesus is not recorded to have said this to anybody else. He told all men to aim at perfection, but he never gave two men the same instructions in regard to the discipline necessary to attain perfection. This man needed to do precisely what Jesus told him to do. His temperament and disposition and gifts were such that it was better for him and for the world that he should be poor. Moreover, the time called for this act of renunciation. There was a place just then and there where his money could be invested to large advantage in extending the kingdom of God. The ideal thing for him to do was to give up his property and enter into the company of the preachers of the new religion. But his duty was not the duty of every one. There are men in every age who ought to be poor. They do the world more good by remaining poor than they could do it by becoming rich. This is true of all teachers and preachers, and of many artists and authors. Teachers can never get rich by their teaching; preachers can never get rich by their preaching. It is better for them and better for the world that they should renounce all expectations of amassing property. It is better for a Milton to write " Paradise Lost," even though he gets only a few dollars for it, than to write

volumes of chaff which will bring in a fortune
to-day and be blown away to-morrow.   Some
men are in honor bound to be poor, just as some
men are under obligations not to marry.   There
may be physical reasons, or temperamental reasons, or family reasons, why a man should remain
single, but what is one man's duty is not the duty
of all.   All men are not to remain unmarried, and
all men are not bound to be poor.   To hold up the
duty of one individual as an obligation binding
on all is a sort of demagogism very common in
our day.   No man in the Scriptures, I suppose, is
so well known to the non-church-going classes as
this man who was told to sell all that he had and
give it to the poor.   He stands as the ideal Christian, and agitators who endeavor to stir up feeling
against the churches place this man in the forefront of all Christ's teaching as the model after
which every man should mould his life.   How
foolish!   If it were God's will that all professing
Christians should have nothing, why did not
Jesus tell John, the beloved disciple, to sell his
house?   He let John keep his house, and Jesus'
mother made that house her home after Jesus'
death.   Why did he not tell the women who supported the apostolic band to sell their property?
The mother of John Mark had a house in Jerusalem, and it was in that house that the prayer-
meetings of the early church were held.   They
could not have gotten on without that house.
Zacchæus declared himself ready to give away

one-half of his possessions, and Jesus never inti-
mated that the other half must go too. Martha
and Mary were women of means, and when one
of them poured two hundred dollars' worth of perfume on Jesus' feet, and Judas growled because
the money should have been given to the poor,
it was Judas who received the reprimand and
Mary who received the eulogy. There is something else to do in this world besides looking
after the poor. Money is well spent in luxuries
when those luxuries are the expression of affection and feed the finer feelings of the world.
Flowers, music, pictures, works of art, all these
are good investments, because they minister to
the higher life of man. Indeed, Jesus everywhere
takes it for granted that his followers are going
to have property. He tells them to give, and
make it their constant practice. How could they
give if they had nothing? He tells them how to
conduct their feasts. How could they give great
dinner parties unless they had houses and means
with which to supply the table? He never asked
men to strip the world bare and naked, and to
go about as parasites and beggars. Because he
himself was poor, it no more follows that all his
disciples must be poor than that all men must be
celibates because he never married.

It is incredible that the founder of Christianity
should have taught that poverty is the highest
ideal of life. A strange world it would be indeed
if all Christians should sell all they possess and

give it away.   Would that solve any of our problems?   Would that elevate humanity?   Would
that relieve the distress of the poor?   No.
Imagine all the Christians of New York City
reduced to beggary, living on the alms of those
who do not believe in Christianity! What a mess
of things that would make.   Christians are not
only expected to own property sufficient for their
own wants, but it is taken for granted that they
are to have sufficient to help along all good
causes which promise to better the condition of
their fellow-men. The New Testament does not
anticipate a world in which the Lord's followers shall be dependent on others, but just the
reverse.

But does not Jesus say that it is with difficulty
that a rich man enters the kingdom of God? Yes.
He said it, and it is the truth, as every rich man
who has ever lived can testify.   Listen to these
words of the elder Vanderbilt : " Why, I have not
an hour's happiness in my life.   Consider : I cannot eat or drink more than other men, I cannot
wear more clothes, I only require one bed to sleep
in.   All the rest is not only superfluous, it is the
cause of perpetual trouble.   My millions cause
me ceaseless anxiety day and night."   Hundreds
of men have said that.   George Hudson, the railroad king, made millions and then lost them.   He
was forced to retire to a little inn at Calais, where
he lived in one room.   " Never," he said,
" throughout the heyday of my prosperity was I

so happy as in that humble retreat at Calais." If the kingdom of God is righteousness and peace and joy, surely it is difficult for a rich man to enter into it. He has a thousand temptations which the poor man knows nothing of. There is a deceitfulness in riches more subtle than that which lurks in poverty. A rich man is constantly tempted to be arbitrary, or domineering, or autocratic, or tyrannical, or self-indulgent, or inhuman, or mean. But, though hard to enter the kingdom, it is not impossible. The language of Jesus was so strong that some standing by supposed he taught that a rich man could not be saved. He at once corrected that impression by saying, " With the assistance of the Spirit of God all things are possible." And then, in order to set the matter once for all right in their minds, he said, " Verily, I say unto you, there is no man that hath left house, or brethren, or sisters, or father, or mother, or wife, or children, or lands, for my sake, and the Gospel's, but he shall receive an hundred fold *now in this time,* houses, and brethren, and sisters, and children, and lands, with persecutions ; and in the world to come eternal life." It is the teaching of Jesus that obedience to God will in the long run bring wealth. " Blessed are the meek, for they shall inherit — not the skies, but — the earth." They shall own the lands and the houses, and hold in their hands the commerce and wealth of the world. And this teaching is being fulfilled before our eyes. We say the world is getting richer, but it is only the Christianized part of it that is increasing in wealth. China, India, Turkey, Africa, these are not growing richer. The nations most obedient to Christ's law are the only nations at present piling up gold. It is God's will that Christians shall some day have all the wealth of the world. We have already learned how to create it; we must now learn how to distribute it. The equitable distribution of wealth is one of the great problems of the future.

This, then, is the attitude of the Founder of our religion. He sympathized with the poor, instructed them, comforted them, ate with them, opened the doors of heaven and told them they might go in. He sympathized also with the rich, associated with them, ate at their banquet tables, enjoyed their luxuries, pointed out to them the way of life. Two of his disciples at least had property, and probably others. It was in the tomb of a rich man that his dead body was laid.

He warned the poor. Poverty is a source of danger. A poor man has many besetting sins. Jesus warned the poor again and again. " Be not anxious," he said that to the peasants of Galilee. Most of his words concerning money were addressed to the poor. " Beware of covetousness, for a man's life consisteth not in the abundance of the things which he possesseth." That is what poor people needed to be told then, that is what they need to be told now. Millions of human beings are deluding themselves with the notion that they would be infinitely happier if they had more things.

> " Honor and shame from no condition rise;
>   Act well your part, there all the honor lies,"

and all the happiness, too.

He warned the rich. Money is a dangerous thing. All good things are. The best things are the most dangerous. A man of wealth is tempted to say, " Soul, take thine ease. Eat, drink, and be merry ! " But Christ says that any man who spends all his money on himself is a fool. A rich man is in danger of losing his social sympathies. Unless he is on his guard his wealth will take him away from his brethren, and he will live in a little, narrow world of his own, surrounded by a few flatterers, who toady to him because of his money. That was the sin of Dives. " He is independently rich," we say. Ah, what a devil lurks in that word " independent." A rich man *is* independent in a sense. He can live where he pleases, travel where he likes, amuse himself as he will. He can say to one man, Come, and to another man, Go, and if a servant crosses his will he can toss him out as though he were a stick or a rag. A rich man need but whistle and a thousand men will run to be his slave. That is the crowning danger of wealth. It has a tendency to break down the sense of dependence, without which religion shrivels and passes away. It is only at the end of life that many a rich man has discerned how dependent after all we all are. In the death-chamber he learns that he cannot buy sleep, or vitality, or peace of mind, or love, or a single breath. He cannot bribe the death angel, or purchase the favor of God. A rich man may be very poor. All rich men are dependent.

The Christian religion has, therefore, for all men of wealth words of warning, exhortation, and counsel. " Thou shalt not steal." The New Testament thunders its anathemas against the thief. Accursed is the dishonest man, whether he steals pennies or millions. Better dress in linsey woolsey and live in a tenement on Tenth Avenue than live in the highest fashion on money gotten by crooked and dishonorable means. If you are a thief your broadcloth may introduce you into good society, but it does not cover your disgrace. If you are a scoundrel, you may come to church, but your religion is a mockery. The world agrees with the poet in saying, " An honest man's the noblest work of God," and thrice contemptible is the man who counts himself a Christian when in his practices he is an unrepentant rogue.

" Thou shalt not gamble " is the eighth commandment, written in another form, for what is gambling but stealing, taking money which you have not earned, from poor dupes, who, like yourself, are crazy to be rich? There are little gamblers who hide behind barred doors, afraid of the police, and of these we hear much in the papers nowadays; and there are big gamblers, who walk the street unshamed at noon, far more dangerous to society, because engaged in a business which demoralizes the world of legitimate trade, and builds up fortunes on the wrecks of ruined homes and lives. If our alleys are infested with gamblers, and even our boys in school are smitten with the gambling fever, what are we going to say to these so long as society throws the robe of respectability round the gamblers of the stock exchange? Young men, listen to this: "They that desire to be rich fall into a temptation and a snare, and many foolish and hurtful lusts, such as drown men in destruction and perdition. For the *love* of money is a root of all kinds of evil, which some reaching after have been led astray from the faith, and have pierced themselves through with many sorrows." That is what Paul says to you, and this is what he says to me: "Charge them that are rich in this present world that they be not high-minded, nor have their hopes set on the uncertainty of riches, but on God who giveth us richly all things to enjoy; that they do good, that they be rich in good works, that they be ready to distribute, willing to communicate; laying up in store for themselves a good foundation against the time to come, that they may lay hold on the life which is life indeed." That one sentence contains the entire gospel of wealth. Wealth is a sacred trust. A rich man is a steward of the Almighty. He has his wealth only in order to use it in upbuilding an ideal social order. He must use it for his own development and the development of his family, that he and they may be rich in culture and in all the graces of the highest life. He must use it to promote the spirit of brotherhood. He must use it to bind men to him. Gold, when properly used, does not drive men apart, but draws them closer together. As Clement of Alexandria said centuries ago, a rich man ought to use his wealth as a staff. By means of it he should assist himself in walking as a son of God. They say that money talks, and so it does. The money of New York Christians ought to be speaking a language which cannot be mistaken. It ought to talk against everything wrong in our social system. It ought to talk against the rookeries and old disease-infested houses of certain districts of our city in which thousands of God's children are obliged to live, until these traps of infamy and death have given way to houses fit for human beings to live in. Our wealth ought to talk against the defects of the present system of taxation. This system is not fair, and so long as it is continued books like those of Henry George and Henry D. Lloyd and Karl Marx and Ferdinand Lasalle will stir men's hearts to mutiny and rage, and we shall live on the edge of a smouldering volcano. Many of us have no conception of the fires that are burning in the hearts of the wage-earning masses of our cities. A few years ago, a rich New Yorker died worth $74,000,000. It was stated in all the papers of the country that for years his personal property tax was on only half a million. A few months ago another rich New Yorker died, supposed to be one of the noblest of our New York Christians, and it was stated in all the papers that at his death he had in his possession seventeen millions in securities subject to assessment and taxation by this city, but had paid a tax on only $400,000 of this amount. When that fact came out there were men in this country who gnashed their teeth and said: " Ah, that is your Christian! That is the sort of man who finds refuge in your church!" It is because of facts like this that one of our leading religious teachers said the other day, " If the rich would cease robbing the common people by evading the payment of honest taxes and by stealing valuable franchises, they would have no reason to fear the unsolicited vote of the masses." If Mr. Felix Adler speaks that way, you may imagine what the socialistic agitators are saying.

Christian men of wealth ought to be leaders in a movement for a modification of our present competitive system. It is better than any system which preceded it, but it has worked, and is working to-day, many disastrous and alarming results. It gives the upper classes more than their share of the wealth, and stirs up in the hearts of the

common people feelings of envy and ineradicable
hatred. When a railroad magnate has an income
of $13,000 a day and his brakemen receive $1.50
a day, although the brakeman has more children
to feed and educate than his master, the ordinary
man is sure to feel that the distribution of profits
is not Christian or fair. The constant giving of
enormous gifts only fans the flame of discontent.
The rich men and women of this country in 1893
gave to philanthropy twenty-nine millions, in
1894 thirty-two millions, in 1895 nearly thirty-
three millions, in 1896 twenty-seven millions, in
1897 forty-five millions, in 1898 thirty-eight
millions, in 1899 sixty-two millions, last year
forty-seven millions — over three hundred millions given away in eight years, outside of the
millions given through the churches for educational, benevolent, and religious purposes. Surely
we are a wonderful people. But these figures only
exasperate the enemies of our present industrial
order. They say: " That money was ours. Those
millionnaires ground it out of us. We are slaves
under the heel of the capitalist." And what is
the Christian church saying against it all?
Leaflets and pamphlets by the million are scattered all over the country, showing how much
the rich few have, and how little the masses possess. What will be the harvest of such seed-
sowing? No man knows. Certainly no men have
resting on them such momentous responsibilities
as our Christian men of wealth. Their work is

large and difficult. They deserve the sympathy of all good men. Giving money away to poor people is comparatively easy, providing one has it to give. But that is not the chief work of rich men in our day. Their work is the reconstruction of society, the extension of the spirit of fraternity into business and all social life, the development of our present industrial order into an order more fully informed with the spirit of God, the shaping of our legislation so as to promote the general peace and prosperity and secure justice for all. It is a good thing for us all that one man should be intrusted with millions if he is only willing to use the power of those millions in correcting injustices, and ushering in a new and better era. Consecrated wealth is a great blessing; wealth in the hands of unscrupulous men is the greatest of dangers, and brings the blackest of curses. Listen to James as he speaks to the unscrupulous rich men of his day: " Go to now, ye rich, weep and howl for your miseries that are coming upon you. Your riches are corrupted, and your garments are moth-eaten." There are men and women in this city to whom such words could rightfully be spoken: men and women whose life is a round of selfish pleasure; whose greatest joy is in vulgar pomp and gorgeous display; who pay no attention to Lazarus at their gates; who degrade society by their frivolity and vices, and trample all high ideals under their feet; who keep poor men and women who minister to their wants waiting sometimes for months for their pay; who look upon all human beings below their social circle as so many slaves, to be used in the carrying out of their selfish plans; who gamble and gossip in their parlors through the winter; and who, when they go to the country in the summer time, descend upon it like a plague, driving their horses and playing their games through the Lord's day, demoralizing the life of the community, and filling the heads of young men and young women of country towns with false conceptions of city morality and low standards of conduct and character. Woe unto the lazy, shallow, silly, selfish, godless rich! The New Testament brands them with the brand of infamy, and hurls at them words that burn like fire. But although Jesus and the apostles speak with such passionate utterance concerning rich men and their wealth, not one of them ever falls into fanaticism. There is in the New Testament none of the sentimentalism of Ruskin, none of the vagaries of Tolstoi, none of the wild and frantic rhetoric of Herron. Rich men are warned, but not one word is said against wealth. Its dangers are pointed out, and so also are its uses. Bad rich men are unflinchingly condemned; good rich men are praised and rewarded. It never exalts poverty into a virtue, or catalogues wealth as a sin. It is wonderfully sensible, beautifully sane. The balance is always maintained, the perspective is always true. It deals with rich men and with poor men in language bold and uncompromising and strong. Its message is as clear as the outline of a star. No one can read it without coming away with the conviction that it is an awful thing to lay up treasure for oneself, and not to be rich toward God.

CHRISTIANITY AND WAR

CHRISTIANITY AND WAR

"Blessed be the Lord my strength, which teacheth my hands to war, and my fingers to fight." — Ps. cxliv. 1.

"Nation shall not lift up sword against nation, neither shall they learn war any more." — Isa. ii. 4.

CHRISTIANITY and War. It is a great theme! There is vast confusion concerning it in the public mind, and therefore every Christian should work himself out into clear conceptions and definite convictions. Christianity and War — that then is our subject. Not Christianity and any particular war, be it South African, Philippine, or Cuban, but just war as a tribunal for the settlement of disputes, as a method of reaching international conclusions, as a means of working out moral purposes and securing moral ends. What shall we say of war? Is it ever right, necessary, Christian? Or is it always and everywhere unnecessary, unchristian, and wrong? The world gives a divided answer.

There are those who say war is always wrong. At the head of this school stands Leo Tolstoi. For years he has been making war upon war. Entering the army at twenty-three, he won distinction as a soldier in the Crimean War, and made himself famous by the publication of " War Sketches."

For thirty-five years of his life he believed in nothing, but at the age of fifty-one he says faith came to him. "I believed," he says, "in the doctrine of Jesus, and my whole life underwent a sudden transformation." For twenty-two years he has been asserting that according to the teaching of Jesus the employment of force to work out moral results is forever unchristian and absolutely wrong. In a recent number of the *North American Review* he discusses what he calls "the root of the evil." After painting a vivid picture of the horrible inequality in social condition existing in all Christian countries, he asks, Why is this? His answer is that a few men have usurped the land, the factory, and the taxes. They are able to do this by means of an army; they are able to raise an army by teaching men "that military service is an excellent and praiseworthy occupation, and murder during war an innocent action." "The root of all evil," he declares, "is the false teaching. Abolish the false teaching, and there will be no more armies. The awful system of human life which now prevails will cease to be when men cease to believe the lie in which they are educated, and believe instead the supreme truth which was revealed to them 1900 years ago, and is clear, simple, and accessible to their reason." Tolstoi is a genius, an artist, a writer of extraordinary power. His ideas are spreading everywhere. His disciples in this country are both numerous and influential. One sees his opinions cropping out in many of the letters published from day to day in our daily papers. One hears his arguments sometimes at religious conferences. At a recent Episcopal Convention a lawyer of this city stoutly contended that war is murder, forever abominable in the eyes of God. Last year a book was published by a Western clergyman entitled, " Put up thy Sword." Its argument is as follows : " War is inhuman, unchristian, unnecessary, and forever wrong. How can a Christian do other than condemn it with all the power of his being! The army is a libel upon our boasted civilization. The navy is a stain upon our seas. No one can be a true Christian and an advocate of war. No true Christian can engage in military service."

The question now is, Is this interpretation of the New Testament correct? Will it stand the test of reason and of the scriptures? If Christ absolutely forbids all use of force, the sooner Christians accept his teaching, the better it will be for ourselves and the world. But if Tolstoi's interpretation is erroneous, it will work mischief both in the church and in society, and the sooner its falsity is exposed the better it will be for us and for all men.

What does the New Testament have to say concerning war? According to the Gospels Jesus never made use of force in dealing with men. He never struck a man, nor resisted a man who struck him. It is amusing to see with what eagerness certain defenders of recent wars have seized upon Christ's cleansing of the temple as a proof that he used force in the securement of moral ends. No other episode in all his life has been used so frequently within the last three years. The fact that the advocates of war are driven to make such constant use of this one incident shows how scanty must be the material of the gospels out of which an argument for war can be constructed. St. John says that Jesus "made a scourge of cords and cast all out of the temple, both the sheep and the oxen." That is, Jesus, picking up a few slender rushes lying on the floor, twisted them into a whip in order that he might start the steers and sheep by waving it over their backs. He might possibly have struck an animal, but that he struck a man is a reckless guess of the biassed imagination. It is incredible! What was the use of striking those men? The poor mercenary wretches skulked away, cowed and whipped by the glances of those burning eyes. It was not by a whip, but by sheer, moral power, that Jesus cleansed the temple — the same power by which the officers that came to arrest him were overcome at the garden gate and fell backward to the ground. There is not a scintilla of evidence that Jesus ever used an ounce of physical force to carry out his plans. As a lamb he was led to the slaughter, and as a sheep before her shearers is dumb, so opened he not his mouth.

Nor did he ever tell his disciples that they might make use of force in carrying on their work. He told them when he sent them forth that men were wolves, but that they must all be lambs. Now wolves fight, but lambs do not. Lambs do not protect themselves. They cannot. He would not allow his disciples to take with them even a walking-stick. " Be harmless as doves," he said. " But, O Master, we will be killed!" " Never mind that," he replied, " do not be afraid of those who kill the body. Fear no one but God." There were times when his disciples wanted to use force, but he always reprimanded them for their belligerent temper. " Shall we call fire down from heaven to burn up this Samaritan village?" they one day asked. " You do not know," he said, " what spirit you are of." Peter on one occasion took matters into his own hands without asking for Jesus' permission. He struck a man with his sword. Jesus said to him, " Put up thy sword, for all they that take the sword shall perish by the sword."

When we study his teaching we find not a sentence from first to last which seems to sanction the use of force by any one. " Ye have heard that it hath been said, An eye for an eye and a tooth for a tooth: but I say unto you that ye resist not evil, but whosoever shall smite thee on thy right cheek turn to him the other also." " Ye have heard that it hath been said, Thou shalt love thy neighbor, and hate thine enemy. But I say unto you, Love your enemies, bless them that curse you, do good to them that hate you, and pray for them which despitefully use you and persecute you." The one sentence which seems to lend any support whatever to the argument of force is the saying, " I came not to send peace on earth, but a sword." That has been quoted a thousand times in recent years by reputable papers and speakers, to prove that Christianity not only justifies war, but renders it necessary. But all such twisting of the Scriptures ought to be shunned and condemned by every man who has any sense of fairness or the slightest regard for the authority of the sacred writings. Jesus goes on at once to explain the meaning of that word " sword." It means discord, contention, aliena- tion, separation. " For I come to set a man at variance against his father, and the daughter against her mother, and the daughter-in-law against her mother-in-law. And a man's foes shall be they of his own household." That is, Christianity, by introducing a new standard of duty, will cause separation even of those bound together by the closest ties. But that Christ's fol- lowers are therefore authorized to kill those who turn away from them, or against them, is both ridiculous and blasphemous. Four books were never written more completely stripped of sen- tences which can be used in support of war than the four Gospels. The Gospels set before us as the ideal man a meek and gentle teacher, one whose advent was heralded by angels who sang of peace, one who does not strive or cry aloud in the streets, one who rides on an ass into Jerusalem as the Prince of Peace, one who when reviled reviled not again, and who died praying for the men who were putting him to death. It is not hard to read the New Testament in such a way as to come out precisely where Tolstoi lands.

But that way of reading the New Testament is after all unfair. There is no book so easily misread as the Bible. One can read the Old Testament in such a way as to get good reasons for slavery and polygamy and a dozen other abominations. One can find arguments in the New Testament against marriage, wealth, learning, liberty, and against a dozen other things known to be rational and good. We must read the New Testament in a large way and with the light of God's providence falling on it, or it will mislead us. Jesus is an idealist. He sets before men the ends at which they are to aim. He tells them what they are to be when the processes of development have reached their consummation. That is what a great teacher must always do. He must set the ideal before men's eyes, and breathe into their hearts the spirit by means of which the ideal can be realized. God's ideals cannot be realized in a day or a year, in a century or in ten centuries. All things are under the law of growth; they pass from stage to stage, and it is only at the end that God's purposes are fulfilled. Jesus never wearied of making this plain in his parables and discourses. Men all around him were impatient. His constant advice was, Wait! And so he never struck the features of his age which a lesser man would have certainly attacked. He never said a word against slavery. It was an awful institution, but the time for its death had not come. It was to be sloughed off by and by, but not cut out just then. The world at that stage of its development was better with slavery than it would have been had some military leader attempted to crush the slave system by a single blow. He never said a word against the Roman Empire. Other men railed and thundered against it, but he never did. It was not an ideal government, but it was better than none. Without it humanity would have fallen into chaos. As Paul put it later on, " The powers that be are ordained of God." They are not ideal, but all things considered they are the expression of the life which the race has attained unto; and consequently they have a place in the unfolding of the divine order. Jesus never struck the Roman army. It was full of barbarous and dissolute men, and was often used as an instrument of tyranny; but it was better than no army, for without it society would have dropped to pieces, and the best men would have been at the mercy of the worst. Paul was always glad to avail himself of the protection of the Roman army. But while he did not hurl thunderbolts against slavery and Rome, he planted principles in the hearts of men which, when they were fully ripened, caused the disappearance of slavery and the dissolution of the Empire. It must never be forgotten that Jesus came into the world to do one specific thing. " I have a baptism to be baptized with; and how am I straitened till it be accomplished!" He made his life narrow in order that it might flow with a current so tremendous that every generation to the end of time might feel the throbbing of its resistless tide. He never said anything about beauty. He never gave encouragement to art. Pictures and statues and architecture and music he passed by as though they did not exist. But he put into the human heart impulses and ideas which have flowered out into the marble of Michael Angelo, and the color of Raphael, and the oratories of Haydn, and the architecture of St. Peter's and St. Paul's. He never said a word concerning education. There is no word of commendation in all the New Testament for a school or a college or a university. He ignored all the institutions created for the training of the intellect. But he put into the mind a few ideas which have borne fruit the wide world over. Our modern system of education is the creation of the Christian religion. He never spoke of patriotism. There is scarcely a sentence from his lips which would lead a man to think that he ought to love his country and that he has any civic duties whatsoever. He seemed to have no interest in the state or state policy, or in state officials, or in state obligations. But he planted a few principles which have worked themselves out into the British Empire and the American Republic. Strange to say, he seldom spoke about the church. According to the Gospels he mentioned it only twice, and then in a hurried way. He never said a word about its organization. How many officials it should have, what shall they be called, what shall be their duties, what sort of creed shall it adopt, all these vital questions he left open, but he breathed into men a spirit which has created an institution the mightiest known to human history. It is because of this limitation which our Lord placed upon himself which has made it possible for every unbalanced mind with a liking for religious speculation to find in the New Testament support for its vagaries, and confirmation of its hallucinations. Christian Science and Tolstoism are the latest of the long line of plausible delusions, both claiming to be the only true interpretation of the New Testament. They are both erroneous and dangerous because the creation of unbalanced minds.

Jesus was a teacher of heart life. He was not an officer of the State, therefore he could not use force. Had he ever used force he would have become at once a brawler and a criminal. That would have ended his career at once. When he ordered those miscreants out of the temple he was not usurping the authority of the State, he was only doing what every Jew had a right to do. But he was doing what no Jew would do because his conscience had been seared. His disciples were to be religious teachers, and consequently had no right to make use of force. It is the state which has the right to use force, and Jesus never spoke of the state. That was a subject outside of his province. If his disciples had forced their way, they would have been promptly suppressed. It was better for a few of them to lose their life than to shut the door in their face by breaking the laws of society. They were ordained to work on the heart. Jesus was king, but not the king of any earthly kingdom. He came not primarily to build up a state, but to create a new disposition in the hearts of men out of which future states should come. As he himself said to Pilate: "My kingdom is not of this world. If my kingdom were of this world, then would my servants fight that I should not be delivered to the Jews." That is, if Jesus' mission on earth had been the immediate creation of a civil order, he would have called on men to use force in order to establish that order. He came into the world for another purpose. "To *this* end was I born, and for this cause came I into the world, that I should bear witness unto the truth." He was a teacher, not a state official. All that he says, therefore, concerning non-resistance and forgiveness of enemies is addressed primarily to the heart of the individual man. Men who follow Jesus must have a peaceable disposition, and must give up the savage principle of retaliation. They must forgive their enemies and bring themselves into subjection to the golden law of love.

But while this is the law for individuals, what is the law for states? States also must come under the law of love, but may not love sometimes employ force? Must a community do away with all the processes and compulsions of government? Must a nation go unarmed and submit to every injustice which its own citizens or foreign states may inflict upon it? Jesus never discussed that question, and we are left for our guidance to the revelation which God has made of his will, in our own reason and in the experience of many generations, and in the general trend and character of New Testament thought.

In an ideal world of course there is no war. An ideal world is under the reign of love. All the prophets from Isaiah to Victor Hugo have seen in vision the time when war shall be no more. The ideal of the Bible is a world ruled by love. That is the ideal of reason. But the world is not yet ideal, and in the long process of development by which it climbs on stepping-stones of its dead self to higher things, is there a place for war? In a perfect world there is no place — how about an imperfect world? In a race developed there is no justification for carnage, but of an undeveloped race, what shall we say? In a Christian world there is no excuse for the instruments of slaughter, but in a world ruled as yet largely by animal impulses and instincts, and just beginning to learn the virtues and graces of the spirit, must all the enginery of force be at once abolished?

Our question, then, is this, In the world as it exists to-day is the use of force to secure moral ends ever necessary, right, or Christian? Let us see. Is it right to secure order and justice in New York City? What makes Manhattan Island a habitable place for decent people — schools and churches? They help, but they alone are not sufficient. We are dependent upon churches and schools *plus* public opinion and the police force. We could not live here without policemen. There are in our city insane men not confined in an asylum. There are dangerous men here, born with defective brains and brutalized by lives of sin. There are ruffians and desperadoes here from the ends of the earth, who would kill a man as readily as they would kill a fly if they dared. We have in our city thousands of men who are kept from outrage and violence only by the firm pressure of government. Take away the police force and we should have pandemonium in less than twenty-four hours. Moral power is good, but it is not sufficient of itself to hold a city together. Moral force must be supplemented by physical force to save us from utter social and political disintegration. What is a policeman but a soldier? His value lies in the fact that he is armed. Wherever he goes he carries a club and a gun. The club is made as inconspicuous as possible, but it is a club nevertheless, with sufficient weight to crack a man's skull. The gun is shortened so that it may be carried in the pocket, but it is a gun nevertheless, and a gun that can kill. Let the word go out that no policeman in New York City shall be permitted henceforth to strike or shoot, and there would be an immediate uprising of the murderers and thieves. We are saved from chaos by the use of force. The seven thousand policemen of this city constitute an army, and they are just as essential to the city as teachers or preachers. Without policemen, teachers and preachers could not do their work.

But more than city policemen are needed. The state as well as the city possesses the right of self-defense. She must protect all her citizens, no matter where they live. There are smaller cities and large towns and small villages and isolated farmhouses, and all these must be protected by the state. It must not be left possible for a band of lawless men to march out of the city and spread devastation over sections of the commonwealth which are unable to protect themselves. The property of individuals and corporations must not be left to the mercy of rioters and mobs. We must have state policemen, a body of men under the command of the Governor, every man armed, every man trained to shoot, every man capable of using steel in putting down frenzied masses of men endangering the property and lives of others. Without the militia our churches and schoolhouses would be at the mercy of the mob. The history of this city contains a solemn warning for us. Again and again there have been the most fearful riots, and had it not been for the use of force the loss of life would have been incalculable, and the city would have been repeatedly burnt to ashes. We are all safer in property and life because there are in various sections of the city great fortresses stocked with guns and ammunition. Those armories are not a libel upon our civilization; they are tangible proof that we believe in the sacredness of property and life, and intend to protect both against the attacks of the enemies of civilization.

If the state must protect itself, so also must the nation. Not one locality must be unguarded, not one citizen must be left exposed. There are regions where the local authority is weak and where the brute element in human nature is strong. These regions must be protected by the government's right hand. The frontiers must be guarded. In other words, the nation must have policemen. A body of national policemen is known as a standing army. Instead of calling them policemen we call them " regulars." I do not see how we can say a standing army is a libel on our civilization unless we are ready to say that the police force of our city is an impertinence and a disgrace. Why should not a nation as well as a city protect itself? We lock our doors and windows every night to keep out those who might come in to take our life — should not a nation lock its doors? Every harbor is a door, and every fort is nothing but a lock.

But if the nation is bound to protect itself upon land, why is it not bound to protect itself upon the sea? Men live these days upon the water, and carry on their business there, and wherever life and property are exposed the government must give protection. Broadway does not stop at the Battery, it runs out and on, across the Atlantic branching into a hundred highways : one running to Glasgow, and another to Liverpool, another to Hamburg, another to Genoa, another to Naples, another to Cairo. The trucks and drays do not stop at the Battery; they change their form when they strike the water, but they carry the goods of our merchants to all the markets of the world. If it is right to have policemen stationed along Broadway as far as the Battery, it is right to have policemen on the water as far as Yokohama and Hong Kong. Fifth Avenue does not stop at Washington Square. It runs out across the water to every European capital. People ride in their carriages from Riverside Drive to Paris or Berlin. The carriage changes its form when it reaches the water, and becomes a Cunarder or something else. And if it is right to have policemen stationed along Fifth Avenue it is not unchristian to have policemen along the Fifth Avenues of the sea. The police force on the sea is known as the navy. Instead of stationing a man every thousand feet it is necessary to group them in bands of five hundred. The platform on which they stand is called a battle ship, or armored cruiser, and as the

distances are long, the revolver of the land policeman is lengthened and enlarged and becomes
known as a Krupp gun. Were it not for these
armed policemen of the sea, every ocean would be
infested with robbers, and it would be unsafe to
trust either our lives or our goods out of sight of
land. Let the word go forth that every vessel
bearing guns has been destroyed, and a great
horde of pirates would swoop down upon our
commerce and convert every ocean into an arena
of outrage and blood. It is hard to see, therefore,
how a navy can justly be called a stain upon the
sea, or why a Christian man should be condemned
for serving his country behind a gun. A Colt
revolver, a Mauser rifle, a Krupp gun, they are all
instruments of force and are made to kill. If they
could not kill they would be of no service to the
world. If the Krupp gun is unnecessary and
unchristian, so also is the rifle, and so also is the
revolver. But we have seen that New York City
cannot possibly dispense with the revolver,
neither can the state dispense with the rifle, nor
the world with the Krupp gun.

If, then, a nation is under obligation to arm
itself in order that the highest ends of government
may be secured, it must follow that a government
has a right to use its arms whenever occasion demands it. In other words, a nation has a right
to engage in war. The state has a right to make
war on a mob, the city has a right to make war on
a riot, the nation has a right under certain cir-

cumstances to strike another nation which persists in trampling upon the rights of humanity and defying the eternal principles of justice. If a nation has no right under any circumstances to strike another nation, then we must assert that the state has no right to quell a band of rioters in the act of destroying property and life, and that the police force has no right to put down a mob in our streets. The principle is the same. It runs through all departments of life. Once admit that force may ever be legitimately used in order to secure moral ends, and you cannot escape the conclusion that a national army and a national navy are institutions essential to the well-being of the race, and that, therefore, instead of contradicting the spirit and nullifying the teachings of Christ, they are instruments in the hands of society by means of which the principles of Jesus of Nazareth are given an opportunity to advance in their conquest over the hearts of men. They are not a libel on our civilization, but an expression of good sense and a frank confession that the race has not yet reached its growth.

If the case is as simple then as it has here been made to appear, how are we to account for the fact that an increasing number of thoughtful and sensible people are crying out with vehemence and bitterness against militarism, and never grow weary of saying that all war is murder. It is because the majority of wars have been without moral justification, and might have been avoided by the exercise of a little patience and forbearance, and because of the enormous expansion of armaments and armies within the last thirty years. The world is to-day the victim of one of the wildest insanities that ever burned in the blood of the brain. Whenever one set of men become extremists, another set of men will go to the opposite extreme and be just as foolish as their opponents. The amount of nonsense talked and written in favor of war within the last few years is sufficient to account for the wrath and excesses of the disciples of Tolstoi. Having considered the unreasonable assumptions of the Tolstoian school, let us now look at some of the sophistries of the other side.

It is asserted constantly that war, after all, is a desirable episode in the life of a nation. It is a moral tonic and stirs up its sluggish blood. It furnishes a school in which young men are developed in all the manly virtues. Without war a nation must inevitably become effeminate and cowardly and weak. Could any argument be more atrocious than that? Has Tolstoi ever said anything crazier than that? A school for the development of virtues — forsooth! Men who want to develop manliness and courage have abundant opportunities without going to war. Let them be true men in any sphere of labor and they will be subjected to as severe a test as any which the battle-field affords. To do one's duty in the days of peace is more difficult than to do it

in the days of war, for the strain is more continuous and the motives to heroic action are less
conspicuous and urgent.   No braver man than
Jesus ever lived, and he never struck a blow.
Saul of Tarsus never joined an army, but he said,
" I have fought a good fight."   If to develop
manhood we must use guns every few years, why
not have a local war?   Why not encourage an
uprising of our dangerous classes?   That would
give us a conflict at our doors, and we should all
have a chance to develop the virile traits of manhood.   It is the men who do not expect to fight
themselves, or to have their home or fortune
ruined, who say with such devilish smoothness,
" War is a good thing."   John Ruskin used to
say to the aristocracy of England, " If war broke
the china on your sideboard you would put an end
to it at once."

But do not blessings follow war?   Yes.   They
follow everything.   They follow famine, pestilence, calamity, crime.   No demon can put his
foot down so hard upon this earth that a flower
will not spring up as soon as his foot is removed.
This is due to the overflowing goodness of God.
He compels the wrath of men to praise him, but
the wrath is not therefore justified.   No matter
what man may do, good will follow.   Let him
burn down the forest and the land will be enriched
by the ashes and ready to bring forth luxurious
harvests.   David committed adultery and murder,
and after his sins there came a beautiful repent-

ance, expressing itself in a heart-breaking poem which has been a solace and inspiration for three thousand years. Blessings spring up in the track of all actions, no matter what they are. The fact that blessings always follow war does not prove that war is a good thing. The Galveston flood was followed by blessings. It opened the hearts of thousands of people, and brought the North and South closer together. Shall we pray for another tidal wave? The famine in India was followed by blessings. It softened the world's heart and strengthened the bonds between Orient and Occident. Shall we ask for another famine? Libby prison was followed by blessings. It bound its inmates together by a brotherhood whose bonds can never be broken — but we want no more Libby prisons. If the half of this city should be burned, the catastrophe would be followed by blessings. What an improvement in our architecture. Think of the men who would secure work! If a pestilence should lay half of our population dead, blessings would follow. What sympathy in the outside world! What a mellowing of the hearts of those of us who might be spared! It would bring a great religious revival. War brings with it great blessings! Yes, and it brings with it direful and immeasurable curses. And a sensible man will ask, Do the blessings outnumber the curses, and might not the blessings have been secured at a less frightful cost? War is never justifiable, no matter what blessings follow it, except as a last terrible, unescapable resort, and as a means of securing an enormous and lasting good not to be obtained in any other possible, honorable way. That condemns nearly all wars that have ever been fought.

Another piece of sophistry is the maxim that in order to preserve the peace we must prepare for war. This is one of those half truths more dangerous than a full-blooded lie. Up to a certain point the maxim is true; beyond that point it is false. What we ought to say is, in order to preserve the peace we must prepare for peace. Multiplying the instruments of war beyond a certain point only stirs up bad feeling, and makes it easier to come to blows. Our fathers wanted to live at peace with our neighbors to the north and so they prepared for peace. They abolished forts and fortifications along the northern boundary, and declared that the great lakes should be a highway for commerce and not stations for ships of war. We prepared for peace and peace we have had for 125 years. But there are men to-day who, bitten by the military mad dog, are alarmed at the imminent danger of an invasion from the north, and would have the whole Canadian border bristling with guns.

It is this kind of talk which so-called military experts frequently indulge in. A military expert is often a man who looks at the world through the bore of a gun. He is frightened by dangers which are created by his own imagination. A nation is doomed as soon as it gives itself up to the leading of its military experts. A military expert has his place. The construction and location and firing of guns, these are technical matters on which he has a right to speak. But on all the larger questions of statesmanship relating to the policy of the nation, and concerning the size of army and navy, he is ordinarily incompetent to pass a trustworthy judgment. It is because the nations of Europe have so largely followed the advice of their military experts that all Europe is in such a deplorable condition. The blind have led the blind, and they are all in the ditch. Specialists in any field are always to be feared whenever they deal with questions outside their own little province. As Huxley says in one of his letters, " Directly a man gets the smallest repute in any branch of science, the world immediately credits him with knowing about ten times as much as he really does." How large an army and navy should this nation have? That is not a question for military experts. That is a question for scholars, and men of wide experience and sound practical judgment. It is for the banker and merchant and college professor, the learned lawyer and cultured doctor and scholarly preacher and keen-eyed statesman, for the men of learning and large outlook and clear vision, who know the history of the world from the settlement of Greece to the capture of Aguinaldo, who are acquainted with the age and know the currents of its manifold life, who believe in the principles of the Son of God and desire to give them the fullest embodiment in the lives and institutions of men — it is for these men to determine just how much military force is essential to protect us against marauders and to enable us to play the part to which the Lord God has called us in the unfolding drama of the world. It is a vast and momentous question, and only Christian scholars and men of affairs of the largest caliber are competent to deal with it. If we leave it to the military experts and a few reckless newspaper scribblers, and a few avaricious firms growing rich by building torpedo boats and battle ships, we may expect to see our army and navy growing larger and larger with the years until they become an unbearable burden, a curse to us and a menace to the world.

What, then, is the duty of a Christian in our day? Should he not be a passionate advocate of peace? Should he not set himself against all bluster and brag, and resist with all his might the tendency to increase military expenditures beyond the limit absolutely demanded by the welfare of the sisterhood of nations? Every increase in our navy strengthens the war party in every parliament of Europe, and every increase of the military burden there drives to this country a new horde of exiles whose very life has been almost ground out of them by the military system, and crushes the millions who cannot get away down into a more pitiful and hopeless degradation. M. Bloch, the distinguished Polish political economist, closes his monumental work on the " Future of War " with the assertion that the consequences of the present expenditure on preparation for war is slow destruction, a destruction that extends not simply to industry and finance, but to the framework of society and the fibre of men's souls. I wish you could all read his six great volumes, and study his awful, frightening pages of statistics. You would then understand why Tolstoi and others cry out in the agony of a great despair. It would make clear why there are socialists and anarchists and nihilists. It would explain why so many of our best-informed and farthest-sighted citizens fear militarism more than any other demon ever let loose from the pit. We have had one great Peace Conference. We must soon have another. At the conference of The Hague an international tribunal was established; at the next conference plans must be adopted for scaling down the magnitude of the armaments which are souring and poisoning and damning the life of Christendom. Militarism is the running sore, the inexcusable blunder, the unspeakable crime, the unpardonable sin, of the Christian world. I believe that the world would be infinitely happier and safer if all the great fighting fleets of battle ships were sunk to the bottom of the sea, and there should be no navy except an international force of cruisers just sufficient to protect commerce from pirates and the possible depredations of half-civilized tribes.   In the great work of redemption America must lead the way.   From the beginning we have been preëminently a nation of peace. That is why God has blessed us above all the nations of the earth.   As little money as possible, consistent with national safety and responsibility, for soldiers and battle ships; as much money as possible for schoolhouses and churches — this is the motto which contains the secret of our wealth and happiness and power, and points out the road along which our feet must travel, if the blessings which we enjoy are to be handed down to our children's children.

That nation does most for men and most for God who does most to carry the world toward the golden time when the nations shall beat their swords into ploughshares, and their spears into pruning-hooks, and all shall acknowledge that the Prince of Peace is King of Kings and Lord of Lords.

> " Glad prophecy ! to this at last,
>   The Reader said, shall all things come.
> Forgotten be the bugle's blast,
>   And battle music of the drum.
> A little while the world may run
>   Its old, mad way, with needle gun,
> And iron-clad, but truth at last shall reign.
> The cradle song of Christ was never sung in vain."

THE BRAMBLE KING

THE BRAMBLE KING

"Come and put your trust in my shadow." — Judges ix. 15.

The Bramble King: How he got his Crown, and how he may be dethroned; or, the Reign of the Boss in American Politics.

THAT is a striking parable recorded in the 9th chapter of the Book of Judges. Gideon is dead, and the men of Israel are in search of his successor. It is not necessary for them to seek long, for among the sons of Gideon there is a scapegrace by the name of Abimelech, who at once lays schemes whereby he may climb to power. He is ready, if necessary, to wade through slaughter to a throne. Seizing all the male members of his father's family, he puts them to death, only one escaping, the youngest of them all, Jotham. This refugee rushes to the top of a neighboring hill, and to the assembled multitude delivers the following picturesque discourse: "Once upon a time the trees went forth to anoint a king over them. And they said unto the olive tree: Reign thou over us. But the olive tree said unto them: Should I leave my fatness, wherewith by me they honor God and man, and go to wave to and fro over the trees? And the trees said to the fig tree: Come thou and reign over us. But the fig tree said unto them: Should I leave my sweetness, and my good fruit, and go to wave to and fro over the trees? And the trees said unto the vine: Come thou and reign over us. And the vine said unto them: Should I leave my wine which cheereth God and man, and go to wave to and fro over the trees? Then said all the trees unto the bramble: Come thou and reign over us. And the bramble said unto the trees: If in truth ye anoint me king over you, then come and put your trust in my shadow; and if not, let fire come out of the bramble, and devour the cedars of Lebanon."

The interpretation of this parable by the men of Israel was not difficult. Jotham had said to them: " O men of Israel, you have been too busy to attend to governmental affairs. One of you has offered one excuse, and another another, and a mere bramble of a man has come forth, saying, Come and put your trust in my shadow. He does not offer you timber or fruit or shade. He has nothing but a shadow, a mere skeleton of a shade; and he says, Come and trust in this, or I will burn down the cedars of Lebanon, the social and political structure of the nation."

It is a parable of perennial freshness and significance. It fits into the political conditions of the last decade of American history. We are living under a government of the people, for the people, and by the people — a government the most difficult of all to manage, and one which requires the continuous thought and sacrifice of all those interested in its perpetuation. This government lays upon the shoulders of every citizen weighty responsibilities. It places in the hands of great cities large influence in the shaping of national policy and destiny. Every city has a government of its own, and by this government the rights and liberties of the people are safeguarded, or sacrificed to the gains of wicked men. A city government goes forth from time to time in search of a king. She calls upon all good citizens to cast their ballots for a man in whose hands the welfare of the city shall be secure. She goes to the merchant and says, " Come thou and use your influence in forming a government that shall be an honor to your city"; and the merchant replies: " I cannot leave my fatness, I am hourly engaged in making money, and by my money I honor God and man. I am too busy to give my thought to politics." The government turns to the professional man and says, " Come thou and make it possible for good men to reign over the lives and property of the people." But the professional man replies: " I cannot leave my sweetness and my good fruit, my clients, patients, pupils, editorial work. I have no time or strength to bestow upon a political campaign." And the government thereupon turns to the elegant man of leisure, saying, " Come thou and do what thou canst toward making the city what it ought to be." But he says: " I cannot come, I am enjoying life here with my friends. I cannot leave my cards and cigars and wine to dabble in political affairs." Whereupon a bramble impudently steps forward, saying, "I will put on the crown; come and put your trust in my shadow." And thus, by the indifference and preoccupation of honest men, the bramble king climbs to power. He has neither timber, nor fruit, nor shade. He is a useless man, and worse, he is dangerous. He is not substantial or fruitful, but he is combustible. He is capable of burning and setting other things on fire. Although only a bramble, he may start a conflagration which will burn the cedars of Lebanon — the fabric of our liberties.

The indifference of many good men to their political obligations and duties in our country is appalling. Many good men do not seem to know that they have such a thing as a political duty. In the home they are good men, faithful husbands, and kind fathers. In the church they are generous, industrious, and reliable. But in the world of politics they are recreant to every duty and false to every trust. Upright and noble-hearted men in a few departments of life, in another department they are nothing but shirks and cowards. Some of these men have come to us from other lands, and have never been naturalized. They came to this country to enjoy the advantages it offers, but they are unwilling to make the slightest sacrifice that the government may be maintained. Many native-born American citizens seldom register. It is too much trouble.

They count themselves good men, but are unwilling to walk six blocks in order to do a service to their country. Others register, but on election day they do not vote. They forget all about it, or go out of town on business or on pleasure, and then come back without the least shamefacedness over the disgraceful thing they have done. So low have we sunken in our conception of civic virtue, and so seared is our conscience, that it is not uncommon to hear good men say: " I know nothing about politics, and I do not want to know anything. I want nothing to do with politicians, or political affairs," — as though such an attitude were evidence of a superior type of virtue, and the crowning excellence of an ideal American citizen! When good men run away from their most sacred obligations, no wonder the bramble king says with haughty insolence, " Come and put your trust in my shadow."

How did we ever get into this deplorable condition? Who is responsible for this wholesale neglect of political responsibilities and duties? The pulpit, I think, is in part to blame. Preachers, as a class, have not instructed their congregations as it was their duty to do, in the principles and aims of government, and concerning the duties which all good men owe to their city and country. There are various explanations for this lamentable neglect. The church has always been disgraced by a few ministers who have never been able to preach politics without degenerating into partisans or demagogues. In the enthusiasm of political excitement they have converted their pulpit into a political rostrum, and have poured out upon their congregations bitter and partisan harangues, which have led sensible men to think that preachers are more successful in dealing with the other world than in discussing the affairs of this. It is an interesting fact in the history of this city that the very first minister who ever preached the Gospel on Manhattan Island was a minister of this stripe. Bogardus was his name, and whenever he touched upon politics he invariably became excited and bitter. So blatant and vindictive was he in his utterances that the Director General found it advisable to station a squad of soldiers outside the church door, so that whenever the obstreperous dominie entered upon one of his political tirades, his voice might be drowned in the roll of the drums. Dominie Bogardus has had many descendants, and some of them have been heard from in recent years. It is because a few unbalanced individuals have degenerated from prophets into partisan pleaders that there has grown up in the church the general feeling that a minister had better let politics alone. And that is true if by politics you mean the discussion of questions purely economic, or the comparative merits of rival candidates; but it is not true if you mean by politics the principles and ends of government, the science and art of ruling men.

But the chief reason why the clergy have held aloof from political duties is not the fear of being classed among the hot-heads, but rather a narrow conception of the Gospel, and a mistaken idea of what the mission of the pulpit really is. It is often said that the business of the preacher is to preach the simple Gospel. If he leaves the simple Gospel, he is forsaking the work he is sent to perform. Many persons are always afraid that the preacher will get away from the simple Gospel. The saloon keeper wants the preacher to stick to the Gospel. What right has a preacher to talk about saloon legislation! Is that the Gospel? In slavery days all friends of slavery desired the preacher to preach the simple Gospel. There is not a tyrant or a knave anywhere who does not say that preachers do best when they preach the simple Gospel. By simple Gospel they mean such vague generalities as the fatherhood of God and the brotherhood of man. So long as they preach beautiful abstractions all is well, but the moment they begin to apply the principles of Jesus to the complicated problems of everyday life, they are giving an exhibition of clerical bad manners. Now, preachers ought to preach the fatherhood of God and the brotherhood of man with all the passion and power of which they are capable, but they are cowards to men, and untrue to God, if they spend all their time in glowing generalities, while the fires of Gehenna are burning at our doors. The simple Gospel is no Gospel at all unless it grapples with demons that are to be smothered and dragons that are to be slain.

But some one says, Did not Paul say: " I am determined to know nothing but Jesus Christ and him crucified "? Those are his precise words. But what do they mean? Did Paul mean to say that he never preached anything but the incarnation and the crucifixion? Did he fill up all the hours in narrating details of Jesus' life and death? Paul had a fashion of crowding infinite contents into his phrases. Many of his sentences are broad enough to cover a world. To find what he meant by " Jesus and him crucified," read his thirteen letters. He has a message for husbands, and a message for wives, and a message for children, and a message for teachers, and a message for servants, and a message for citizens. He deals with traditions and customs and problems, and takes in the whole scope of human life in all its complexities and entanglements. He is determined to know nothing but Jesus Christ and him crucified, and so he gathers up the whole world and views all in the light of Christ's love. Nothing could be insignificant or unclean to him in a world for which the Son of God had died. And so, while he was the man who said he would " know nothing but Jesus Christ and him crucified," he was also the man who said that " the powers that be are ordained of God." In the 13th chapter of Romans he is discussing political obligations and duties. He says the state is divine.

It is a part of God's divine order. The church is divine, but it is not more divine than the state. The officers of the state are ministers of God. Mark the breadth of the man. We have narrowed the meaning of " ministers of God." We confine the great phrase to a little set of men who stand in the pulpits. Paul knew no such limitations. Preachers are not the only ministers of God. Civil officers are all ministers of God. And it is the duty of Christians to see to it, not only that worthy men stand in the pulpit, but that worthy men be intrusted with governmental affairs. The state is divine, and it is to be supported by the devotion of Christians, and redeemed by their life.

But some one says Jesus never touched politics. He came to save men from their sins, and not to teach men how to run a government. The assertion is plausible, but fallacious. It is the argument of those who cling to an exploded interpretation of the Gospel. According to this interpretation, the world is a sinking ship. The ship with most of its passengers is going down, and all that we can hope to do is to save a few of those on board, and get them safely to the eternal shore. But that interpretation is belated. Men of vision now see that the world is the subject of redemption, that society is to be saved, and that, instead of confining our attention to a few individual passengers, we are to save the ship and all who are on board. Civil government then comes into the plan of redemption, and Christians, if faithful to their calling, must be citizens intent on bringing their government into subjection to the laws of Christ.

The fact that Jesus did not deal with political questions has given sceptics a chance to criticise and scoff. They say his failure to instruct men concerning civic duties is an evidence of his one-sidedness as a teacher. " His insight into human life was not deep. His message was not comprehensive. He failed to teach a complete and perfect morality because he left essential elements out. His was a narrow view of life, and his teaching is mischievous because hopelessly one-sided. The New Testament is good as far as it goes, but it must be supplemented if we are to have a book worthy of being made a guide-book for a nation." That is the arraignment which has been brought against the carpenter of Nazareth, and if it is unanswerable then Jesus is no longer fit to be our leader in the complications and entanglements of our modern life.

But there is an answer for all this. Jesus' life was brief, and he never did unnecessary things. He did not dwell upon those elemental truths which had been established in the human mind. He did not teach any of the simple and elementary principles of conduct. Plato and Aristotle taught many things which Jesus never touched. He never said, Be sober, or be just, or be brave. Men knew all that without being told. He never taught the duty of patriotism because it is one of

the elemental emotions of our human nature, and
had worked itself out into prominence and power
in human history. Horace had said that it is
beautiful to die for one's country, and the entire
pagan world had said, Amen. Cicero had said,
" Dear are parents, dear are children, dear are
friends and relations; but all affections to all men
are embraced in country alone." There was no
dissenting voice from that. But of all the nations
of the ancient world there was no nation so pas-
sionately and wildly patriotic as the Jews. Their
patriotism was a consuming fire. It was always
threatening to pass over from being a virtue into
a blind and destructive vice. They loved their
country with such intensity of devotion as to
render them contemptuous of all other lands. No
river was like the Jordan, and no sea was so beautiful as Galilee. There was only one city in all
the world, and that was dear Jerusalem. The
men around Jesus were boiling with patriotic fer-
vor. They listened constantly for a word to
start them against Rome. Palestine was a magazine of gunpowder, and if Jesus had dropped the
match, Christianity would have been burned up in
its cradle. Jesus was silent in regard to patriotism
because he did not care to speak of lessons which
the world had already learned. " I came," he
said, " to fulfil." " I came not to tell you things
you already know, but to call your attention to
things which you have dropped and almost forgotten." And if you ask why did Jesus never

speak of civic duties, the answer is: The.Jews in the first century had no civic duties. Why should Jesus have spoken about things which had no existence. Palestine was a tributary province of the Roman empire. She lay helpless beneath the feet of a tyrant. Her people had no political rights, and hence no political obligations or duties. He might have stirred up an insurrection, and struck a few feeble blows against the mailed hand which clutched Judea by the throat, but he was too far-sighted to do that. He rather chose to drop into the air a few simple principles which when fully developed in human hearts would melt the shackles of Oriental despotism, and create in distant ages far away the liberties of the British Empire, and give birth to a republic in a spacious land which Christopher Columbus in the fulness of time was to pick up out of the Western Sea.

But if Jesus was silent in regard to political obligations and duties, the Hebrew prophets never were. In their day Palestine was free, and the people were responsible for national policies and progress. All the great prophets were enthusiastic politicians. Their discourses are crammed with political discussions. No one can read the prophecies of the Old Testament with the understanding, unless he is acquainted with the political issues and combinations of their times. The greater the prophet the more deeply he was immersed in politics. Who are the tallest of the prophets? Isaiah and Jeremiah. And these are the greatest of all Jewish politicians from the days of Moses to the days of Nehemiah. When men say, as they sometimes do, that a minister has no right to preach politics, he is passing judgment on the very men whose political discourses are incorporated into our Bible. If one were allowed to prophesy concerning the coming century, I should not hesitate to say that the preaching of the American pulpit will be increasingly political. The American pulpit is a half century behind the English Nonconformist pulpit in its influence on municipal reform and national affairs. The English pulpit is a power in every national and local election. To be sure there are men in England who still cling to the old conception. Only the other day General Booth issued an order advising all Salvationists to take no part in the general election, but Dr. John Clifford of London, one of the most influential clergymen now alive, declared amid thunders of applause before a great convention of ministers that he hoped every Salvationist in England would start an instantaneous revolt against the command of the General. John Clifford has the Hebrew ideal of the mission of the prophet of the Lord, and indicates, I believe, the direction in which the pulpit in the future is going to move.

But if ministers have erred, laymen have not been blameless. They have in large numbers shirked their duties shamefully. Some of them have done it in ignorance. They have not realized what they have done. Others have done it through indolence. They have shrunk back from political service because it was disagreeable. Others have been unworthy citizens because of sheer selfishness. Immersed in business, they have given themselves to their own interests, and have ignored completely those larger duties upon whose faithful performance the perpetuation of the republic depends. They have used their city as a commercial convenience. They have made it their rule to put into it as little as possible, and take the most possible out of it. They have treated the city as though it were a cow. They have filled their own little pail with milk, and then have retired into their house to drink it, not caring what became of the cow. Shame on the man who enjoys the protection and liberties of our government, and makes no sacrifices by means of which the government shall be strengthened and enriched.

And what is the result? Lamentable enough. Our cities are notorious the wide world over. Mr. Bryce, one of the keenest-eyed and most genial of all our foreign critics, says that the government of cities is the one conspicuous failure of the United States. Mr. Albert Shaw has not hesitated to declare that our cities are the worst governed cities in Christendom. No one has ventured to dispute his assertion. The bramble king has gotten his crown, and the question before us is, how may he be dethroned?

Certainly not by pessimistic whines. We have altogether too much whining in our modern life. We have too many men who are experts in the art of uttering lamentations. Nothing is ever cured by pessimistic moans. The late Senator Ingalls once said that " the purification of politics is an iridescent dream," and for his assertion he was berated and denounced. But I am not sure that Mr. Ingalls meant what he said. I am inclined to think that he wrote that sentence in order to get in that adjective " iridescent." It is not every day that a man can use such an adjective as that. It is a peacock of a word, and spreads its feathers before our eyes in gorgeous style, and Mr. Ingalls must have felt a secret joy when he got that fine word nicely embedded in his sentence. But whether the senator meant what he said or not, there is no doubt that many of our people believe that the political world is hopelessly corrupted. It is an Augean stable which no Hercules will ever cleanse. It is a kingdom which belongs to Satan, and which can never be redeemed. Believing this they lie down and cry! But bramble kings care nothing for the cries of men who act like babies.

Nor can he be dethroned by denunciations. Nothing comes easier for many men than denunciation. They are masters of the vocabulary of scorn, and are never quite so happy as when pouring contempt on some antagonist or foe. There are times when denunciation is not only proper but effective. Jesus lived in such a time. When he faced the Pharisees he hurled at them sentences which were thunderbolts that cleansed the air. There was a time for denunciation in the years preceding the civil war. When so many good men were fumbling in their Bibles for sentences with which to bolster up the institution of slavery, it was fortunate for the nation that we had a prophet of the Lord, Wendell Phillips, whose sentences were like brilliant steel, and who jabbed and slashed with merciless genius the rhinoceros hide of Daniel Webster and the other great men who having eyes could not see. It is well now and then to-day for some one who knows how to do it, to beat the Christian church with lashes because of her shameful indifference to the ravages of the liquor traffic. Does not a church need to be cudgelled and shot through with the lightnings of wrath that will go to sleep in the presence of one of the deadliest evils known to human history? And so there may be times when men may be justified in hurling thunderbolts at the bramble king. But no man should attempt to do this unless he can do it well. When every little whipper-snapper of a reformer sets himself up as Jupiter and begins to throw thunderbolts, the whole business becomes wearisome and disgusting. The lightning flashes of a great man may clear the air and show us the way out of our bondage and darkness, but the fulminations of Tom and Dick and Jack are like the evanescent glow of fire-flies whose momentary glimmerings only reveal the darkness of the night. After all, denunciation will not carry us very far. It generates heat in the person who indulges in it, but throws no light on our path to political redemption. All this snapping and snarling and scolding is a nuisance which ought to be abated. The bramble king is to be dethroned, not by sneers, but by ballots; not by pelting him with adjectives, but by undermining his authority by votes. A bramble king cannot be blasted by a sneer. The side that wins is the side that has the votes. Nothing, therefore, is effective that does not increase the number of right-minded voters. What we want is more Christianity in our politics. We have too much vitriol, and not enough sacrifice; too much denunciatory talk, and not enough redemptive work. If some of the gentlemen who spend several nights every week in eating luxurious dinners, and who curse the bramble king while they pick their teeth and fill the air with impotent lamentations over the mischief of universal suffrage, were only willing to take off their coats and go to work upon a great campaign of education and reconstruction, the bramble king might some day lose his crown. One thing is certain, and that is that all this sputtering and hurling of thunderbolts, of which we have at present more than enough, will never prevail against a bramble king.

Go into politics. Do not say that politics is dirty, for if you do you will compel us to think you are a Pharisee. No duty is too dirty for the whitest of God's saints to take hold of. The muddier the pool, the more urgent is your duty to get into it, and cleanse it by the purity of your Christian life. Do not say that it is disagreeable, that you will be misunderstood and maligned and hated. If you say that, you will lead us to think you are a coward. We are in this world, not to be understood, but to do our duty, and we can afford to wait for our reward until we reach the world where we shall know as we are known. Do not say you have no time. If you say that, we shall know you are selfish.

Go into politics, young men. What will our republic do if our young men give all their leisure time to amusement and sport? The young doctor while he is waiting for patients, and the young lawyer while he is waiting for clients, and the young clerk while he is waiting for promotion, ought to be learning the structure of our government and getting practical lessons in the manipulation of its political machinery. All college men ought to go into politics. The indifference of many college men to political duty is a shame and a danger. "The republic was founded by scholars," says Lowell, "and it can be defended only by the self-sacrificing devotion of scholars." If good men sit at home complaining that things do not go right, then, as George William Curtis used to say: "It is not a government mastered by ignorance; it is a government betrayed by intelligence. It is not the victory of the slums; it is the surrender of the schools. It is not that bad men are politically shrewd; it is that good men are political infidels and cowards." Men of wealth ought to go into politics. What better thing can a rich man buy than time, and to what better use can he put time than filling it with work for the political salvation of his city, commonwealth, and nation?

All Christians ought to be in politics. No man can be a good Christian unless he is a good man, and no man can be a good man unless he is a good citizen, and no American citizen can be a good citizen unless he does his duty at the polls. The ballot was won by the bloody sweat of centuries, and he who fails to use it is recreant to his highest duty and false to his most sacred trust. A ballot! A piece of paper! As sacred as a page torn from the Bible! Think what it cost. Think of the men who died that we might take it between our fingers. Think of what can be accomplished by that piece of paper. Health can be safeguarded, crime can be reduced, the weak and the poor can be protected, justice can be established and righteousness made possible. What is the ballot? It is a sword with which great evils can be hacked to pieces. It is a battering-ram for beating down established wrongs. It is a cannon ball by which oppression can be ground to powder. It is a nerve in the great hand of the people by whose pressure and guidance institutions are moulded and national destinies are fixed.

> " A weapon that comes down as still
> As snowflakes fall upon the sod ;
> But executes a freeman's will,
> As lightning does the will of God."

TEMPTATION FROM THE MOUN-
TAIN TOP

TEMPTATION FROM THE MOUN-
TAIN TOP[1]

"The devil taketh him up into an exceeding high mountain and showeth him all the kingdoms of the world and the glory of them; and saith unto him, All these things will I give thee, if thou wilt fall down and worship me." — Matt. iv. 8.

THAT is the devil's masterpiece. He can never do anything shrewder than that. He is an adept in concocting temptations seductive and subtle, but when he offers, on only one condition, the kingdoms of the world and the glory of them, his ingenuity can go no farther. He had already tempted Jesus in many ways and every assault had been repelled. As a last resort he now takes him up into an exceeding high mountain and shows him all the kingdoms of the world and the glory of them. " All these things will I give thee " — so ran the honeyed and tempting offer. " Get thee hence, Satan! " was the hot and vehement response. And then the devil left him. Of course he did. There was nothing more for him to do. There are limits beyond which even the devil cannot go.

But the devil left him only for a season. Again and again throughout the life of Jesus the devil returned and always with the same old offer of the kingdoms. If the Son of Man is to fall at all, he must be pierced by this particular poisoned arrow. And so the devil comes under many different disguises. He speaks to him through the lips of his own brethren. "If thou do these things shew thyself to the world." In other words, there are kingdoms down in old Judea which you ought to master, why not go down and take possession of them? He speaks to him through the lips of his dearest friend, Simon Peter. "Be it far from thee, Lord: this shall not be unto thee!" And in a flash the old response leaps forth: "Get thee behind me, Satan!" It was the old devil in a new disguise. The devil speaks to him through the crowd which follows him, crying lustily, "Hosanna!" and always clamorous to make him king. The spirit of the leaders, the spirit of the masses, the spirit of the age, was always at his side, pointing to the kingdoms of the world and the glory of them, and saying, "All these things will I give thee, if thou wilt fall down and worship me." You know the answer. There it stands — the cross!

> ". . . Towering o'er the wrecks of time,
>   All the light of sacred story
>   Gathers round its head sublime."

THE LOVE OF POWER

The temptation was an appeal to the love of power. The love of power is innate in man. It is born with every child that comes into the world.

" Mother, just watch me and see me do this," cries the urchin as he exhibits his mastery over some new kingdom of activity which he has recently entered and conquered. Every healthy schoolboy has in him the instincts of a Napoleon. This love of power never forsakes us. Unhappy we, if it did. We are created in God's image. With his nature in us, it is natural that we should desire to perform and master and extend the borders of our dominion.

This love of power is in itself not evil. The instinct is God-implanted. The man who does not wish to extend the limit of his influence, and increase the measure of his resources, is not a full-toned and normal man. The merchant, the scholar, the poet, the orator, the statesman, the farmer, the general, every one of them has his eyes on kingdoms and the glory of them, and one of the rich pleasures of life lies in mastering these kingdoms and bringing them under the dominion of the soul.

But along with this passion for power must go the temptation to acquire power by compromising with evil. Every man has at some time or other felt the edge of this temptation. The merchant knows what it is, so does the physician, so does the lawyer, so does the preacher, so do we all. Success is what we all desire, but how to secure success, ah! there's the rub. Success may be won in many ways, and some ways are not the ways of righteousness. We see the kingdoms and the

glory of them, and in our impatience we grasp
for them without asking if our methods will bear
the scrutiny of the eyes of the Almighty.

And the temptation becomes more subtle and
powerful in proportion as a man's aims are high
and noble. If a man is eager to bless the world, if
he is in possession of truth which he is sure will
widen and glorify hearts and homes, if he is the
leader of a movement on whose ultimate outcome
the welfare of millions hangs, the temptation to
impatience, and to adopt measures such as the
world has tried and found efficient, becomes well-
nigh irresistible. The ambition to gain the kingdoms is legitimate. The conquest of them has in
it no sin at all. But to use earthly instead of
heavenly means in conquering the kingdoms, this
is a temptation before which the strongest of our
race have fallen. To hasten the triumph of a
heavenly principle by compromising with evil is
the most common, and the most subtle, and the
most nearly unconquerable temptation which the
human mind can know.

THE TRIUMPH OF JESUS

Hence the significance of the triumph of Jesus.
He was tempted not because he was weak, but
bcause he was strong, and had in him the energy
of all robust and conquering men. He was
tempted not because his heart was evil, but because his heart was good. His zeal was so intense,

and his desire to bring the world to God was so consuming, that he could not possibly escape the thought, Why not hasten the good work by falling in with popular conceptions, and making use of methods universally adopted? O what a temptation was that! The world needed a Messiah. The world had settled in its mind the sort of Messiah that was needed. All the statesmen and clergymen and scholars and jurists were a unit in their ideal of the world's deliverer. The people clung to the ideal furnished by their leaders. The world was groaning and travailing in pain, waiting for a Saviour. Under such circumstances, why not cater just a little to the prejudices of the leaders, why not pander just a little to the wishes of the crowd, why not bend just a little toward the standards of the age, in order to establish *God's* kingdom, and hasten the day when man's agony should cease and God's glory begin. Fascinating was the offer, but it was rejected. To go one way meant praise, popularity, honor, immediate success. To go the other way meant derision, isolation, calumny, ignominy, shame, and death. And with the two ways plain before him, he chose the long and narrow and rugged path that led to distant but unending triumph by way of the cross.

THE IDEAL MAN

There is only one New Testament in the world. Only one ideal man has ever lived. History is a

record of men who, when taken into an exceeding
high mountain and shown the kingdoms of the
world and the glory of them, have immediately
succumbed. What a roll of world-conquerors history presents, whom their contemporaries counted
great, but who are now seen to have been colossal
failures. Through slaughter they waded to a
throne to found a dynasty soon to perish. What
a host of statesmen in every nation have gained
the kingdoms and lost their honor. How many
merchant princes have become masters of large
areas in the world of trade, only to be conscious
on their dying bed that they had been defeated on
the spot where the Son of Man had stood and conquered. The merchant, to increase his business,
makes use of methods he knows are wrong, and
excuses himself by the thought that such methods
are common to the whole commercial world. The
politician, to advance his party and make sure the
triumph of his policy, allows his lieutenants to
make use of underhand methods, and though himself a man of honor, he winks at dishonorable
procedures. The ecclesiastic, in order to defend
the truth, lies for it, and pushes forward the kingdom of holiness by methods altogether unclean.
So it has been from the beginning.

THE TRAGEDY OF HUMAN HISTORY

As men fall, so do institutions fall. The direst
tragedy of human history is the fall of the Chris-

tian Church. It was the third of Christ's temptations which caused the overthrow of his bride.
She began her life single-eyed and spotless. At
once the Prince of Darkness made war upon her.
In Jerusalem he endeavored to quench her spirit
by taunts and ridicule, and later on he tried to
strangle her by judicial persecution. The first
three centuries of the Christian era were centuries
of furious opposition. The new religion was
obliged to make a desperate struggle for a foot-
hold on the earth. There seemed to be no room
for her anywhere. The Roman emperors from
Nero to Diocletian endeavored to stamp out the
accursed sect by the use of every cruelty known
to the wicked heart of hate. Men and women
were slandered, imprisoned, whipped, tortured,
outraged, slain, worried to death by dogs, torn to
pieces by wild beasts, affixed to crosses in public
places, burned at stakes to light up the royal gardens when the sun had set. But neither Nero, nor
Domitian, nor Trajan, nor Hadrian, nor Decius,
nor Valerian, nor Diocletian, was able to destroy
the Church against which the Lord had said the
gates of Hades should nevermore prevail. She
was despised and rejected of men. Tacitus and
Pliny passed her by with a curt word of contempt; Lucian smiled sarcastically upon her;
Celsus and Porphyry poured upon her their vials
of sarcasm and abuse. But not all the scoffers
and sceptics of the Roman Empire caused her to
budge from the position she had taken at the foot

of the cross. Heresies, insidious and almost innumerable, sprang up within and without, and heretical teachers of great genius and vast learning endeavored to wreck the structure whose foundations the apostles had laid. But neither Cerinthus, nor Basilides, nor Valentinus, nor Saturninus, nor Marcion, nor the whole pack of dreamers and theorists with which the first centuries swarmed, were able to add to or subtract from the faith once for all delivered to the saints. Ebionism, Gnosticism, and Manachœism, Judaism, Romanism, and Heathenism, all united their forces and did their worst. They fought in vain. Through these three centuries of fire the Church remained true to her Lord. The Church in the catacombs was invulnerable and triumphant.

THE FALL OF THE CHURCH

At last, when all other devices had been tried and abandoned, the Church was led into an exceeding high mountain, and there shown the kingdoms of the world and the glory of them. The vision was too fascinating to be resisted. The Church of God fell. She fell on the mountain. The prospect of ruling over the vast pagan world in imperial pomp blinded her eyes and froze her heart. She adopted the luxurious robes of the Roman court, invoked the authority of the Roman law, used when deemed necessary the Roman sword, built up her organization along the lines projected by the genius of Roman statesmen, used the Roman emperor as a crutch by whose aid she walked up the steps of the throne, and placed the chief of her bishops at last in the charmed chair of the Cæsars. O what a fall was there! From the catacombs to the throne! It was like the fall of Lucifer. From that fall came the Dark Ages, and the Inquisition, and the intolerable, inexpressible, innumerable villanies and tyrannies which stained the pages of a thousand years of Christian history. From that fall came the despotism under which nations shrivelled and rotted, and whose iron grip no one was able to loosen until Martin Luther came. The greatest calamity in human history — what is it? The Romanization of the Christian Church! Do you want to know why the Church is to-day all divided and discordant, split into three great sections, neither one of which will commune with the others? It is because centuries ago the leaders of the Church, eager for empire, consented to use the forces of the world for the extension of the Kingdom of the Lord. "We will compel them to come in," shouted the Roman prelates as they whipped heretic and barbarian into the fold. By their impatience to hasten the day of the world's redemption, they retarded it uncounted thousands of years. The lust for universal dominion in the hearts of political and ecclesiastical leaders is the most insidious and most dangerous force against which the ages are obliged to contend.

THE SITUATION OF OUR REPUBLIC

Nations, like men at times, go up into exceeding high mountains and behold the kingdoms of the world in a moment of time. Into such a mountain in these recent days our Republic has been carried. It is with us as it was with the Son of God. He was swept by the Holy Spirit onward to be tempted of the devil. He was entering a new epoch in his life. A great work lay just before him. His imagination was stirred to unwonted activity, and all the currents of his life flowed with a new momentum. In this highly wrought condition of nerve and spirit, new yearnings, strange ambitions, lofty dreams, seized and held him. Vast possibilities opened before him. Conflicting suggestions thronged upon his soul. The world lay at his feet. He felt himself to be its rightful lord. How to enter into his dominion was the problem which crushed him almost to the earth. The decision was reached only after tremendous struggle. Out of the wrestling he staggered, weakened and fainting, to be ministered unto by angels.

We as a nation are passing through a crucial experience. We are at war. We feel we were driven into the war by the spirit of the Lord. But the war furnishes an arena in which we must suffer temptation of the devil. No high experience is ever possible without attendant dangers. We are to-day stimulated to unnatural life. All our senses are abnormally acute. We see and dream as we never did in the quiet days of peace. Visions flit before us. New ambitions seize us. New responsibilities and duties awe and alarm us. Possibilities vague and alluring charm us into a delicious intoxication. Temptations robed in garments of light stalk before us. Conceptions and enterprises of which we have heretofore been unconscious stir within us and give us a strange unrest. We are passing through a national crisis. The crisis is crowded with perils, subtle and deadly. We feel we are on the verge of a new era. A great work lies just ahead of us. A new century at the threshold stirs the imagination and fills us with mighty dreams. Now is the time to be careful. Now is the time to think deeply, soberly, reverently, of our duties, and in the fear of God to ask ourselves by what road will our nation reach the place provided for it in the councils of the Almighty, by what policy will it best advance the interests of the kingdom of our King?

War always brings out the best and the worst in the human heart. It is not surprising, therefore, that in these recent weeks there has been an outburst of the savagery which underlies all civilization. The thirst for revenge, the flippant regard for human life, the ghoulish delight in slaughter, the cold-blooded ambition to test the destructiveness of guns, the brag and the swagger of the braggadocio and the ruffian, all this has been washed up before our eyes on the shore of

our barbaric press, out of that great unclean sea
— the unregenerated heart. The acres of bom-
bast and gush, falsehood and fury, which have
been published within the last thirty days, have
given us new insight into the depths of the ruin
of human nature, and have revealed with startling
distinctness the vastness of the work which the
Church of God is given to accomplish.

THE PASSION FOR EMPIRE

And along with this passion for revenge has
come the far more dangerous passion for empire.
To tempt Jesus of Nazareth it was necessary to
show him all the kingdoms of the earth and the
glory of them. To tempt many Americans it is
necessary to show them only a few islands of the
sea. The victory in the harbor of Manila has
roused in thousands the old devil of love of conquest, and already ambitious editors are counting
up with glee the islands which will form the string
of spoils with which we shall come off laden from
the war. Our modern editor takes up islands as
a very little thing.

Nor is this lust of empire confined to the impet-
uous statesmen who furnish copy for our sensa-
tional papers. It is pervading all classes of our
people. Reputable editors are writing editorials
on "Imperial America," and men high up in
Church and State, to whom the people naturally
look for counsel and guidance, are speaking in

patronizing tones of Washington's outgrown ideas, and are asserting that the time is ripe for territorial expansion and the adoption of a policy impressively imperial. The spirit of conquest is in the air. The pride of power is on us. The avarice for domain, finely cloaked under religious and patriotic phrases, appeals to us with all the subtlety and persuasiveness of a devil. Now is the time for every man to think. We must not lose our heads simply because we are on a mountain top. We must not be swayed by the clamor and sophistry of an ignorant and irresponsible press. We must not be imposed on by phrases such as " Manifold destiny," " Providential openings," " God's manifest decrees." Men have always used such phrases to induce the world to move in the direction in which they wished it to go. We will give slight weight to the puerile argument that because we extended our domain across a continent we should therefore extend it around the world. We will not believe that it is necessary for us to hold a foot of land whose possession will jeopardize or embarrass the great experiment of popular government which we are working out for the nations and ages. What is our responsibility to any island compared with our responsibility to the vast future? We will ask, not what can we do to impress Europe, but what is our duty? We will think over our home problems. We will recall our inability to govern the Red Man at our door, and will blush once

more as we remember that our efforts in this direction have filled a century with dishonor.

SOME PROBLEMS NOW BEFORE US

We will ponder the fact that the negro problem
cries aloud for solution, and is one of the most
difficult and dangerous problems which any
nation on earth is obliged to meet. We will think
of our great cities, whose reputation smells to
heaven, and makes us a byword and reproach
among the nations of the earth. We will call up
before us the faces of our Congressmen, and remind ourselves once more that it is an open
question whether we are able as yet to send to
Washington men mature and great enough to
grapple successfully with our pressing and complicated financial and industrial problems. And
we will not forget that every island added to our
dominions necessitates a larger navy, and that we
are gradually but surely, in the opinion of many,
passing into the relentless grip of the militarism
of the Old World, and that too in spite of the fact
that militarism is the greatest of all existing
curses, and the most needless and most intolerable
of all historic scourges. We will not be charmed
out of our senses by that proud and fatal phrase,
" Imperial America." Imperial — away with it!
I do not like the sound of it. It has in it the sound
of a death knell. It is a devil of a word which has
lured many a nation to its ruin. Run your eye
along the tombstones of the nations which have

been imperial — Assyria, Egypt, Babylon, Macedon, Rome. Look into the faces of the great imperialists from Alexander the Great to Napoleon III.! All of them with their "purples rent asunder, disinherited of thunder." Imperial America? Never! Let us make it Christian America.

"A GREAT CHRISTIAN POWER"

Men are exulting everywhere that we have become at *last* a great world power. We amounted to nothing until the victory in the harbor of Manila!

> "O Judgment, thou art fled to brutish beasts,
> And men have lost their reason."

He is a Rip Van Winkle of an American who had to be aroused from his sleep by a cannon shot to learn that the Republic of the West is a great world power. America has been a great world power for years. How did she become such? By her army? No. By her navy? No. By dabbling in diplomacy? No. By colonies and dependencies? No. By the cultivation of the arts of peace. By attending to her own business. By building colleges and schools and churches. By developing free institutions. We started poor and without a friend. We were counted the offscouring of the world. We are to-day one of the richest of all nations. In thirty years of this century we created and accumulated forty-nine thousand millions of dollars, more than the entire wealth of Great Britain. We can to-day buy up the aggregate wealth of the United Kingdom and have twenty billion dollars left to make purchases elsewhere. We have not fooled away our time in drilling and marching. We have worked. We have not squandered our money on armies and navies. We have built it into schools. And to-day we are a power in the world. It is absurd to think that a nation cannot be a great world power without an immense army. "A great naval power" — that in many a circle is a phrase to conjure with. "A great Christian power" to my ears sounds better.

NOT A HERMIT NATION

But the question may be asked, Is it right for us to be a hermit among the nations, an international recluse? Should we hold aloof from the world's affairs, "in impotence of fancied power" hiding behind the barriers of our protecting seas, and quietly go on making money and allowing other peoples to suffer and to rot? No! No nation lives to itself and no nation dies to itself. Whether they live or die, they are the Lord's. We want the earth for our ideas and our religion. The ambition is altogether legitimate. But we must not be impatient. The deadliest of all national sins is impatience. Christ urged his disciples to possess their souls in patience. His kingdom cannot be set up in a day. It grows. It is like a grain of mustard seed — small at first, great later on. It is like corn — first the blade, and then the ear, and then the full corn in the ear. It is like leaven. It must be given time to work. Christianity is under the laws of growth. If it is forced it becomes something else. Democracy and Christianity are alike in this, they cannot be set down upon a people. They must be the product of a long evolution in the nation's interior life. Our work is not to thrust republican institutions on unprepared peoples by the aid of the cannon, but to create the atmosphere in which freedom and brotherhood and peace shall blossom the wide world over. America isolated? No! Her spirit for years has walked up and down the earth. Where is there a land which her influence has not reached? The perfume of her garments has gone through all the earth. Her merchants trade in every market. Her missionaries labor under every flag. Her ideas have touched and thrilled the hearts of men under every sun. She has done more for freedom and human happiness and peace within the last hundred years than any other nation in the world. She is a power in the evolution of the race. And yet some men never knew it till a gun was fired in the harbor of Manila!

OUR RELATIONS WITH ENGLAND

Our greatest temptation to-day comes from England. She is at once our greatest inspiration, and also our most dangerous friend. The popular imagination always paints its ideals in colors drawn from a concrete example held before the eyes. That is what misled the Hebrew people. They knew no kings but those of Egypt, Babylon, Persia, and Rome, and they could conceive of no other kind. They saw the Messiah always through the glory of Oriental courts. They crucified Jesus because he did not tally with the type of king the world had agreed to reckon great. The Church of the fourth and fifth and sixth centuries was misled by the Roman Empire. The empire was the synonym of power, the ideal of majesty, the consummate flower of human genius. Rome was the Eternal City. And so Christian leaders shaped their ideals of the Christian Church from the mistress of the world. Dazzled by imperial glory, they could conceive of no city of God that did not reproduce the structure and features of the city of the Cæsars. We are in danger of committing the same fatal blunder. England is to us the great nation of the earth. London is mightier than Rome ever was. England has dependencies — why should not we? England has an imperial policy — why should not we? England has a mighty navy — why should not we? England has accomplished vast good by her battle ships and army — why should we not follow her example? Easily deluded is the mind of man. A battle ship is more attractive even yet to millions than the man who hangs on the cross. But that Man on the cross sways the future! He alone holds a sceptre that shall not be broken. After the towers of Westminster Abbey have crumbled in ruins and been mingled with the dust of its immortal dead, the Kingdom of Christ will still be young. Of the increase of his government there shall be no end. It is earnestly questioned whether England has not already reached the zenith of her greatness. As Captain Mahan says, " She is gorged with land and her statesmen are weary of looking after it." She has dependencies, but as Disraeli long ago asserted, they are a millstone around her neck. She has a mighty navy, but dearly does she pay for it. Upon her army and navy over one-third of her vast revenues are annually expended, while her paupers increase with the years. She has naval power, but she is without a friend upon the planet. Nations fear her; they do not love her. She has taken possession of many lands, but her methods have so embittered the hearts of many of her subjects that they never can accept the Gospel at her hands. The preacher who follows the wheels of the powder cart need not be surprised to find hearts barred against him. Saul of Tarsus made swifter progress in the work of redeeming the world than any Englishman can ever make. Saul of Tarsus was never preceded by bayonets or cannon. I am familiar with all the arguments which military men are expert in using, but after all I venture to think that the methods of Jesus of Nazareth are best. The world has never yet seen a Christian nation — a nation based on love. No nation has ever yet tried to live the Gospel. " Increase your guns if you want peace." So say many of the wisest men of our age. I cannot believe that the Son of God agrees with them.

AN EXAMPLE TO OURSELVES

There is no nation on the earth whose example it is safe for us to follow. It is to the everlasting glory of our fathers that they turned their back on the ideals and traditions of Europe, and with an audacity grandly sublime sought the principles of the ideal government in the dreams of hearts that had been cleansed by the spirit of Christ. All that we have done has been possible only because they with magnificent courage refused to be hampered by the policies and precedents of the past, and struck boldly into an experiment that seemed to them to have the sanction and authority of God. We have gone our own way from the beginning. We should continue in it to the end. We must be true to our own traditions. We must remain a peculiar people. Many are disturbed because the courts of Europe do not think highly of us. What of it? Mr. Richard Olney says, " We stand without a friend among the great powers of the world, and we impress them as a nation of sympathizers, and sermonizers, and swaggerers." What of it? We have been misunderstood and maligned from the beginning. We can scarcely expect supporters of monarchies and aristocracies and vast armies to appreciate and adore the nation which is doing more than any other power under heaven to undermine the foundations of all despotisms and overthrow the pretensions and tyrannies of all aristocracies. Let them sneer. Germans and Frenchmen sneer at the man who will not when challenged defend his honor in a duel. Let them sneer. Inhabitants of certain islands scoff at a man too fastidious to eat his neighbor's flesh. Let them scoff. Men sneered at Jesus all the way from Nazareth to Golgotha. They sneered at him while he was dying. He let them sneer. The world on the other hand applauded Napoleon. Men called him "Napoleon the Great." But Napoleon the Great one day became Napoleon the helpless, and on the island of St. Helena, his prison home, he made this frank confession: "Alexander, Cæsar, Charlemagne, and myself founded great empires; but upon what did the creations of our genius depend? Upon force. Jesus alone founded his empire upon love, and to this very day millions would die for him."

This is my ambition for America — that we may found our empire upon love; that we may spend our money on churches and schools, libraries and hospitals; that we may build ourselves four-square in righteousness, so that wherever an American citizen may go upon the earth he will be honored and loved, not because of our battle ships, but because he represents a nation which has nothing but justice and kindness for all races of men.

> "O Beautiful ! my Country ! ours once more !
> Smoothing thy gold of war-dishevelled hair
> O'er such sweet brows as never other wore,
> And letting thy set lips,
> Freed from wrath's pale eclipse,
> The rosy edges of their smile lay bare,
> What words divine of lover or of poet
> Could tell our love and make thee know it,
> Among the nations bright beyond compare ?
> What were our lives without thee?
> What all our lives to save thee ?
> We reck not what we gave thee ;
> We will not dare to doubt thee,
> But ask whatever else, and we will dare ! "

THE HARVEST COMING GRADUALLY

THE HARVEST COMING
GRADUALLY

(Mark iv. 23–30.)

I want to study with you one of Jesus' parables.
It is probably the most neglected of all the parables he ever spoke. St. Matthew did not record
it in his Gospel, although Matthew was fond of
parables. St. Luke did not include it in his Gospel, although St. Luke had a liking for spiritual
truth expressed in pictures. St. Mark is the only
one of the four evangelists who thought it worth
while to narrate this parable, and this is somewhat
surprising, for Mark did not seem to care much
for parables, choosing rather to tell us what
mighty things Jesus did. But for some reason or
other he took a fancy to this parable, and set it as
a gem in his Gospel, there to shine forevermore.

The parable has been neglected throughout
Christian history. Many of those who have made
a special study of the parables, and have written
books about them, have neglected this parable altogether. Many writers who have attempted to
deal with it have treated it with scant courtesy,
and in a hurried, unsatisfactory manner. Such

men as Arnot and Trench attempt to expound it, but they do it in a slovenly fashion, as though they said, " Stand back, little parable, you are not worth much anyhow." Indeed, many writers on the parables have not given sufficient attention to this parable to know really what it teaches. Its very name is an indication of the bad treatment which it has received. It is commonly known as " the parable of the seed growing secretly," but that is not its name at all. The object of the parable is not to teach that the kingdom of God grows secretly. The great words in the parable are not " he knoweth not how." Those words are simply incidental. They are a part of the parable's fringe. The climax of the parable is this sentence: " First the blade, then the ear, and after that the full corn in the ear." The object of the parable is to teach not the secrecy of growth, but the gradualness of it, and therefore, the name is not " the seed secretly growing," but rather " the harvest coming gradually."

It is a parable which fits in with the temper of this age. One of the great words in the modern world is " growth." Throughout the 18th century men looked upon the universe as a vast machine. It was a mechanism created by an infinite mechanic. When Paley wished to prove the existence of God he compared the universe to a watch in which every wheel was finely cut and nicely placed, and worked harmoniously with every other wheel. Such exquisite mechanism,

Paley said, proved the existence of a divine arti-
ficer. But the modern world has thrown away
Paley's watch. Thinking men no longer consider
the universe as a machine, but as an organism. It
is not a bit of machinery cut out of dead matter,
but a thing that grows. The universe has grown
to be what it is. It has climbed upward through a
long process of development. From the beginning
until now, it has been held in the grip of the unchanging laws of growth. Not only has the earth
grown, but everything upon it has grown. All
human things have life in them, and pass through
stages of advancement. Languages have grown,
and so have governments, and so have all the arts,
and so has religion. Everything that lives has
roots, and for the last fifty years men have been
engaged in studying the roots of things. Jesus
taught that the spiritual life is a growing thing.
" Consider the lilies of the field, how they grow,"
he said. " You men and women who want to
know how to live ought to watch growing things,
and get encouragement and admonition out of
them." " The kingdom of heaven is like unto a
mustard seed. It is very small, but it has vitality.
Plant it and give it time, and it will grow." " The
kingdom of heaven is like unto leaven. Leaven is
a living thing. It is aggressive, industrious, ex-
pansive, and it will never rest until the whole
lump has been leavened." " The kingdom of
heaven is like unto seed cast into the ground.
A man sows it and then goes to bed and gets up

in the morning and goes about his work, and the seed keeps right on growing." " For the earth brings forth fruit of herself; first the blade, then the ear, after that the full corn in the ear."

This is one of the most encouraging of all Jesus' parables. There is no other parable, unless it be the parable of the Prodigal Son, which has in it greater stores of consolation. It heartens us and braces us, and throws light upon many a mystery over which we have stumbled. It saves from discouragement and depression. Many a Christian does not grow because he is depressed. It is impossible to grow under a cloud. His depression in many cases rises from a false conception of the nature of the Christian life. It is possible for a man to expect too much of himself. He cannot expect too much of himself at the end of the age, but he may expect too much of himself to-day. No man can dream a dream too high of that which he may some day be. " Now are we the sons of God, and it doth not yet appear what we shall be." But while it is impossible to expect too much of ourselves to-morrow, it is very common to expect too much of ourselves to-day. A man starts out to be a Christian. The ideal Christ floats before him, infinite in patience, self-control, and love. The man looks at Christ and says: " I am going to follow him. I will be his faithful follower. I will be patient." But before the first week has run its course he has become impatient. He has allowed himself to be nagged and fretted

into a fever of impatience. And he says: " I am
not a Christian, I was not converted, I did not
start right. No genuine Christian could ever be
so impatient as I have been." Another man starts
out to be a Christian, saying: " I have a fearful
temper, but I am going to exercise self-control. I
have given myself to Christ, and he has promised
to keep me henceforth. I will be calm." But before the first month is ended he has burst into a
paroxysm of temper, worse, if anything, than any
explosion that occurred in the old days. He says:
" There is no use in my trying to be a Christian.
I am not a Christian. I am nothing but a hypocrite. I will make no further pretences." Another
man starts out and tries to live the law of love.
He reads Jesus' words concerning love, and comes
into the church saying, " I will love my fellow-
Christians." But as the months come and go, on
examining his heart he sees that there is nothing
in it that can rightfully be called Christian love.
He does not love his fellow-Christians. He loves
his friends, but he does not love church members
because they are members of the Christian family.
Here and there he sees a person whom he has
never liked, and the very sight of them causes the
old feeling of disgust and revulsion to surge up
in him and he says: " I am not a Christian. No
Christian could ever have such feelings as those
that are boiling now in me." Many a man, confused and humiliated by such experiences, has
gone back and walked no more with Jesus.

Oh, discouraged Christians, read the parable of the harvest coming gradually. No man can become a perfected saint in a week, or a month, or a year. A man may become a Christian in a moment, because a Christian is a pupil, a learner, an apprentice — but no one can become a saint, perfect in holiness and love, in an hour or a year. "First the blade," that is all that is possible at first, "then the ear," and a long time afterward — "the corn." Sympathies are mellowed with the increase of the seasons. The will is strengthened only by repeated holy choices. The mind is widened by the process of the suns. Do not be discouraged because you are not what you know you ought to be, but take to heart the exhortation of the Psalmist: "Wait on the Lord."

The parable will also save us from confusion and humiliation caused by modern criticism. A terrific storm of criticism is beating at present upon the Christian church. Everything about it is subjected to ridicule and scorn. Many Christians are dumbfounded by this criticism, and scarcely know what to think and say. Here and there one finds a Christian who is almost ashamed to confess that he is a member of the Christian church, excusing himself for his position by saying that he joined the church before he knew what he was doing. It ought to be borne in mind that criticism of the church is nothing new. Peter had not more than gotten his head through the door of the upper chamber when somebody in the streets of Jerusalem sneered at him. The church on the day of its birth was smitten on the cheek. From that day until this there has never been a day when it has not been misrepresented, maligned, hated, and cursed. Let no one, therefore, be distressed as though some new and unparalleled calamity had overtaken the church. It has been kicked and cuffed and abused through all the centuries, and will be thus hardly treated for centuries to come.

A great many men just now are making sport of the Bible. That was a task in which Robert G. Ingersoll was an expert. He ran through the Old Testament, and picked out all the dark and fearful things he could find there, and held them up as evidence that Christians were great fools. And what a collection any man can make if he is so disposed. Polygamy, slavery, butchery, retaliation, bigotry, and meannesses of a hundred kinds, all these are in the Old Testament, and they have furnished food for scoffers and sceptics for the last two thousand years. Every now and then some minister who counts himself liberal attempts to play the part of Ingersoll, and shows up the crudities and blunders of the Old Testament in a ridiculous light. By doing this he thinks he will increase his own congregation, and lead the world to think that orthodox Christians are superstitious and benighted, and God's truth and light have come to liberal Christians alone. All such men ought to read the parable of the harvest coming gradually. The Bible is a living thing. It has grown to be what it is. It was not flung upon the earth from the heavens, but it came up out of the hearts of sinning, struggling, aspiring men. It did not come as the Book of Mormon is said to have come to Joseph Smith, nor as the Koran is said to have come to Mahomet. It came as growing things all come: " First the blade, then the ear, and after that the full corn in the ear." The spiritual life did not start upon the earth full-orbed. Man did not reach an adequate conception of the Almighty at a single bound. Man's conscience did not become full-statured in a day, or a year. "First the blade, then the ear, and after that the full corn in the ear." The Hebrew people in the early stages of their career were like all other peoples, narrow and crude and carnal. Many of their conceptions of God were erroneous. They sometimes thought he said things to them which he never said. They sometimes mistook their own inclinations and impulses for the voice of the Almighty. We are not bound by any of their misconceptions. We are not called upon to eulogize or defend any of their blunders or sins. All that was immature and imperfect in their thought and life has been outgrown. Jesus says that God's law never changes. Not one jot or tittle of it shall ever pass away. But there are parts of the Old Testament that shall pass away, and have passed away, because they never were the law of God. They were the law of men. " It was said by those of old time thus and thus, but I say unto you," and as he spoke a page of the Old Testament grew dim. " I say unto you," and another page of the Old Testament faded. " I say unto you," and another page vanished. Everything that is in the Old Testament that does not tally with the standards of Jesus is considered by us Christians as husks, old garments to be cast away. The Hebrew people at the beginning sanctioned polygamy and slavery, and many another action condemned by the ethical standards of to-day, because they were ignorant and young, and understood but faintly the laws of spiritual life. But back there in those dark ages the blade was growing, which by and by passed into the ear, and in the New Testament we find the full corn in the ear. The Old Testament ought to be an interesting and precious book to every thinking man because it is a book of beginnings. It tells how spiritual life in the midst of weeds and thorns began to grow, and how it rose higher and higher until at last it burst into that celestial flower, Jesus of Nazareth. I am surprised that intelligent people in any American city should be willing to listen either to a lecturer or preacher who is so shallow and unfair as to attempt to make sport of the frailties and failings which the world was guilty of in its youth. As well pour scorn upon a cornfield because at first it is a field of blades, as pour ridicule upon the Hebrew race because its spiritual life at the beginning was feeble and small.

Next to the Bible the preachers come in for the largest amount of criticism and abuse. They are being attacked just now on every side. Newspapers and magazines, lecturers and declaimers, business men and professional men, seem to be vying with one another in their efforts to prove that the ministers are an ignorant and incompetent set. The burden of the accusation in the majority of cases seems to be that preachers are too slow. They do not seem to be keeping up with the progress of the times. Other men are doing wonders, while the ministers are doing little or nothing. Now it is not difficult to see what has given rise to this impression. The criticism is born of the spirit of impatience. We are living in an age in which there is a great deal of rapid movement. The rapidity of movement has been made possible by the harnessing of the forces of nature and the application of mechanical principles. The numerous inventions and discoveries that have been made within the last hundred years have increased the power of men enormously. One pair of hands will do the work that it formerly took five hundred pairs of hands to do. It is possible in many departments for one man to accomplish in a single day more than a man could once perform in an entire year. This use of the forces of nature has made it possible to work miracles in every department of life in which the forces of nature can be made use of. We can travel across the ocean quickly. We can bridge rivers, tunnel mountains, build vast railroads, in an amazingly short space of time. We can turn out goods from our factories and mills with a rapidity that is astounding. We can run up a twenty-story building in a few months. Everywhere we see this rapidity of action. Vast businesses can be built up in a few years. Great fortunes can be amassed, cities can be built almost in a day. This power of working miracles, and working them quickly, begets in men a spirit of feverish impatience, unwilling to brook delay. It is not surprising, therefore, that we should find men demanding rapid action in other departments of life. Men do not see why the same swiftness of results which is possible in the material world should not be possible in the mental world, and everywhere we find men making use of forcing processes. Read the advertisements of to-day and you will see that there are short cuts to everything. The art of music can be mastered in ten lessons, and so can the art of elocution. Men can learn to speak and write German, or French, or Italian in ten weeks. Doctors and lawyers can be made in a few months. The age is furiously impatient, and cannot wait for the tedious processes of growth.

It is not surprising, therefore, that the world should feel that preachers are slow. When men all around are doing gigantic things, and doing them with marvellous rapidity, why cannot the preachers do big things, and do them swiftly? A few years ago a bright young man became the head of a journal, and by ability and push he succeeded in running up the subscription list of that journal to several hundreds of thousands. The journal was voted a great success, and the young man at the head of it was praised as a wonderful man, and almost immediately he began to lecture the preachers. He felt that he was able to give them points. If he by his bright brain could induce hundreds of thousands of people to read his journal, why should not preachers be able to do far more than they were doing? But his criticism was gratuitous and unfair. There are many men in the American pulpit as bright as he is, but they have an entirely different work to do. It is one thing to induce a few hundred thousand people to read a magazine containing bright articles about the latest fashions, and it is a totally different thing to induce people to put on the robes that will enable them to stand unashamed at the marriage feast of the Lamb. The other day a distinguished New Yorker attempted to tell what is the matter with the Christian church, and to give advice to the ministers. He has had behind him one of the greatest millionnaires in the world, and because of the enormous capital at his disposal he has been able to do wonders in the railroad world. He has been able to bring things to pass, and to bring them to pass quickly. He has bridged rivers and tunnelled hills, and ordered great gangs of men here and there, and all this has given him such a sense of power that he no doubt feels that

if he were a preacher, he would lift up one corner
of the world. But it is one thing to dig in earth
and cut out stone and buy steel rails, and throw
up an embankment along which an express train
can run, and it is a totally different thing to throw
up a highway for our God.

The minister is the one man in modern society
who has not been helped in the least by any of the
inventions or discoveries of the last hundred
years. The architect can build a house in a fraction of the time formerly required. The manu-
facturer can set his machinery running, and turn
out a thousand boxes or bales of goods with incredible celerity. The newspaper proprietor can
set his great cylinder presses running, and keep
them thundering through the nights and the days,
and can throw his newspaper before the eyes of a
million people. But the preacher is as naked and
helpless to-day as he was when Saul of Tarsus
stood on Mars Hill and was insulted by the sar-
castic Athenians, who said, " Good day, we will
hear you again." All that the preacher has is his
tongue. That is all he had two thousand years
ago. It is not possible for him to do any more
than St. Paul did, simply stand before men and
say, " We pray you in Christ's stead, be ye reconciled to God."

The only man in the modern world with whom
the preacher may be compared is the farmer. A
preacher is a farmer. He is a sower of seed. Part
of the seed which he sows falls upon hearts that

are beaten hard by the thoughts and pleasures of the world. That seed brings forth no fruit. It is not the preacher's fault. Another part of the seed falls upon soil that is rocky. That is not the preacher's fault. Another part of the seed falls into thorny soil. And that is not his fault. Another part falls into soil that is good, but even in good soil the seed must have time to grow. And it must pass through the various stages of development which the Almighty has appointed. " First the blade, then the ear, and after that the corn." The preacher cannot do things quickly. He is appointed to do slow, discouraging, heart-breaking work. The processes of growth cannot be accelerated. Steam — what does wheat care for steam? It takes wheat just as long to grow in the twentieth century as was required in the days of Herodotus. All the inventions of the last century have not accelerated the rate of wheat in the least. Electricity — what does corn care for electricity! Corn grows now just at it grew in the days of Washington. You cannot change the laws of growth by your inventions and discoveries. Nor can you change the laws of the soul by your impatience and your petulance. Goodness grows just as slowly now as it did in the days of Methuselah. From the beginning until now, the law has been, " First the blade, then the ear, and after that the full corn in the ear."

But the entire church is criticised by the world

of to-day. "I have no use for the church," said a man the other day, and he was simply spokesman for ten thousand men. Miserable, narrow, hypocritical church, away with it! That is the feeling which is met with in many a circle. When we ask what is the matter with the church, the answer comes back: Look at its ignorance, its narrowness, its vanity, its bigotry, its censoriousness, and its selfishness. Give us a church made up of saints, and then it will be worthy of our respect and support.

But how unreasonable all this criticism is. How can you have a church without ignorance in it? Impossible! What is the use then of whining about the church's ignorance? How can you have a church in this world without narrowness in it and bigotry? Bigotry is not a creation of Christianity, it is a part of human nature. It comes into the church because human nature comes in. How can you have a church without selfishness in it? Selfishness is not the product of Christianity, it is an element in human nature. But is this all you can see in the church, ignorance, bigotry, vanity, selfishness? If that is all you can see, you are blind. Can you not see any virtues sprouting? Can you not see any graces growing? The Christian church is not a museum of perfected saints, it is a growing field in which the spiritual life is ripening. The Christian church takes human beings of all ages, of all grades and all textures and all attainments, and subjects them to certain influences which are adapted to develop in them the graces of the spirit. On every Lord's day they are brought together that they may be subjected to the dew of spiritual songs and the spray of Christian prayers and the light of Christian instruction. Little by little souls ripen, and grow mellow, and become ready for the harvest. Every church has in it members whose spiritual life is only in the blade. But there are others in whose souls spiritual life is in the ear, and every church has in it a few saints in whose spiritual life there is complete corn in the ear. But we do not keep these with us long. When the harvest is ripened, God puts forth his sickle and takes these mature souls to himself.

The church of to-day is criticised not only because of the immaturity of its members, but because of its impotency in solving problems and conquering evils. What is the church doing? is a cry that is heard on every side. And the people who shout out those words use an inflection which says, the church is doing nothing. See the wars! Why does not the church stop all wars? Look at the liquor traffic! How awful is its degradation and curse! Why does not the church banish the liquor traffic? See the injustice that is wreaked upon defenceless women by sharpers and rogues in our own city and in all cities! Why does not the church put an end to this? See the corruption in politics! Why does not the church drive out the rascals, and usher in an era of pure government? See the gigantic evils lifting up their bold heads on every side! Why does not the church strike them to the earth? If the church is a divine institution, let her show her divinity by stepping forth and conquering things that hurt humanity. It all sounds plausible, but it is foolish. It was the same sort of question which arose in the heart of John the Baptist when he was imprisoned in the fortress of Machærus. Jesus was in Palestine. Jesus was the eternal Son of God. He was the Saviour of the world. He came to redeem the world. He said he could call twelve legions of angels to his assistance. He said he was the Messiah. And the Messiah, so all the prophets had said, would set the Hebrew nation free, but Jesus did not seem to fulfil his mission. Jerusalem was rotten, and it remained rotten. He did not purify it. White-headed hypocrites sat in the Sanhedrin, and he did not cast them out. Throughout Judea and Galilee vices and evils flourished and grew strong, and he did not kill them. The nation bowed under the Roman yoke, and he never lifted a finger to strike it off. So far as John's disciples could see he was simply frittering away his time eating and drinking with a few obscure people, telling interesting stories to a dozen insignificant men. John's soul burns within him, and at last he sends some of his disciples to Jesus, saying, " Art thou he that was to come, or are we to look for another? " As much as to say: " If you are the Son of God, why do you not do something? If you are going to re-deem the world, why do you not do it now?" Jesus sent back this reply, " Tell John that here and there a leper has been cleansed, that here and there a blind man sees, that here and there a lame man is walking, and that the poor have the Gospel preached to them." In other words, tell him that the good work has begun. The Gospel is a seed, and the seed is being planted, and by and by there will be a golden harvest. That is the answer which we must give to all the critics and all the sceptics. That is the all-sufficient answer. When men taunt us with the impotency of the church, and say, Why does it not do this and that and the other thing? let us say, Here and there a lame man is walking, a blind man is seeing, a leper has been cleansed, a life has been transfigured, a home has been filled with the atmosphere of heaven, all who are poor in spirit and hungry for spiritual truth are having the Gospel preached to them. The seed is being planted, and the harvest will come later on. When men say the church could do this and that if it only would, they take it for granted the church is full-statured. They do not realize that the church is as yet noth-ing but a blade. Men say, Why does not the church stop war? Because the church is not made up of men who have reached the stature of Jesus Christ. If the church of America were made up of full-grown men with the spiritual insight of Jesus, then the church could take every American city and shake the rascals off their thrones of power, and cleanse civic life of its pollutions. And if the church in Europe were made up of men who had reached their growth, who had insight and spiritual enthusiasm, the church would take hold of the men responsible for the military expenditures of Europe and would say to them, We have had enough of this nonsense, we will allow the people to be oppressed no longer by your useless navies and your enormous armies. If the church had reached its growth, it could perform all sorts of miracles, but the church is only in its infancy. It is in the first stage of its spiritual development. If it took God millions of years to get the rocks of this earth to suit him, who knows how many millions of years he will consume in developing a church which shall be without spot or blemish or wrinkle, or any such thing? The church has cast out many a demon, and it will cast out all the demons if you give it time.

Let us give our parable to those who criticise Foreign Missions. There are some men who are always carping at foreign missions because the returns are so tardy, and so small. Men say, Just think of it — we have been sending missionaries across the seas for a hundred years, and what have we achieved? Every now and then we find some man wasting his time by calculating how many dollars it costs to convert one Pagan soul. What has the church done in foreign lands? It has planted seed. If there was not a blade visible in all the Pagan world, the work of the century would not be lost. The church is never losing time when it is planting seed. But the seed has sprouted, and all over the Pagan world there are blades giving promise of abundant harvests. What are you going to do with a man who on the day after the farmer has planted his wheat, goes out and looks over the fence and says, I think the farmer has thrown his seed and his labor away! But that man is not so great a dunce as is the man who looks out over the Pagan world and says, "The Pagan nations have not yet become Christian, and I think that all money contributed to foreign missions is simply so much money thrown away!"

Be patient! Spiritual life is a seed, and because it is a seed it grows. It will grow in your own life, it will grow in the life of your church, of your nation, of the world. If the seed is once planted, the future is certain. The harvest will not come in a day, but it will come. The stages of growth are tedious and long, but they follow one another in the sequence which has been determined by God. "First the blade, then the ear, and after that the full corn in the ear." The world in which we are now living is a world of beginnings. We shall see no completions until this corruption shall have put on incorruption, and this mortal shall have put on immortality.